PARAMILITARY FORCES OF INDIA

PARAMILITARY FORCES OF INDIA

Lt. Colonel M. D. Sharma

PUBLICATIONS

KALPAZ PUBLICATIONS
DELHI - 110052

Paramilitary Forces of India

Rs. 690

ISBN: 81-7835-708-9

Published in 2008 in India by
Kalpaz Publications
C - 30, Satyawati Nagar,
Delhi - 110052
E-mail: kalpaz@hotmail.com
Phone: 9212729499

Printed at : Excel Prints, Naraina, New Delhi.

Contents

PART – VI
PARAMILITARY FORCES UNDER STATE GOVERNMENTS

PART – VII
ORGANIZATIONS ASSISTING PARAMILITARY FORCES

Preface

India is a big country with a dominant position in world affairs. With its large area, diversity and kilometres of borders, India needs specialized forces that can maintain law and order in disturbed areas and keep vigilance on borders. In today's circumstances the security and safety of our countrymen is not only into the hands of Indian army. The security of Indian borders and internal matters are being looked after by brave men working in other security forces which are termed as Para-Military Forces.

Throughout their history, the Paramilitary Forces have existed as a small but professionally effective organizations. They have been able to achieve the tasks set for them by the government of the day. Today, they are vastly developed but still professional in attitude.

This book focuses primarily on the Paramilitary Forces as they are today with inclusion of their history, origin, organization, duties and functions, role and future. It also covers the context within which today's Paramilitary Forces have been raised and gives some of the flavour of their heritage in war and peace. It shows many of the problems and issues faced by the Paramilitary Forces today. It discusses the broad policies within which the Paramilitary Forces must operate, the rationale for those policies and the specific objectives desired as policy outcomes. It discusses the command and control of the Paramilitary Forces, the relationships between advisers and their staffs. It also examines the range of activities undertaken in the name of counterinsurgency and also international peacekeeping under UN and other auspices. Each service's structure, equipment and operating procedures are examined in some detail. This book covers all paramilitary organizations and other organizations that provide assistance to these forces.

In formulation of this book, the author has freely consulted large number of sources so no authenticity is claimed. Author is especially thankful to all those persons who helped in shaping this book in its final form. Suggestions for further improvement of this book are not only welcome but also greatly appreciated.

PART – I
INTRODUCTION

1

Introduction to Paramilitary Forces of India

Paramilitary Forces are those forces whose purpose and functions are like those of a professional military force, but which are not regarded as having the same status. The term Para means 'beside' in Greek. We can define Paramilitary Forces as "Forces or groups that are distinct from the regular armed forces of country, but resembling them in organization, equipment, training, or mission". The word Paramilitary is subjective, depending on what is considered similar to a military force, and what status a force is considered to have. The definition of Paramilitary Forces differs according to the context. For example, in Ireland, Paramilitary means any illegally armed group with a political purpose, but in Colombia, Paramilitary refers specifically to illegally armed groups which are considered right-wing.

Concept of Indian Paramilitary Forces

In India, Paramilitary Forces are those government organizations that help military forces, help in disaster management and control civil agitations. The Paramilitary Forces of India are those agencies of the Ministry of Defence or the Ministry of Home Affairs, which act as armed forces auxiliaries and are considered part of the Indian armed forces. The Paramilitary Forces of India are world's second largest after the Chinese People's Armed Police which has 1.5 million personnel. In 2007, the total strength of the Paramilitary Force was more than 1.5 million.

Main responsibility of protecting our country lies on the shoulders of soldiers of Indian Armed Forces, but apart from courageous efforts of Indian soldiers, the security of India, particularly border security and internal matters are also being dealt by some other courageous men. They are termed as Paramilitary Forces. There are a number of Paramilitary

Forces with a wide variety of roles. These miscellaneous forces broadly follow the role of gendarmerie and carry out counterinsurgency or anti-terrorist missions. These forces also help in maintaining law and order in disturbed areas and provide help during calamities. The Paramilitary Forces of India is regarded as one of the most powerful among other Paramilitary Forces.

In India there are twelve Paramilitary organizations under various Ministries and State Governments. These are Coast Guard Organization, Assam Rifles, Border Security Force, Central Industrial Security Force, Central Reserve Police Force, Indo-Tibetan Border Police, Rashtriya Rifles (National Rifles), National Security Guards, Special Frontier Force and Railway Protection Force. At the state level there is Home Guard Organization, which is controlled by the State Governments. Beside these there are organizations to assist Paramilitary Forces such as National Cadet Corps, Border Road Organization and Territorial Army.

Present Scenario

Presently our Paramilitary Forces are engaged in large number of operations ranging from counterinsurgency to disaster management. In comparison to civilian police forces, Paramilitary Forces may provide a more disciplined force whose military capabilities make them more capable of dealing with all types of violence. On the other hand, the necessity of a more stringent selection process for military service, especially in terms of physical prowess and health, restricts the pool of potential recruits in comparison to those a civilian police force could select from.

Paramilitary Forces may also provide various military or police services. For instance, the Paramilitary Forces are used in border patrolling, crowd and riot control, counter-terrorism, policing at sea, control and security at airports, official buildings, honorary services, VIP protection, rescue and security of important industrial sites.

Paramilitary Forces play an important role re-establishing law and order in conflict areas, a task which is suited to their purpose, training and capabilities. Paramilitary Forces are also used in peacekeeping operations, for instance in the Sri Lanka, Bosnia and in Kosovo. Their primary mission is internal security.

Insurgency: Sixty years after independence, the India finds itself leading a broad alliance of Paramilitary forces engaged in peacemaking, nation-building, and counterinsurgency warfare. Little attention has been paid to the theory and practice of counterinsurgency warfare in conventional studies. Discussions of the so-called revolution in paramilitary affairs and associated technologies for battlefield surveillance and precision targeting dominated planning discourse in the 1990s. Nation-building and peacekeeping discussions rarely addressed counterinsurgency warfare, perhaps because nation-building operations during the 1990s did not confront a determined, violent insurgency.

Meanwhile, with knowledge about counterinsurgency warfare waning among policymakers, resurgent terrorism scholarship and counterterrorism policy initiatives avoided the issue of a strategic terrorist campaign to destabilize nation-building. More recently, vague historical references and misplaced analogies to have muddled discussions of the counterinsurgency effort. Lessons and insights from past low-intensity wars deserve revisiting. They provide perspective as well as context for what may be a defining period for the Indian war on terrorism. What lessons from past counterinsurgencies can inform current efforts? What theoretical and operational issues are available to aid coalition activities? This exploration of why counterinsurgencies fail avoids the experience, a subject that continues to evoke images and arguments that could possibly overshadow the central purpose—that is, discussing the lessons of previous counterinsurgencies and their applicability to Indian strategy. A systematic approach is needed.

Counterinsurgencies require an interlocking system of actions—political, economic, psychological and military. The only way to avoid pitfalls is to fight the specially adapted organization that is common to almost all subversive, violent movements seeking to overthrow the status quo. Presumably steeped in counterinsurgency warfare, CRPF and other units operating against terrorists have learned the lessons of past modern wars. They will not simply sweep towns. This won't defeat an organized insurgency. Instead, the enemy's organization must be targeted to defeat the clandestine organization attempting to impose its will on the people.

Four elements typically encompass an insurgency: cell-networks that maintain secrecy; terror used to foster insecurity among the population and drive them to the movement for protection; multifaceted attempts to cultivate support in the general population, often by undermining the new regime; and attacks against the government. Only by identifying and destroying the infrastructure of the subversive organization can the fledgling government persevere. Stated another way, just as the traditional war is not fought with the individual soldier or platoon in mind but rather the state's capacity and will to continue hostilities, modern war seeks to destroy the organization as a whole and not simply its violent arm or peripheral organs. After comparing the relative resources of the insurgent and government forces, the guerrilla's greatest advantages are his perfect knowledge of an area (which he himself has chosen) and its potential, and the support given him by the inhabitants. To turn this defeat into a victory, the counterinsurgent must recognize that this total dependence upon terrain and population is also the guerrilla's weak point. Three actions are needed: separate the guerrilla from the population that supports him; occupy the zones that the guerrillas previously operated from, making them dangerous for him and turning the people against the guerrilla movement; and coordinate actions over a wide area and for a long enough time that the guerrilla is denied access to the population centres that could support him. This requires an extremely capable intelligence infrastructure endowed with human sources and deep cultural knowledge. Indeed, intelligence is the key. Despite unparalleled improvements in intelligence, the India does not seem to have the depth and breadth required in human intelligence and cultural intelligence arenas.

Intelligence is one of several crucial enablers for defeating an insurgent. Others included a secure area to operate from, sources in the general population and government, maintaining the initiative, and careful management of propaganda. A critical step in any counterinsurgency campaign is the creation of a tight organization to counter the enemy's organizational advantages. Created from the bottom up, based on a full appreciation for the tactical situation, a successful counterinsurgency organization must depart from its standard operational approach to warfare. For example, campaign planning should include a system to account for every citizen, coordination with the political effort to designate a hierarchical network of groups headed by pro-government chiefs, and a system to monitor the activities of guerrilla sympathizers.

This entails a census, the issuing of photo-identification cards, and a countrywide intelligence system. The ultimate goal is to separate the fish from the sea, leaving it exposed to the state's spear. In India it is clearly difficult to weed out insurgents while protecting the forces ability to win the trust of the people and downplay its image as an occupying force. Whenever the commoner feels threatened or afraid, the guerrilla has the upper hand. Protecting basic liberties must be balanced with weeding out subversive elements and threats to stability. Some means and methods are historically ineffective. Routine patrols, isolated ambushes, large-scale sweeps, and even outposts tend to be wasted activities. Of these, outposts are useful when they keep roads and lines of communication open. But none of these activities establishes lines of battle. In previous counterinsurgencies, success required long occupation, something requiring a degree of political will that the current forces may not have.

Present Challenges: Militancy has existed in various forms, mainly in Jammu and Kashmir, the Indian-controlled side of the disputed territory. Kashmir has been the target of a campaign of militancy by all sides in the conflict. Thousands of lives have been lost since 1989 due to the intensified insurgency. Casualties include civilians, Indian security forces, and Kashmiri and non-Kashmiri militants which are supported by Pakistan. The Inter-Services Intelligence of Pakistan has been accused by India of supporting and training mujahideen to fight in Afghanistan and Kashmir.

Though there had been instances of sporadic conflict in many regions for many years, intensified attacks occurred in the late 1980s, when mujahideen fighters from Afghanistan slowly infiltrated the region, allegedly with Pakistan's help, following the end of the Soviet-Afghan War in 1989. Since then, violence has increased significantly in strength. Many separatists have carried out attacks on Indian civilians and Indian army installations in response to what they see as Indian army occupation.

India claims most of the separatist militant groups are based in Pakistan and Pakistan-administered Kashmir. Some like the All Parties Hurriyat Conference and the Jammu and Kashmir Liberation Front, demand an independent Kashmir. Other militant groups such as Lashkar-e-Toiba and Jaish-e-Mohammed favour a Pakistani-Kashmir. These groups have contacts with Taliban and Bin Laden. Both the organizations no longer operate under these names after they were banned by the Indian and Pakistani government, and by other countries including the US and UK. Of the larger militant groups, the Hizbul Mujahideen, a militant organization based in Indian administered Kashmir, unlike other groups, has only kept its name. Despite casualties, the militants are still believed to number thousands rather than hundreds. Several new separatist organizations have also emerged. According to US Intelligence, Al-Qaeda also has a main base in Pakistani Kashmir and is helping to foment terrorism in Jammu and Kashmir.

It is hard to determine the total number of casualties. According to a report by the Government of India in the year 2000, 31, 000 Indian civilians had lost their lives due to the insurgency. Human rights groups and local NGOs put the total figure at more than 84, 000 (2005 figure). Militancy had reached its peak in 1994 when the region saw more than 6, 043 incidents and has since declined. However, Kashmir continues to remain as the most volatile region in the world with an average of 2, 500 incidents every year. According to an Indian estimate in 2005 there were about 2, 000 militants in the Kashmir valley alone; 1, 200 of them belong to the Hizbul Mujahideen. Not all Kashmiri separatists and militant organizations share the same ideology. Some fight in the name of religion, some are pro-Pakistan and some favour an independent Kashmir.

India claims it is the presence of these numerous anti-India insurgent groups that has compelled New Delhi to deploy massive number of troops in Indian administered Jammu and Kashmir for the task of counter insurgency. New Delhi has never made an official count, but military analysts estimate that anywhere from 30, 000 to nearly 33, 000 security personnel are most likely involved, supported by thousands of Indian paramilitary groups such as the Rashtriya rifles, and the Romeo Force (all part of Indian army).

Over the last two years, a militant group, Lashkar-e-Toiba has split into two factions: Al Mansurin and Al Nasirin. Another new group reported to have emerged is the Save Kashmir Movement. Harkat-ul-Mujahideen (formerly known as Harkat-ul-Ansar) and Lashkar-e-Toiba are believed to be operating from Muzaffarabad, Azad Kashmir and Muridke, Pakistan respectively. Other less well known groups are the Freedom Force and Farzandan-e-Milat. A smaller group, Al-Badr, has been active in Kashmir for many years and is still believed to be functioning. All Parties Hurriyat Conference, an organization that uses moderate means to press for the rights of the Kashmiris, is often considered as the mediator between New Delhi and insurgent groups.

Not much is known about collaboration between the various groups, but most say they are members of an alliance known as the United Jihad Council (UJC). The two groups which India says were behind the December 2001 attack on the Indian parliament in New Delhi — known then as Jaish-e-Mohammed and Lashkar-e-Toiba are believed to be members of the UJC. India says that it was Jaish-e-Mohammed that attacked the Jammu and Kashmir State Assembly in Srinagar in October 2001. It is also known that the Jaish-e-Mohammed was responsible for the hijacking of Indian Airlines Flight IC-814 to Kandahar, which forced the Government of India to release Maulana Masood Azhar, the chief of the Jaish-e-Mohammed. Recruits from various parts of the world have been sent to Pakistan-administered Kashmir for training and advice.

The emergence of radical Islamist groups in Kashmir over the last decade has added a new dimension to the ongoing conflict in the region. It has led to a rapid transformation in the terms of discourse in which the conflict is represented, by India, Pakistan and by many Kashmiris themselves. The current stage in the Kashmir conflict can be dated to 1989, when the Jammu and Kashmir Liberation Front (JKLF) inaugurated an armed uprising against Indian rule. By the mid-1990s, however, the JKLF had been increasingly taken over by Pakistan-based Islamist groups. The wiping out of many of its cadres in confrontation with the Indian armed forces, the withdrawal of Pakistani support and the growing realisation of the need for peaceful, as opposed to military, means for the eventual resolution of the Kashmir dispute, seem to be among the major reasons for the gradual decline of the JKLF as a military force in Kashmir, despite the fact that its goal of an independent Kashmir still commands the support of many Kashmiri Muslims. On the other hand, military and other forms of support from the Pakistani establishment, from private jihadist groups in Pakistan and elsewhere, in addition to a passionate zeal for what is seen as a 'holy' cause, account, in large measure, for the gradual take-over of the armed struggle in Kashmir by militant Islamist groups, mainly based in Pakistan and led, for the most part, by Pakistani nationals.

Despite the active involvement of Islamist groups in the on-going struggle in Kashmir, little written has been written about them from a scholarly and detached point of view. Here we seek to provide an account of the ideology, organization and development of one of the leading Islamist groups active in Kashmir today, the Lashkar-i Tayyeba. Of the several Pakistan-based Islamist groups active in Kashmir today, the Lashkar is, by far, the most well-organized, well-trained and heavily armed. From the mid-1990s, this once little known group has emerged today as the most serious challenge to the Indian armed forces, being responsible for several attacks in Kashmir, killing a large number of Indian soldiers as well as civilians, both Hindu as well as Muslim.

India's northeast is a geopolitically strategic region. It comprises eight states — Assam, Arunachal Pradesh, Nagaland, Manipur, Tripura, Mizoram, Meghalaya and Sikkim and is spread over a 262, 179 square kilometres area. The eight states contain a total population of 39 million. India's northeast connects with five countries-Bangladesh, Bhutan, Myanmar, China and Nepal by a 4, 500 kilometres international border; the region, however, connects to India only through a narrow and tenuous land corridor measuring merely 22 kilometres.

A fact that further jeopardizes mainland India's links with the region is the thriving militancy in most of the northeast states. The demands of the different militant groups range from autonomy within the provisions of the Indian constitution to outright secession. Such militant movements started early with India's independence in 1947. At one point, more than 120 militant groups operated in India's northeast. In recent years, the Indian government has had some success in achieving stability in the region, using tactics from negotiations to military operations to rooting out militants. Nevertheless, the region remains a potential tinderbox.

Militants in India's northeast once enjoyed vast popular support since they, in their formative years, voiced genuine grievances of the people such as poor governance, alienation, lack of development and an apathetic attitude from the central government in New Delhi; in recent years, however, this influence has been reduced. Nevertheless, in most of the states in the northeast, anti-government militants retain significant nuisance value and often indulge in successful strikes against government interests.

Nagaland, then part of the larger state of Assam, was the first to experience militancy. Long before the British left India, Nagas considered themselves to be independent and petitioned the British to declare them as an independent country. After being snubbed by both the British and the new regime in New Delhi, Nagas, under the leadership of the Naga National Council (N.N.C.), headed by A.Z. Phizo, declared independence. In his declaration, Phizo argued that in a plebiscite held in Nagaland in May 1951, more than 99 percent of voters favoured independence. The veracity of the plebiscite remains debatable.

Subsequently, the N.N.C. split into different factions and its breakaway faction, the National Socialist Council of Nagaland (N.S.C.N.) also broke into two factions; those factions were the Isak-Muivah faction (N.S.C.N.-I.M.) and the Khaplang faction (N.S.C.N.-K.). These organizations have continued separate violent struggles for Nagaland's independence.

Similarly, Mizoram, which was a part of the state of Assam before it was granted statehood in 1987, experienced militancy after the Union government failed to respond positively to its demand for assistance during the massive Mautam famine. The Mizo National Front (M.N.F.), led by the legendary leader Laldenga, launched the movement on February 28, 1966 and demanded independence for Mizoram.

In Tripura, the smallest of the north-eastern states, migration of Hindus from the British-ruled East Bengal, which subsequently became East Pakistan and then Bangladesh, is believed to have been responsible for reducing the indigenous tribal people in the state to minority status; this development sparked a violent backlash among the indigenous people. Starting in 1970, militant groups sprang up in the state demanding the restoration of the tribal rights from the Bengali population, who are accused of dominating the political and economic affairs of Tripura state.

Migration from Bangladesh, a fact that is refuted by that country, was the source of militancy in the state of Assam as well. A movement that started demanding the deportation of the illegal migrants also witnessed the birth of the militant outfit the United Liberation Front of Asom (U.L.F.A.) in 1979. Following U.L.F.A.'s example, a number of militant groups, each claiming to represent the aspirations of different tribal communities in the state, formed. Prominent among these groups are the Bodo Liberation Tigers, the National Democratic Front of Bodoland (N.D.F.B.), the United People's Democratic Solidarity (U.P.D.S.) and the Dima Halim Daogah.

In the state of Manipur, militancy originated in protest against the forcible merger of the former Manipur Kingdom with India. In 1964, the United National Liberation Front formed with an avowed objective of ending the discrimination against Manipur, which was accorded statehood only in 1972, nearly 23 years after its merger. Subsequently, a number of militant organizations have formed with each representing the cause of different tribes, sometimes more than one outfit espousing the same cause.

Analysts indicate that most of the militant outfits in the region have been quick to transform themselves into purely terrorist entities, bereft of their original objectives and ideology. For example, U.L.F.A. in Assam, which originated as a reaction to Bangladeshi migration into the state, has found shelter in Bangladesh and, through a publication in the 1990s, has repudiated its earlier anti-Bangladeshi position. Militant outfits in Tripura, the National Liberation Front of Tripura (N.L.F.T.) and the All Tripura Tiger Force espousing the tribal cause have indulged in a number of attacks on the tribal population. Militant groups in certain states also have clashed among themselves. For example, in Nagaland, most fatalities are recorded as a result of the infighting between the two factions of the N.S.C.N., rather than from government forces.

With small arms being easily available in the region and in the neighbouring countries, capabilities of even relatively smaller groups to challenge state authority have dramatically grown over the years. As a result, militant groups have successfully transformed themselves into huge abduction and extortion rackets collecting regular contributions from the public, government servants and the business houses. With little protection available from the state government, people have often found it convenient to bribe the militant groups for peace, rather than risk death and abduction.

Role of Paramilitary Forces in Counterinsurgency: Operations using the Paramilitary Forces remain the preferred mode of official response to contain militancy. A strong military presence has been the feature of all the militancy-affected states in the region. The Union government, as a matter of policy, reimburses security-related expenditure incurred by the states. It also has an ongoing program for the modernization of the state police forces that sometimes possess weapons of lesser sophistication than the militants. Interestingly, in all of effected areas, the ratio of policemen per 10, 000 people is far above the national average.

Military operations in affected areas, where the army reportedly launched air strikes to neutralize the terrorist cadres, resulted in several fatalities and displacement among the civilian population. Military operations in Nagaland, too, resulted in civilian fatalities and large-scale displacement. However, such operations have not been able to post conclusive gains against militancy in any of the states. In states like Manipur, militants have been able to carve out vast stretches of "liberated zones" where only their laws and dictates hold sway.

In 2005, with 410 militancy-related deaths, Manipur was the second most violent state in the country behind Jammu and Kashmir. Fencing the 4, 095 kilometre (2, 545 miles) long Indo-Bangladesh border, pitted as the solution to the problems of cross-border militancy as well as illegal migration, has progressed at a tardy pace.

While the government's military options have achieved only minimal results, lack of development continues to alienate the people of the region further from the mainstream. The region has also received little attention from either the national or the international media. Achievements by a separate ministry created by the Indian government for the development of the region remain minimal. With the current trend, the region is expected to remain volatile for the foreseeable future.

Civil Operations

Civil Operations of Paramilitary forces refers to the use of capabilities across a range of operations that fall short of outright war. Operations other than war focus on deterring war, resolving conflict, promoting peace, and supporting civil authorities in response to domestic crises. It may involve elements of both combat and non-combat operations in peacetime, conflict, and war situations. Its purposes may include deterring potential aggressors, protecting national interests, supporting the United Nations or providing humanitarian assistance.

Some of these operations are:

- Combatting Terrorism: This includes antiterrorism and counterterrorism. Antiterrorism programs are defensive measures taken to reduce vulnerability to terrorist acts and form the foundation for effectively combating terrorism. Counterterrorism is offensive measures taken to prevent, deter and respond to terrorism, which provides response measures that include pre-emptive, retaliatory, and rescue operations.
- Anti-smuggling operations
- Humanitarian assistance: These operations relieve or reduce the results of natural or manmade disasters or other endemic conditions such as human pain, disease, hunger, or hardship in regions.
- Support to civil authorities: These operations can consist of temporary augmentation of air traffic controllers and postal workers during strikes, restoration of law and order after a riot, protection of life and property, or providing relief in the aftermath of natural disaster.
- Non-combatant Evacuation Operations.

Recent paramilitary interventions in Kashmir, North-east has sparked controversy by using humanitarian aid to further paramilitary goals. In 1999, forces set up refugee camps for fleeing Kashmiris. Despite the heated rhetoric concerning militarized charity, paramilitary and humanitarian actors offer little examination of its effects. Studies reveal three types of interaction, which are humanitarian soldiers, aid workers as government agents, and the humanitarian placebo. In the absence of adequate security, humanitarian soldiers cannot create stability or meet local humanitarian needs. Additionally, aid organizations face the reality of non-neutrality, and may be considered as de facto government agents, if they operate in close proximity to forces.

Recent paramilitary interventions have sparked controversy by using humanitarian aid to advance paramilitary goals. The prevailing discussion of paramilitary involvement in humanitarian activity usually fails to differentiate among the various types of interactions that occur. Our analysis distinguishes two main ways that humanitarian action can function as a force multiplier during a paramilitary intervention. In the first type of interaction, the paramilitary engages in humanitarian activity as part of a strategic plan. In the second type, the reverse occurs—humanitarian organizations fulfil paramilitary or political goals for sponsoring governments. The third form of interaction—what is termed as humanitarian placebo effect—results when government deploy humanitarian organizations in lieu of political or paramilitary engagement. All three types of interaction can politicize humanitarian assistance, regardless of intentions.

Two main insights emerge from the analysis of paramilitary and humanitarian interaction in recent interventions. The first is that humanitarian action undertaken in an insecure environment can actually intensify violence and endanger civilians. The identity of the aid givers—paramilitary or humanitarian—is less important than the need for security as a prerequisite to providing aid. This may be unpalatable to paramilitary planners who hope that reconstruction activity can create a secure environment. It cannot. The strategic use of humanitarian assistance cannot fill a security vacuum, and may well exacerbate insecurity. In an active conflict, combatants will view humanitarian assistance as a political, and even paramilitary, resource.

Second, this confirms that neutrality is impossible during many paramilitary interventions. Neutrality is an ideal, not a reality. When aid workers operate in close proximity to Western Paramilitary Forces, all sides will inevitably view the aid workers as political actors. For their own safety, and that of the aid recipients, humanitarian organizations are now forced to consider the potential political ramifications of humanitarian action, even if they would prefer to avoid politics altogether.

Recent paramilitary interventions have featured government provision of humanitarian assistance to civilians, even while the same government conducts paramilitary attacks. Among its practitioners, paramilitary involvement in aid provision, sometimes known as "hearts and minds" operations, is thought to increase stability, win local allies, and bolster international legitimacy. Paramilitary expertise in logistics and planning leads to an often unspoken assumption that paramilitary provision of aid will efficiently meet civilian needs. Strict adherence to humanitarian ideals of neutrality and impartiality are seen as a hindrance to effectiveness, rather than integral to success. Although aid workers express resentment of the paramilitary role in humanitarian activity, there is little understanding of the actual effects of paramilitary provision of aid on security and humanitarian conditions.

Critiques of the humanitarian soldier model often fail to differentiate among the various roles the paramilitary plays in providing aid. One can see that the least controversial intervention occurs when a Paramilitary Force responds to a natural disaster without using force. For example, the use of CRPF to aid flood victims. The rescue mission did not require the use of force and was viewed as strictly humanitarian. Governments also deploy the paramilitary in the service of humanitarian goals during crises such as the massive flood in Orissa in 2006. During that crisis, aid agencies relied on paramilitary logistical expertise to cope with the problem.

Tensions between aid organizations and Paramilitary Forces rise when both groups are operating in the same arena, but for different purposes. When paramilitary provision of aid seems driven by strategic goals, such as the recent interventions, aid agencies bristle at the infringement on their "turf" and the perversion of humanitarian principles of neutrality and impartiality.

Three high-profile interventions in Kashmir, north-east and naxalite areas demonstrate increasing paramilitary reliance on humanitarian action. A number of aspects of this crisis differentiate it from the current conflicts. Additionally, the humanitarian and paramilitary campaigns occurred in different geographical areas.

Aid workers are also worried by the increasing danger surrounding their work. Humanitarian organizations are sharply divided about the proper role for security forces. Attacks against aid workers, including abduction and killings, have effectively curtailed the activities of NGOs.

Security threats have forced radical changes on the standard operating procedures for the remaining aid organizations. Most organizations have essentially gone underground—removing identification from their vehicles and offices and attempting anonymity in their daily activities. In other crises, NGOs rely on their reputations as neutral charitable organizations to protect them. They emblazon their logos on cars, t-shirts, banners, and provisions. Publicity also is used for fundraising campaigns for Western publics. Some paramilitary planners view security and economic development as a chicken and egg problem. It is thought that better economic development and services will decrease security threats and pacify the population. This reasoning has led forces to attempt humanitarian and economic development work. The continued attacks on infrastructure reveal the fallacy of that logic. The attackers actually view increased electricity output and oil exports as threats rather than inducements. Without adequate security, such economic and humanitarian measures are doomed.

Recent trends in antiterrorism policy stress preventing state failure and alleviating poverty as valuable tools to combat the spread of Terror. This thinking has led paramilitary planners to embrace humanitarian assistance and development aid as counterterrorism strategies. For example, the paramilitary has undertaken public works projects in remote villages as a way to build support, as well as keep the area under surveillance for terrorist activity. Local leaders in the villages expressed a mixture of suspicion and gratitude at the paramilitary presence. Like other traditional hearts and minds operations, initiatives seek to pacify a potentially hostile population by demonstrating the goodwill and power of the donor.

Aid workers are generally highly critical of paramilitary provision of humanitarian aid. Many humanitarian organizations argue that humanitarian soldiers violate the principles of neutrality and impartiality. NGOs also worry that armed humanitarian operations do not meet civilian needs efficiently and ignore potentially deserving recipients who do not fit the strategic goals of the aid distribution.

Humanitarian soldiers certainly cannot claim neutrality, especially when they are part of an ongoing paramilitary intervention such as in Afghanistan. But an essential question is whether the lack of neutrality means that soldiers cannot meet humanitarian goals. It is not sufficient to cite the breach of the principles of neutrality and impartiality as evidence that humanitarian soldiers create negative outcomes. It is also inadequate, if not misleading, for humanitarian organizations to claim that their neutral and impartial intentions lead to non-political outcomes. Regardless of intentions, injecting resources into a conflict zone affects the actions and calculations of the combatants.

Proponents of paramilitary aid provision point out that in some instances the environment is too risky for aid workers to operate. Many NGOs respond that in such dangerous situations, the paramilitary actors should devote their efforts to creating secure conditions for the humanitarians to work. The solution to an insecure environment is not using soldiers as aid workers but a division of responsibility in which the paramilitary provides security and the NGOs provide humanitarian assistance.

The ongoing insecurity indicates that paramilitary provision of humanitarian aid is an expensive distraction from the core mission of stabilizing those states. If even Paramilitary Forces cannot perform humanitarian tasks adequately while under constant threat of attack, certainly aid workers cannot. No matter who provides humanitarian assistance to a needy population-soldiers or aid workers-security is a prerequisite for success. It is unrealistic to expect the inverse: humanitarian assistance will not achieve security. Perhaps over time, improved humanitarian conditions will aid stability or economic growth. But humanitarian aid is an inappropriate tool for quelling rebellion or imposing law and order. In the absence of security, humanitarian resources can actually encourage violence—especially when they are appropriated by militants.

Reconstruction & Rehabilitation Operations

The convergence between paramilitary and nonparamilitary tasks has accelerated over the past ten years as forces seek to defeat the insurgencies in Kashmir and North-East. One result of this convergence is an increased role for Paramilitary Forces in the conduct of humanitarian missions previously viewed as the sole preserve of nongovernmental organizations. This transition is reflected in a greater emphasis on reconstruction activities by the paramilitary in contemporary operations.

To some extent, most paramilitary organizations involved in Kashmir and North-East now appreciate the requirement for paramilitary units to conduct reconstruction operations as part of their normal missions. At the strategic level, the government have established offices for developing a more coherent approach to building activities. Reconstruction Teams established over the last several years are evidence of this. These may have a limited impact in some higher threat areas because of a lack of sufficient, integral intelligence, surveillance, and reconnaissance and force protection assets.

A more robust approach to paramilitary-led reconstruction operations would see organizations with increased mobility, a strengthened capability, and enhanced security. This self-contained capability will allow for the conduct of reconstruction operations where and when required. If the indigenous capacity is weak and nongovernmental organizations are unable to work securely, such an organization can make a significant contribution to shaping the opinions and perceptions of the local population. We examine here the contribution of paramilitary-led reconstruction operations as part of a unified counterinsurgency campaign. These operations require the precise, discriminate application of nonkinetic effects to support the overall campaign plan in an effort to defeat contemporary and future insurgencies. Such operations require the allocation of significant combat support elements such as engineers and civil affairs, and should be synchronized within a joint, interagency application of national resources in support of the counterinsurgency effort. The ultimate aim of these operations is to coerce or persuade target populations to support friendly forces over insurgents.

Reconstruction operations play a vital role within the broader conduct of a counterinsurgency campaign. In many respects, the effects of reconstruction activities will have a more enduring influence than tactical, nonkinetic operations. This is not to minimize the importance of robust combat forces; there will always be a need to target certain insurgent elements for destruction. But the population-centric nature of counterinsurgency means that kinetic operations may often play a supporting role for other nation-building activities. The ability of the counterinsurgent to achieve the right balance between precise, discriminate kinetic and non-kinetic actions will have a major impact on how successfully local populations can be influenced.

Given the number of civilian agencies and the depth of their capabilities and experience, some may question the rationale for an expanded role for paramilitary organizations in reconstruction operations. The harsh reality is that in many areas such as Leh, tenuous security conditions prevent many aid groups and other government agencies from establishing a presence. In some instances these aid organizations are deliberately targeted by insurgent groups in an effort to prevent them from gaining a foothold and becoming effective in assisting the local populace. In spite of these negative influences, the need for reconstruction operations in support of security missions remains. This capacity is best provided by highly capable organizations that possess an integral mobility and protection capability permitting the conduct of reconstruction operations with minimal interference from insurgents. Only paramilitary organizations, particularly paramilitary engineers, possess the ability to conduct reconstruction activities while concurrently providing robust self-protection.

Paramilitary-led reconstruction operations provide time and space for indigenous capacity to backfill existing paramilitary programs and functions. They also allow for the eventual integration of nongovernmental and aid organizations. This is not to say that reconstruction operations occur only after kinetic operations have terminated. The key to any successful counterinsurgency campaign is the commencement of reconstruction activities from the very beginning of the campaign. Such campaigns and their accompanying strategies require some cultural adjustment in most western paramilitary organizations. In traditional, conventional operations, the enemy is the object. Their defeat or destruction is the key goal of Paramilitary Forces. Consequently, forces combat units have primacy on the battlefield and are supported by a range of combat support and combat service support organizations. In complex insurgencies, however, when opposed by insurgents, the population is the object. As a consequence, the main effort becomes the effects generated by those paramilitary (combat support and service support) organizations that are best suited to provide support to population operations and the rebuilding of indigenous capacity. Security operations, conducted by combat units, should be integrated into these population support operations.

The conduct of large-scale reconstruction operations by paramilitary organizations may require a reallocation of resources from kinetic security operations into what has traditionally been support roles, such as construction and civil liaison. While undertaking reconstruction, paramilitary engineers may also teach the local populace basic trade skills and the planning and conduct of construction tasks, while ensuring that the indigenous capacity to execute such skills and tasks is constantly improving. Providing skills improvement to the local population is an effective way to assist disrupted populations in helping themselves and is a key element of any exit strategy.

In the conduct of reconstruction operations, both the populace and the nascent indigenous government often require additional support. This should be done concurrently, both to enhance the legitimacy of the government and to maintain the credibility of the Paramilitary Forces performing the reconstruction operations in the eyes of the local populace. This two-tiered approach could be described as a top-down—bottom-up approach. Such an approach is best exemplified by the conduct of concurrent operations to rebuild government institutions and infrastructure (top-down), while at the same time conducting small-scale missions to assist the people in individual towns and villages (bottom-up) based on community priorities.

Reconstruction undertaken in the top-down category should wherever possible be based on the priorities of provincial officials. This requires detailed consultation and interaction with local inhabitants and their representatives. It also requires the development of a relationship where both sides are able to build trust and candidly discuss the projects that will benefit the local populace, not just those benefiting local officials. These projects will normally be significant in their scale and scope, for example, the wide-scale construction of schools, roads, or healthcare facilities. The duration of these projects will probably take a fairly long time and should involve significant contributions from local contractors.

Consultation with local officials and other interested parties will be a critical aspect of prioritizing the reconstruction projects. It is worth establishing a formal mechanism, involving all stakeholders, to facilitate community and government consultation. This interaction should include regular meetings with officials and local inhabitants to work out the details of individual projects, ensuring that what will be delivered is what the locals need.

It is also worth considering the adoption of a minimum level of local labour content for every contract signed with local construction companies. The threefold aim of such a plan is to keep locals employed in constructive endeavours, foster the transfer of work skills, and inject money into the local economy. To enhance employment opportunities for local people, a benchmark percentage of local labour should be set for every project. This can be reinforced by making it a contractual obligation. When contractors fail to meet this benchmark, they should not be allowed onto worksites. If contractors identify during the tendering process that the technical nature of a project would prevent them reaching this minimum level of local labour involvement, that fact should be part of the contract negotiations.

Bottom-up reconstruction requires detailed consultation with local officials, not just at the provincial level but at the community level. Once again, the quality of this interaction with community leaders depends on the trust that is established with the various paramilitary elements. The importance of these bottom-up operations is twofold. First, they provide an immediate and tangible justification for the presence of foreign Paramilitary Forces. If local people see immediate benefits resultant of this presence, they are less likely to provide support to insurgents. The second advantage of this type of project (also known as quick-impact projects) is that they provide time and space for the completion of the larger scale—and longer duration—reconstruction projects in the top-down category.

The second part of this conceptual model for paramilitary-led reconstruction operations is a dual focus on physical and intellectual (capacity-building) reconstruction. As impressive as new hospitals, clinics, schools, bridges, and other infrastructure may be, the capacity of local people to staff this infrastructure and maintain it in the long-term is of overwhelming importance. Consequently, reconstruction operations need to undertake capacity-building—paramilitary and civilian training and education—as a foundation for the entry of a broader range of government agencies to assume these functions once the security situation permits. It should be emphasized, however, that capacity-building cannot wait until other government agencies are totally mobilized—these actions should be undertaken from the beginning of any paramilitary operation. This will ensure, once again, the local populace will see a tangible benefit from the presence of Paramilitary Forces. It should also ensure that those that may be tempted to support any insurgents have other options.

A consistent theme in the approach of government and nongovernmental organizations to nation-building is capacity-building. The significant contribution this type of activity may provide is often underappreciated. Training in basic trade courses can also be undertaken by paramilitary units. Not only will this contribute to increased basic skills among the local youth, it can also play an important role in information operations. Mentoring of local officials by experts (paramilitary) should also be undertaken. Selective recruiting or contracting of experienced experts in such areas as education, economics, and municipal planning and administration may significantly improve the capacity of the local populace to improve civil infrastructure. Investing in basic capacity-building activities enhances the ability of the local population to play a positive role in the reconstruction of infrastructure and communities.

A critical element of this strategy requires support to capacity-building enablers. A logical step is to combine physical construction with indigenous capacity-building through the development of educational infrastructure. The construction of infrastructure such as schools to train the paramilitary, healthcare professionals, and training centres is an example. If this training is reinforced through the partnering of paramilitary, police, and government organizations with friendly Paramilitary Forces from the sponsoring countries, the training is likely to be more enduring.

By overlaying these two approaches, a simple but durable paramilitary concept for guiding the conduct of reconstruction operations is enabled. Such an approach ensures that reconstruction projects not only have an immediate impact, but capacity-building that may be incorporated into each project ensures a whole of life approach for the maintenance, training, and development of management skills by government officials.

Paramilitary-led reconstruction operations play a key role in a cohesive approach to the conduct of successful counterinsurgency operations. Such an approach requires the precise, discriminate application of nonkinetic effects in support of a unified campaign plan. The conduct of reconstruction operations does not negate the requirement for robust combat forces. Kinetic operations, however, play a supporting role in population-centric, counterinsurgency warfare. The ability of the counterinsurgent to achieve the proper balance between precise, discriminate kinetic and non-kinetic actions will have a major impact on how successfully local populations are influenced.

Ensuring paramilitary reconstruction operations are based on sound intelligence is one key to success. The integration of intelligence ensures precision; that projects are conducted where and when they are needed. It also provides discrimination; that deployments to small villages for community projects are supporting the right people while negating any bias toward a particular ethnic or tribal group. Likewise, the synchronization of reconstruction operations with NGOs and other government agencies will play a central role in the success of these operations.

The paramilitary's involvement in reconstruction operations, and the manner in which they are conducted, provide a highly capable, complementary function to the array of kinetic means currently employed in Kashmir and other areas. The mix of construction and internal security is a powerful combination capable of supporting the conduct of kinetic activities in a counterinsurgency environment. Every insurgency is unique; however, paramilitary-led reconstruction operations do provide the counterinsurgent with a powerful tool to shift support of the populace away from insurgents. Possessing the ability to destroy the enemy and make them irrelevant to the population through reconstruction operations is a powerful tool in any synchronized counterinsurgency strategy.

REFERENCES

Annual Report 2005-2006, Ministry of Home Affairs, Government of India.

Annual Report 2006-2007, Ministry of Home Affairs, Government of India.

Chaudhuri, K. C.: History of Ancient India, Central, Calcutta, 1982.

CIA World Factbook 2005: India.

Coffee Land News, Jan. 2000.

Frontline, Aug. 28, 1999.

General K. V. Krishna Rao: Prepare or Perish - A Study of National Security, Lancer, 1991.

India Today, Oct. 11, 1999.

Indian Defence Review, Jan. 1993.

Indian Defence Review, July 1991

Indian Express, Aug. 12, 1997.

Indian Express, Dec. 16, 1997

Indian Express, Dec. 06, 1999.

Indian Express, July 24, 1999.

Indian Express, July 06, 1999.

Indian Express, May 01, 2000.

Indian Express, May 18, 1999.

Indian Express, May 08, 1999.

Jacob, JRF (Lt. Gen), IDR, The defence scene and the budget: An appraisal.

Joshi, Manoj, The lost rebellion.

Praval K. C.: Indian Army After Independence, Lancer, 1987.

Ken Conboy: Elite Forces of India and Pakistan, Osprey, 1992.

Kundu A.: Militarism in India: The Army and Civil Society in Consensus.

Lieutenant General Depinder Singh: IPKF in Sri Lanka, Trishul, 1992.

Lieutenant General Sardeshpande, UYSM, AVSM (Retd),

Assignment Jaffna, Lancer, 1992.

V. P. Malhotra: Encyclopaedia of Indian Army, Anmol, New Delhi 2006.

Mohan M. Mathews, India: Facts and Figures, Sterling Publishers Pvt. Ltd., 2002.

Nayar, KK, (Vice Admiral), Amar Jawan - A Book of Remembrance, India Book House.

The Daily Excelsior, July 30, 1999.

The Daily Excelsior, Oct. 15, 1999.

The Doon City Cronicle, June 1999.

The Hindu, Jan. 27, 1997.

The Times of India, 18 Nov. 1984.

The Tribune, Aug. 20, 1998.

The Tribune, July 16, 1999.

Vayu Aerospace Review, VI, 1993.

2

Ministerial Classification of Paramilitary Forces of India

In India there are twelve Paramilitary organizations under various Ministries and State Governments. Paramilitary Forces under Ministry of Defence is Coast Guard Organization. Paramilitary Forces under Ministry of Home Affairs are Assam Rifles, Border Security Force, Central Industrial Security Force, Central Reserve Police Force, Indo-Tibetan Border Police and Rashtriya Rifles (National Rifles). Paramilitary Forces under Prime Minister Office are National Security Guards and Special Frontier Force. Paramilitary Forces under Ministry of Railway is Railway Protection Force. At the state level there is Home Guard Organization, which is controlled by the State Governments. Beside these there are organizations to assist Paramilitary Forces such as National Cadet Corps and Border Roads Organization.

Paramilitary Forces under Ministry of Defence

Coast Guard Organization: The origin of Coast Guard began in 1977. It was the outcome of an understanding that had been growing for some time in India for the need to employ national laws in the waters under national jurisdiction and make sure safety of life and property at sea. It was also considered that these law enforcement tasks should be undertaken by a service suitably capable of and based on the models of the Coast Guards of nations like USA and UK leaving the navy to use the fleet for its wartime role.

A committee was constituted under the chairmanship of Mr K.F. Rustamji in September 1974 to study the problem of seaborne smuggling and setting up a Coast Guard type of organization. This committee suggested the setting up of a Coast Guard Service modelled on the navy for universal supervision and patrolling of seas in peace time under administrative cover of Ministry of Defence. The Maritime Zones of India Act was approved on 25 August 1976. Under this Act, India claimed 2.1 million square kilometre of sea area in which it has the special rights for exploration and exploitation of resources at sea. Following this, a cabinet resolution was passed by which an temporary Coast Guard Organization came into being on 01 February 1977. The Coast Guard in its present shape was formally inaugurated on 18 August 1978 as an independent armed force with the enactment of the Coast Guard Act 1978 by the Parliament with its motto as "Vayam Rakshamah" meaning "We Protect".

Coast Guard Started its operation in year 1978 as an armed Paramilitary force. The general running, direction and control of the Coast Guard is exercised by the Director General of Coast Guard. Its charter of duties includes; Safety and protection of offshore installations and artificial islands, Providing protection to fishermen in distress, Protection of maritime environment, Assisting customs in anti-smuggling operations, Enforcement of MZI (Maritime Zones of India) Act, Safety of life and property at sea.

Total coastline of India is divided into three Coast Guard Regions: Western region, Eastern region and Andaman and Nicobar Islands region. The regional headquarters are located at Mumbai, Chennai and Port Blair. These regions are managed by their respective Commanders.

These regions are further separated into eleven Coast Guard districts based on our maritime states. There are Four on the east coast, namely Chennai, Vishakhapatnam, Paradip and Haldia There are five district headquarters on the west coast, namely Porbandar, Mumbai, Goa, New Mangalore and Kochi and two district headquarters in Andaman and Nicobar Islands, namely, Diglipur and Campbell Bay. In addition, there are Coast Guard stations and air enclaves at different locations. The Coast Guard is headed by a Director-General stationed at its headquarters in New Delhi.

Coast Guard started with two frigates and five seaward defence boats (SDBs) and with passing time, the service has developed into a full-fledged maritime organization with nine offshore patrol vessels (OPVs), two advanced offshore patrol vessels (AOPVs), twenty-four fast patrol vessels (FPVs), fifteen interceptor boats (IBs), seventeen Dornier aircrafts and fifteen Chetak Helicopters. Thus we can see the quick progress Coast Guard made in the last 28 years.

The Coast Guard is the main organization for enforcing national rules and regulations in the maritime zones of India and provides diverse services to the nation and marine community. It ensures safety and protection of the artificial islands, offshore installations and other structure in our maritime zones. It provides protection to fishermen and also assists them at sea while in distress. It preserves and protects our maritime environment including prevention and control of maritime pollution. It assists department of custom and other authorities in anti-smuggling operations. It enforces MZI Acts. It initiates measures for the safety of life and property at sea.

Thus we can see that Coast Guard is an organization with multi-mission public service agenda with long-term as well as short-term calculated goals. Most of its duties are related to fishermen and their livelihoods. But it can be deployed for law and treaty enforcement, as well as for humanitarian, environmental and military goals. The strategic role of the Coast Guard is to guard the maritime zones from illegal activities including penetration through maritime routes, and environmental damage, and provide humanitarian and scientific assistance within the maritime domain.

Paramilitary Forces under Ministry of Home Affairs

The Ministry for Home Affairs controls most of the Paramilitary Forces. The police are a civil authority subordinate to the executive, represented in the union government by the prime minister and in the states by the chief minister, and their respective councils of ministers. Prominent among the union police forces are Border Security Force (BSF), Central Reserve Police Force (CRPF), Central Industrial Security Force (CISF) and the Indo-Tibetan Border Police (ITBP), Rashtriya Rifles and Assam Rifles.

Each of these forces is headed by a Director/Director-General with the status of a three-star General in the army. Increased use of Paramilitary Forces against separatist insurgencies and communal unrest has given the home ministry increasing day-to-day control over law and order operations. The central government provides guidance and support through use of national Paramilitary Forces and in law has ultimate responsibility for protecting the fundamental rights guaranteed under the Constitution. The bulk of the Indian police is comprised of forces in the states.

Each state has its own force headed by a Director-General of police (DGP) who is equivalent in rank to his counterpart in the union government forces. A number of additional Directors-General or Inspectors-General of Police (IGP) who look after various portfolios, such as personnel, law & order, crime, armed police, training, and technical services are located at the state police headquarters and report straight to the DGP. Major cities in a state are headed by a commissioner of police (CP) who, again, reports to the DGP.

Assam Rifles: Assam Rifles is a Paramilitary organization of the ministry of home affairs working under the operational control of the army. Until 1947, the force comprised of only five battalions and was part of civil police under the Inspector General of Police, Assam. After independence a full-fledged Inspector General was appointed as head of the force, the first being Mr HG Bartley. Since 1948 the Inspector General has traditionally been an army officer on deputation.

There was little cultural or other contact between the mainland of India and the north-eastern corner of the sub-continent before nineteenth century. It was not until the early nineteenth century that Assam was drawn into the mainstream of India. Today the former area of Assam have been regrouped politically in seven different states of India, namely Meghalaya, Assam, Mizoram, Arunachal Pradesh, Tripura, Nagaland and Manipur. The "Sentinels of the North-East" aptly epitomizes the role of the Assam Rifles.

The story of this force begins with British attempt to extend their rule into the North-Eastern tracts of India in the latter part of eighteenth century and early nineteenth century. A small force of 750 combatants, called the Cachar Levy, was raised in the year 1835. This small force was ill equipped, ill armed and was conceived as an armed police unit to guard the settlements and tea estates against ravages by local tribes. The title of the force has undergone many changes; Cachar Levy, Assam Military Police, Frontier Police and so on. From its very inception, the force has been actively involved in various operations and the jawans have grown up amidst expeditions and combat.

During World War I, the force provided as many as 23 officers and 3, 174 soldiers to gorkha regiments of the Indian army besides whom they fought in Europe and the Middle East. After World War I, the Assam Rifles undertook many expeditions into remote tribal areas of the North-East and some trans-border expeditions into Burma. During World War II, Assam Rifles covered itself with glory with the exemplary performance of its platoons. They fought far into Burmese territory behind the enemy lines and later fought doggedly in the defence boxes established along the line from Kohima to Ukhrul.

During Indo-China war, force fought bravely. They thus provided the desired delay to enable the Indian army to reach their battle locations. The Assam Rifles once again proved that they were entirely dependable.

Today, the force comprises of the Directorate General Assam Rifles at Shilong, the controlling headquarters, one inspector general headquarters, seven range headquarters and thirty one battalions deployed all over the North-Eastern region. It has its own training centre for training recruits drawn from various parts of the country. The Assam Rifles has obtained an all India responsibility as a central Paramilitary force. Its battalions are employed all over India and also in UN peace keeping Missions.

Presently, force is deployed primarily in the north-east. It helps administration in the maintenance of law and order, assisting the army in counter insurgency duties, and the common welfare of the locals and development of the inaccessible areas.

Border Security Force: From the time of independence in 1947 to 1965, our international boundaries were guarded by the local armed police battalions of every border state. When Pakistan attacked India, the inadequacies of the existing border management setup in coping with external armed aggression were exposed. The central government then sanctioned the formation of the Border Security Force (BSF), a unified, central agency with the specific function of guarding India's international boundaries. The BSF was seen in action in the Indo-Pakistani War of 1971 in areas where the army was thinly spread. A notable battle in which BSF troops performed well was the Battle of Longewala in western India.

When insurgency started in Jammu and Kashmir state in 1989, the existing security set-up struggled to cope with the spiralling violence. The Government then decided to induct the BSF. Formed to guard India's external boundaries, the BSF has additional task of tackling insurgency within the country, along with the Indian army. After initially suffering heavy casualties to hit-and-run terrorist attacks by jihadists, the BSF successfully set up an intelligence network in Jammu & Kashmir with the help of local civilians opposed to the jihad. Steadily, the BSF began to reap the rewards and successfully liquidated and arrested a large number of militants.

The BSF, in its 41 years of existence, has emerged as an elite force of the country having excelled with distinction in the 1971 war with Pakistan. Its ethos is "Any task, any time, any where" and the BSF has proved itself and done proud to its motto "Duty Unto Death".

The main role of BSF is security of border of India. The functions of the BSF can be divided in two parts; During Peacetime and During War Time. During Peacetime its function is to promote a sense of security among the people living in the border areas, to prevent trans border crimes, unauthorized entry into or exit from the territory of India, to prevent smuggling and any other illegal activity, holding ground in less threatened sectors, Protection of vital installations, assistance in control of refugees and anti-infiltration duties in specified areas. In the last few years the BSF has, in addition to their duties, been deployed for counter insurgency and internal security duties. One of its major role today is border fencing, flood lighting and construction of border roads.

BSF contributes every year a number of personnel for services for UN Mission in Kosovo and Bosnia. During the Kargil conflict in May-July 1999, the BSF remained on the heights of the mountains and defended the integrity of the country with all the might at its command in unison with the Army. BSF personnel have been performing internal security duty in Manipur for the last two years and have been successfully fighting insurgency in those areas. During the earthquake in Gujarat on 26 January 2001, the BSF was the first to reach out to help the distressed people. During the communal disturbances in Gujarat recently, BSF personnel went all out to restore amity and brotherhood among the people. The BSF took over the erection of the border fencing in Jammu & Kashmir and it was successful in its task despite all attempts of Pakistan to scuttle our efforts. The BSF has been defending the borders along with the army and checking infiltration on the borders during the current standoff with Pakistan.

Central Industrial Security Force: Central Industrial Security Force was established under the Central Industrial Security Force Act of 10 March 1969. It consists of approximately 90, 000 personnel whose main duty is to guard public-sector areas. The Central Industrial Security Force is responsible for security services at ports and other transportation facilities, as well as various other facilities.

The Central Industrial Security Force had encountered some problems in past. In 1996, the Madras Port Trust board approved a plan for disbanding the Central Industrial Security Force (CISF) at the Madras port, and creating the port's own security force by either borrowing from the State police force or by recruiting directly or by other means.

But Government passed a law stating that all the government-run institutions, including public sector undertakings [PSUs], are required to employ guards from Central Industrial Security Force. At times of general elections to Lok Sabha and to the Legislative Assemblies, the State Governments generally seek assistance of the central government offices and departments located in the states for deployment of their employees in connection with the conduct of elections. The civil employees of Central Industrial Security Force may also assist in election duty. The physical security of India's nuclear installations is managed by the Central Industrial Security Force (CISF).

The CISF provides security cover to 267 PSUs located all over the country. This list comprises vital industrial sectors like atomic power plants, space installations, defence production units, mints, oil fields and refineries, major ports, heavy engineering, steel plants, barrages, fertilizer units, airports and hydro electric/thermal power plants. Most of these installations are located in difficult terrains of the country with extreme climates. Besides providing protection, safety, and security to Industrial undertaking/installations, CISF also offers protection against fire hazards. CISF also provides consultancy services for security of private industries and organizations.

CISF is only Paramilitary force in India having a highly specialised, trained and fully equipped fire wing. The first fire wing unit with a strength of 53 personnel was inducted in Cochin. Till date, the fire wing has 81 units. The present strength of the Fire Wing is 5028 personnel. The fire wing which is an integral part of Central Industrial Security Force is the largest, well trained and equipped fire fighting force in the government sector.

It is known as an outstanding fire fighting force having an enviable record. It is providing fire coverage to establishments varying from power plants, refineries, petro-chemicals, fertilizers, steel plants surface transport, heavy industries, space application centre etc. Fire wing induction in the undertaking is not limited to providing manpower to fight fire alone. It also ensures availability of proper and adequate devices for fire prevention and fire fighting along with the fire fighting staff.

Central Reserve Police Force: CRPF was originally created as CRP(Crown Representative Police) in 1939, with 2 battalions. Its primary duty at that time was to protect the British residents in sensitive areas. In 1949, it was renamed CRPF under the CRPF Act. The Sixties saw major expansion of CRPF in which many state reserve police battalions were merged with CRPF. CRPF has been active against foreign invasion and domestic insurgency.

The Central Reserve Police Force is an armed force of the union of India, with the basic role of striking reserve to assist the state/union territories in police operations to maintain law and order and contain insurgency. Its role is that of a catalyst in maintaining law & order, and returns to barracks once this objective is achieved. The force is also being used for various police duties in various states. It is all India in character, both in deployment and in its composition. Due to its unique capability to quickly adapt to various situational requirements, and also, to work in perfect harmony with the state police, CRPF has, over the years, acquired the distinction of being perhaps the most acceptable force, by the people and the State administrations. Broad range of duties performed by the CRPF is; Crowd control, Riot control, Counter millitancy/insurgency operations, Dealing with left wing extremism, Overall co-ordination of large scale security arrangement specially with regard to elections in distrubed areas, Protection of VIPs and vital installations, Checking environmental de-gradation and protection of local flora and fauna, Fighting aggression during war time, Participating in UN peace keeping mission, Rescue and relief operations at the time of natural calamities.

Besides law and order and counter insurgency duties, the role of CRPF in the general elections has been very significant and vital. This is especially true for the trouble torn states of J&K, Bihar and States of North-East. During the parliamentary elections of September 1999, the CRPF played a major role in the security arrangements. One of the vital roles of the CRPF, which is not very evident, is guarding vital central govt. installations such as airport, power houses, bridges, doordarshan kendras, all India radio stations, residence of governors and chief ministers, nationalised banks and other government establishments in insurgency affected states.

The CRPF is ensuring the safety of the democratic institutions, and preventing the take over of civil society by the militants in highly disturbed areas. This contribution of the CRPF, though not very visible, is nonetheless very vital. 7.5% of the force is deployed for the security of VIPs mostly in northeastern States, J&K, Bihar and Andhra Pradesh, which include governors, chief ministers, ministers, MPs and MLAs of J&K, Assam, Arunachal Pradesh, Manipur and Nagaland, Tripura and Mizoram.

CRPF is also providing security at the residence/office of prime minister of India, various union ministers and MPs and other dignitaries. 17.5% of the force is deputed for guarding the important installations of central and state govenment mostly in insurgency affected areas which includes secretariats, doordarshan kendras, telephone exchanges, banks, hydroelectric projects, jails etc. CRPF is also deployed for the security of parliament house.

Indo-Tibetan Border Police: The Indo Tibetan Border Police is a Paramilitary Force formed in 1962 for security along the Indo-Tibetan Border. ITBP is a multi-dimensional force. Presently, battalions of ITBP are deployed on border guarding duties from Karakoram Pass in Ladakh to Diphu La in Arunachal Pradesh covering India China Border. ITBP is basically a mountain trained force and most of the officers & men are professionally trained mountaineers and skiers. They have scaled more than 140 Himalayan peaks including Mt. Everest three times.

ITBP Batallions are also deployed on anti terrorism duties and VIP security duties in startegic locations and with VIPs in Delhi and Srinagar. ITBP conducts long range and short range patrols to keep an effective vigil on inaccessible and unmanned areas on the border. To maintain optimum operational efficiency of troops, periodical tactical exercises are conducted independently as well as jointly with army.

One role of ITBP is dısaster management. Being the first responder for natural disaster in Himalayas, ITBP was the first to establish eight regional response centres in HP, Uttaranchal and North-East and carried out numerous rescue and relief operations in various disaster situations, which took place in various parts of the country. ITBP has already trained personnel in disaster management including 98 personnel in radiological and chemical/biological emergencies. ITBP has established a national centre for training in search, rescue & disaster response at Bhanu, Haryana which is imparting training to personnel of ITBP and other paramilitary/ state police forces. There is also a training centre for the dogs at basic training centre situated at Bhanu.

ITBP commandos are also providing security to Indian embassy at Kabul, Consulate General Jalalabad and Khandar in Afghanistan. ITBP are also providing security to border road organization personnel for their Delaram – Zaranj road construction project in Afghanistan. ITBP has also excelled in UN peacekeeping operation. The force personnel have been deployed for peacekeeping operations in Angola, Namibia, Cambodia, Bosnia & Herzegovina, Mozambique and Kosovo. Presently ITBP is deployed in United Nation Mission in Congo.. ITBP is also providing security to the pilgrims during annual Kailash Mansarovar pilgrimage (yatra). ITBP provides communication, security and medical cover to the yatries from Gunji to Lipulekh Pass and back to Gunji in co-ordination with Kumaon Mandal Vikas Nigam.

ITBP mans forward border posts at altitudes ranging from 9000 feet to 18000 feet. Most of the forward posts remain cut off by the surface route during winter months. The border posts are exposed to the fury and violence of the nature like snow blizzards, avalanches, landslides, besides the hazards of high altitude and extreme cold where temperature normally remains below minus 40 degrees Celsius. The force, besides guarding the border, is heavily engaged in fighting terrorism in the state of Jammu & Kashmir, where it has displayed exemplary nerve and gallantry. ITBP personnel affectionately called "Himveers" also provide security cover to installations and to VIPs in Delhi.each year ITBP personnel are deployed to UN peace keeping missions in Kosovo, Angola & western Sahara and Sierra Leone.

Rashtriya Rifles: Rashtriya Rifles (RR) was established in year 1990. The Rashtriya Rifles was raised for the exclusive role of fighting insurgency in Kashmir. The 36-battalion, a light elite counterinsurgency force was formed specifically to compensate for inadequate local police and increasingly well-armed insurgents in Kashmir.

For formation of this legendary force, many sacrifices have been made by various organizations and individuals. The manpower for raising of the RR force was drawn from the units of the regular Army. These units operated with reduced manpower till deficiency was made up. The reserves of the army was used for equipping newly raised RR battalions.

Hundreds of school children have been taken on various RR sponsored educational-cum-cultural tours to various historical places in India. Other successes of this force include elimination of over 2700 militants since its raising, capture of large quantities of arms, ammunition and warlike stores, causing confusion and disarray amidst various militant cadres and improving the quality of life of the local public. The total strength of Rashtriya Rifles is five force headquarters, 17 sector headquarters and 66 Rashtriya Rifles battalions in year 2005.

The reputation of Rashtriya Rifles as a specialised anti-terrorist force has a tremendous impact on the militant's psyche who avoids any kind of direct confrontation with RR troops. Secondly, due to the proactive nature of operations conducted by well-trained and well-equipped troops, militants lost a number of their cadres, arms and equipment which was a grave setback to them. Such pressures against the militants have been continuously maintained by RR troops in a relentless manner.

The motivation of all ranks to perform better has it roots in various factors such as a sense of pride to get selected in a special force with a separate identity, dress and organization. Each individual is given here the opportunity to prove his mettle in operational field. As there is more permanence in the deployment of RR formations and units, they have a better rapport with the locals to gain more authentic flow of intelligence. As a result of all these factors, the junior leaders of RR battalions are able to take greater risks, often at the cost of their own lives to attain their operational goals.

They always lead from the front, thereby setting an example for others to emulate. The fact that they have neutralized more than 7000 terrorists, captured more than 6000 weapons of all types and won more than 2000 honours and awards speaks volumes of this organization. Faced with internal security challenges in Kashmir and elsewhere, the Indian army is interested in reducing its overall strength and using available revenue for force modernization. Some Indian spokesmen have suggested that increasing the use of light army forces, such as the Rashtriya Rifles, to fulfil missions in Kashmir and elsewhere could reduce the need for regular army forces in an internal-security role and help realize cuts. Such a move would better correspond to the real security issues with which India must deal.

Paramilitary Forces under Prime Minister Office

There are some special Paramilitary forces which are directly under the control of Prime Minister Office such as National Security Guards and Special Frontier Force. These are specialized forces having totally different roles than other Paramilitary forces.

National Security Guards: The National Security Guard was set up in 1984 as a federal contingency deployment force to deal with all aspects of terrorism in the country. So the most important role of this force is to fight terrorism in whatever form it may assume in areas where activity of terrorists assumes serious proportions, and the state police and other central police forces cannot cope up with the situation.

The National Security Guard is a force specially equipped and trained to deal with specific situations and is therefore used only in exceptional situations. The force is not designed to supplant the functions of the state police forces or other Paramilitary Forces of the Union of India. The NSG is modelled on the pattern of the SAS of the UK and GSG-9 of Germany.

It is a task-oriented force and has two complementary elements in the form of the Special Action Group (SAG) comprising army personnel and the Special Ranger Groups (SRG), comprising personnel drawn from the central Paramilitary Forces/state police forces.

All the personnel in SPG are on deputation. The SPG commandos were first used to combat terrorism in the Indian state of Punjab in 1985. They have now evolved into a counter-terrorist unit and have been continuing major combat operations in Jammu and Kashmir. The NSG has been publicly deployed only rarely, with most of its operations remaining classified. Its most recent deployment was operation Vajrashakti to end the Akshardham temple siege in Gandhinagar, Gujarat.

The NSG is a federal contingency deployment force to handle anti-hijack operations, rescue operations and to provide support to the central Paramilitary forces in dealing with anti-terrorist activities in whatever shape they may take place in different parts of the country. Some of its main functions are; Neutralization of terrorist threat in any specific area, building, vital installation, Engaging terrorists in a specific situation in order to neutralize them, Handling hijack situation involving piracy in the air or land and water, Rescue of hostages in kidnap situations, Security of high risk VIPs, Anti - sabotage checks of venues of visits/public meeting of VVIPs, Data collection on bomb explosions, Training of state police personnel in anti-terrorism, VIP security, PSO duties and Bomb detection and disposal, Sky marshal duties in domestic and international flights.

Special Frontier Force: Tibetans have been an element of the Indian army for as long as it has existed. Independent formations of Tibetan units patrolled the lands they were native to. During the time of the British, the Army began to employ Tibetans as spies, intelligence agents, and even covert militia in northern India and Tibet proper. At the time of independence, the northern hills of India remained the most isolated and strategically overlooked territory of India. When Tibet was invaded by the People's Republic of China, India was in no position to intervene militarily. After the Chinese invasion of Tibet, CIA and the Indian Intelligence Bureau established Mustang Base in Nepal, which trained Tibetans in guerrilla warfare. The Mustang rebels were used to rescue his holiness the Dalai Lama from Chinese captivity, into exile in India.

SFF is responsible for counter-terrorism duties, with teams in a constant state of alert. The forces rotate through this role on a six-monthly basis. Special group teams regularly conduct CT operations in the troubled Kashmir against militants on specific intelligence inputs. SFF also specializes in long range reconnaissance patrols.These pathfinders must be able to remain hidden under the nose of the enemy for days or weeks on an end. The outfit was trained to do this against the Chinese but in actual fact used the technique to great success in the Pakistan administered Kashmir and Punjab.

SFF were the pioneers at close protection (CP) duties in India, having developed many of the protocols themselves unique to the Indian sub-continent. Over the years, the Special Group has shared their expertise with a few friendly nations like Maldives and Nepal, training their own special forces. The government also gets political benefits from such arrangements.

Paramilitary Forces under Ministry of Railways

Railway Protection Force: The original name of Railway Protection Force was the Railway Watch & Ward. It was formed in 1882 when the railway companies appointed their own chowkidars for each department. This arrangement was found to be on the whole fairly satisfactory till there was a steep rise in the incidence of thefts of goods entrusted to railways for carriage which led to the government of India to appoint a committee to enquire into causes thereof and suggest a remedy.

This situation was not peculiar to railway premises only but was a part of the general crime situation in the country. The Watch & Ward units were found to be hopelessly inadequate for the purpose for which they were intended. The government of India, therefore, instituted a special enquiry through Director, Intelligence Bureau (Ministry of home affairs) who in his report in 1954 forcefully brought out the necessity of organising the Watch & Ward on a statutory basis.

It was decided in consultation with the ministry of home affairs that there should be an integrated well organized force on the model of the police with adequate supervisory staff specially trained to meet the particular aspects of crime that were relevant to railway property to work in the particular aspects of crime that were relevant to railway property to work in close collaboration and act as a second line to the states police with whom, under the constitution, policing on railways rested.

This led to the R. P. F. Bill for the better protection and security of railway property being passed into the Railway Protection Force Act, 1957, which led to the formation of Railway Protection Force.

The main duties and functions of Railway Protection Force is to: protect and safeguard railway property, passenger area and passenger, remove any obstruction in the movement of railway property or passenger area and to perform any act conducive to the better protection and security of railway property, passenger area and passengers.

Paramilitary Forces under State Governments

Home Guard Organization: The Home Guard was originally raised in 1946 in accordance with the Home Guards Acts and Rules of States/ Union Territories, under the ministry of home affairs. Home Guards Organization in Maharashtra came into existence in 1952 under the name of Home Defence. Maharashtra Home Guards assisted central government in organizing the Home Guards and Civil Defence creditably during external aggression in 1962. At this time the Home Defence came into limelight by changing the name from Home Defence to Civil Defence.

The role of the Home Guard is to service as a supporting force to the police in maintenance of law, order and internal security, help the community in any kind of emergency such as an air-raid, an earthquake, etc. help in the maintenance of essential services, promote communal harmony, assist civil administration in protecting weaker sections, participate in socio-economic and welfare activities and perform civil defence duties.

The Home Guards are also trained in fire fighting. Home Guards are of two types; rural and urban. In Border States, Border Wing Home Guard battalions have also been raised, which serve as an auxiliary to the Border Security Force (BSF). The total unauthorised strength of the Home Guards in the country is at 472, 000; however the actual strength is at 416, 000 personnel. The organization is spread over in all states and union territories except in Arunachal Pradesh and Kerala.

They are enrolled from various cross sections of people such as engineers, doctors, lawyers, teachers, employees of public & private sector organizations, college & university students, agricultural & industrial workers, etc. who can give their spare time for betterment of the community. All citizens of India, who are in the age group of 18-50, are eligible to become members of the Home Guard. Normal tenure of membership in Home Guards is three to five years.

A member of Home Guard, whenever called up for duty or training, is paid allowance at prescribed rates to meet out pocket expenses. Members of Home Guard with three years services in the organization are trained in the Police in maintenance of law and order, prevention of crime, anti-dacoit measures, border patrolling, flood relief, fire fighting, prohibition, elections and social welfare activities. In the event of a national emergency, some portion of civil defence work is also entrusted to the Home Guard. The Ministry of Home Affairs formulates the policy in respect of role, target, raising, training, equipping, establishment and other important matters of the Home Guard. Expenditure on Home Guard is generally shared between the centre and state governments as per the existing financial policy.

The functions of Home Guards are to; serve as auxiliary to the police and generally help in maintaining internal security, help the community in any kind of emergency—such as on air-raid precautions or on any natural calamity, function as an emergency force intended for special tasks directly or indirectly connected with the defence of the country, maintain functional units to provide essential services such as motor transport, Engineering groups, fire brigade, nursing and first aid, operation of power supply, water installations and communication systems etc. Marine units function as an Indian Coast Guard auxiliary. The Fire Wing assists the Indian Fire Service.

Organizations Assisting Paramilitary Forces

National Cadet Corps: National Cadet Corps (NCC) was created in 1949. The motto of the NCC is "Unity and Discipline". The Headquarters of the NCC is in New Delhi and is commanded by a Director-General of the rank of Lieutenant General. The NCC is administered directly by the ministry of defence. The Director General has a staff which is drawn from the three services; Army, Navy and Air Force.

The NCC is divided into 16 directorates, similar to brigades, in which each state or group of states forms a directorate. The smaller states and union territories are attached with directorates of the bigger states. Each directorate is under the command of an officer equivalent to the rank of a Brigadier. The directorates are further sub-divided into groups, which varies according to the size of the state, each under the command of an officer equivalent to the rank of Colonel. Groups consist of NCC battalions and NCC Air Force & Naval units. Other than the Commanding Officer, each Group Headquarter has an administrative officer and a training officer with ranks of either a Lieutenant Colonel or a Major.

The functions of NCC are to; serve as back-up in maintaining internal security at the root level, help the community in any kind of emergency such as natural calamity, function as an emergency force intended for special tasks such as nursing and first aid.

Aim of NCC is to develop qualities of character, courage, comradeship, discipline, leadership, secular outlook, spirit of adventure and the ideals of selfless service amongst the youth of the country, to create a human resource of organized, trained and motivated youth, to provide leadership in all walks of life and be always available for the service of the nation and to provide a suitable environment to motivate the youth to take up a career in the armed forces.

Border Roads Organization: The Border Roads Organization was constituted in 1960 under the chairmanship of Prime Minister Jawaharlal Nehru, as an inter-ministerial organization. BRO is led by the Director General of Border Roads (DGBR) as it Executive Head who is of the rank of Lieutenant General.

The BRO is also provided a General Reserve Engineer Force (GREF) as the execution force under the Ministry of Surface Transport. GREF comprises engineers from civil engineering, electrical & mechanical engineering disciplines from reputed engineering colleges after selection through Union Public Service Commission (UPSC) by clearing engineering services examination at all India level, administrative officers, supervisors and other trades of personnel. Its operations also run in other countries such as Afghanistan. The organization carries out construction and development works comprising air fields building projects, canlonments, Defence works etc. BRO is popularly known as General Reserve Engineer Force and it commenced its work with Army Engineer Groups. Its main functions and duties are to develop & maintain the operational road infrastructure of general staff in the border areas, to contribute to the socio-economic development of the border states, to develop & maintain roads to keep LOC through in original sectors and re-deployed sectors, To execute additional tasks as laid down by the government contributing to the war effort.

REFERENCES

World Military Aircraft Inventory: Aerospace Source Book 2007, Aviation Week & Space Technology, Jan. 15, 2007.

Annual Defence Ministry Report, 1996.

Annual Defence Ministry Report, 1983.

Bamzai, Prithvi Nath Kaul: Kashmir and Power Politics: From Lake Success to Tashkent, Metropolitan Book Co., Delhi, 1966

Bharat Rakshak Monitor Article.

Bose, Sumantra: The Kashmir Challenge, Sage, New Delhi, 1997.

Deep Waters: Life in the Coast Guard.

Dte General, Assam Rifles, Shillong.

Dte General, BSF, New Delhi.

Dte General, CISF, New Delhi.

Dte General, CRPF, New Delhi.

Dte General, Indian Coast Guard, New Delhi.

Employment News.

George Perkovich: India's Nuclear Bomb, UC Berkeley, 1999.

Harold Wilensky: Organizational Intelligence, Basic Books, New York, 1967.

Hazarika, Sanjoy. 1996. Strangers In The Mist, Viking.

Kargil Committee Report: Executive Summary.

Marston, Daniel P. and Sundaram, Chandar S. A.: Military History of India and South Asia : From the East India Company to the Nuclear Era, Pentagon Press, New Delhi, 2008.

Ministry of Defence.

Ministry of Home Affairs.

Nibedon, Nirmal. 1985. Night Of the Guerrillas, New Delhi: Lancer Books.

Raj Chengappa,"Weapons of Peace", Harper Collins, Delhi, India, 2000.

Russell Smith: The Unknown CIA: My three decades with the Agency, Berkeley Books, 1992.

Sainik Samachar.

Deccan Herald, July 10, 1987.

Indian Defence Review. June 1999.

Times New Delhi, Nov. 25, 2000.

The Assam Tribune July 14, 2001.

Ananda Bazar Patrika, Apr. 11, 2004.

The Hindu, April 11, 2006.

The Hindu, Mar. 21, 2008.

Frontier India Defence & Strategic News Service, 16 May 2008.

PART – II
PARAMILITARY FORCES UNDER MINISTRY OF DEFENCE

3

Indian Coast Guard

"Vayam Rakshaamah"

Introduction

With a coastline of over 7, 500 kilometres and an Exclusive Economic Zone of 2.3 million square kilometres, India occupies an important geo-strategic position in the Indian Ocean. The peninsula juts out for almost 1000 nautical miles thereby providing it an extended sea frontage. Ninety seven per cent of India's trade is moved by sea. There are 11 major and 167 minor ports.

Indian waters are home to important sea-lanes that serve as the umbilical cord of the economies of several countries in the Asia Pacific, North and South America. They carry critical energy resources from the Persian Gulf as also provide an economical maritime trade route. The Malacca Strait is witness to heavy maritime traffic and on an average 200 ships pass through this strategic choke point. The marshalling point for the mercantile traffic, entering or leaving the strait, lies in the Andaman

Sea. India lies astride this critical sea-lane and is therefore strategically located to monitor the entire maritime activity in the area. Any event or contingency in the area or among its maritime littorals, having maritime connotations has direct implications for its security.

Order at sea, respect for laws and conventions and peaceful regulation of seaborne trade are some of the central themes of the maritime world. Over the years, the international system of maritime project has shown a remarkable degree of toughness and strength in challenging destabilising forces. In the past, a majority of maritime security problems were either political or military in nature and were solved through direct diplomatic negotiations or through action.

Today, however, our maritime security needs have become far more complex and demand newer methods to deal with them. The maritime security environment is being challenged from several directions. Some of these are piracy, gun running, drug smuggling, illegal migration, environmental pollution, maritime boundary disputes and illegal fishing. None is independent of each other and failure in one often leads to failure in others.

The jurisdiction of India over its maritime zones generally diminishes the further an incident or issue occurs from the coast. Our maritime zones as they exist today are Internal Waters, Territorial Sea, Contiguous Zone, EEZ and Continental Shelf.

The waters lying on the landward side of straight territorial sea baselines drawn along irregular parts of the coast are Internal Waters. These include the gulfs or bays whose points of entrance are less than twenty four nautical miles wide, as well as the bays or gulfs which exceed the twenty four nautical miles at their entrance but have been historically regarded as internal. A State exercises full sovereignty over internal waters. Prima facie, a ship, by entering the internal waters of a foreign state (unless in distress and obliged to do so), places itself within the territorial jurisdiction of that state and therefore subject to the operation of its laws and the competence of its courts. It also places itself under the protection of the jurisdiction.

The outer limit of the territorial sea is 12 nautical miles (NM) seaward of the baseline. A State has sovereignty over the territorial sea. It may therefore impose comprehensive controls in this area, with the one major exception that it must respect the right of innocent passage of foreign vessels. As a general rule criminal jurisdiction is not exercised on board a foreign ship passing through the territorial sea in order to arrest any person or to conduct any investigation in connection with any crime committed on board the ship during its passage. The exceptions to this are Contiguous zone and Exclusive economic zone (EEZ).

Contiguous zone is the area between 12 NM and 24 NM seaward of the baseline. In the contiguous zone, the coastal State may take limited enforcement measures in relation to customs, fiscal, sanitary and immigration matters.

Exclusive economic zone (EEZ) is the area between the lines 12 NM and 200 NM seaward of the territorial sea baselines. In this area the coastal State has sovereign rights to explore and exploit the living and non-living resources, and a corresponding obligation to protect and conserve the marine environment.

Continental shelf is the area between 12 NM and 200 NM seaward of the territorial sea baseline (that is, much of the same area as the EEZ) and any areas of physical continental shelf beyond 200 NM. Coastal States have sovereign rights to explore and exploit the living and non-living resources of the shelf as well as a corresponding obligation to protect and conserve the resources of the continental shelf.

Keeping in view above situation, the Indian navy and coast guard are responsible for maintaining maritime order in the Indian EEZ. They are well equipped in terms of surface ships and maritime aircraft to undertake patrolling and surveillance of the sea areas. The naval forces also include special helicopters for deployment of quick reaction forces, marine commandos, diving teams and damage control units. The Indian Coast Guard has grown over the years and plays a dominant role in policing Indian waters with patrol vessels, interceptor boats and aircraft. In addition marine customs and police forces play an important role in handling criminal acts in and off Indian ports.

History

Need: The Sea borne smuggling across the seas was out of control towards the end of 1960s threatening the economy of our country. The five Customs patrol craft operated by the Indian Navy for the Central Board of Excise & Customs were inadequate to deter the smugglers.

To augment the anti-smuggling effort, as an interim measure, 13 confiscated dhows were inducted despite their inherent limitations, to support the existing fleet. However, this entire force level was only a little bit effective to contain the large-scale smuggling activity.

The problem of checking sea-borne smuggling traffic was heightened by:

- Extended coastline without any efficient coverage.
- Widespread fishing close to the shores complicated the recognition of illicit traffic, particularly when there was no efficient system in force for registering the fishing boats.
- Need to interrupt illegal vessels within the territorial waters.
- High speed vessels being used by the smugglers.

In the environment of large scale sea–borne smuggling, the Cabinet Secretariat constituted a study group under the chairmanship of Dr. BD Nag Chaudhari with Air Chief Marshal O. P. Mehra and Admiral RD Katari amongst others on 23 January 1970, to examine and report on:

- Number and type of petrol vessels needed to meet the immediate requirements of anti-smuggling task.
- Sources of supply and their availability in the world market to meet the operational requirement.
- Suitability of hovercraft, helicopter and other aircraft for anti-smuggling operations.

The Committee in its report put in August 1971 recommended that there is an immediate need to build our anti-smuggling capabilities on a three-tier system -Indigenous construction and early acquisition of surface craft for anti-smuggling measures.

Hovercraft, in the role of fast interceptor was the choice for immediate augmenting of there limited anti-smuggling capabilities till the new fast surface crafts were acquired. Acquisition of surveillance aircraft in a phased programme could be similarly geared up at a convenient stage. On 03 May 1973, a meeting under the chairmanship of Shri VC Shukla, the Minister for Defence Production, was held to expedite the acquisition of suitable boats for the Customs.

The requirement of two types of patrol boat was felt – a large size patrol boat with 1000 NM range and a max speed of 30 knots, fitted with light armament and capacity for 16 crew and a small boat of higher speed, fitted with light armament, to carry 12 crew. In the inter-ministerial meeting, it was agreed that the medium boats should also be acquired in pursuance of the recommendations of the Committee. In a subsequent meeting with the Ministry of Defence Production on 22 November 1973, the customs indicated a requirement of 20 modified SDB Mark-II type for their department.

Origin: It was however, not until 1974 that a serious official consideration was given to this problem when the Defence Secretary spelled out the need for setting up of a Coast Guard type national organization. In essence the Defence Secretary's note brought out that an organization for ensuring safety of life and property at sea and for law enforcement in the waters under there jurisdiction had not kept pace with the substantial increase in maritime activity in there surrounding seas. The note had further suggested that a suitable inter-ministerial body could examine the adequacy of the existing organizations and the possibility of closer coordination between their activities either by merging some or establishing a central organization like a Coast Guard.

In this context, the Chief of the Naval Staff had also stressed the need for greater inter-ministerial coordination in the maritime field to avoid duplication of effort and for dovetailing measures to ensure that the national objectives are attained by an integrated approach. It was also felt that the law enforcement activities should not be undertaken by the Navy, which would inevitably detract them from their operational role and interfere with their training. Further, deployment of sophisticated warships and manpower trained for specialised roles, on law enforcement tasks on a continuos basis in peace time neither was nor considered cost-effective.

In the wake of the amendment to the Maintenance of Internal Security Act to provide for preventive detention for offences relating to smuggling and foreign exchange violations, a concerted drive was launched to combat smuggling. In this context, in September 1974, the Committee of Secretaries under the Chairmanship of the Cabinet Secretary appointed a committee to examine the shortcomings in there anti-smuggling and other maritime activities and suggest the measures to protect India's marine resources and the creation of the Coast Guard. The committee was to be chaired by Shri KF Rustamji, Special Secretary, Ministry of Home Affairs with Vice Admiral VA Kamath, PVSM, Vice Chief of Naval Staff and Shri Jasjit Singh, Chairman, Central Board of Excise and Customs amongst its members.

The Rustamji Committee in its report submitted on 31 July 1975 strongly recommended the setting up of a Coast Guard type organization for general superintendence and policing of there sea areas in peacetime. The committee's view had become even more pressing by virtue of the discovery of oil in there offshore areas. This committee also recommended that the Coast Guard Service should be patterned on the Navy and work under the Ministry of Defence (MoD). The recommendations of the Rustamji Committee were considered and accepted by the Secretaries on 07 January 1976. The committee, however, decided that the new organization should function under the Ministry of Home Affairs (MHA). The decision was subsequently reviewed at the level of the Prime Minister and it was decided to place it under the Ministry of Defence(MoD).

The Ministry of Defence (MoD) thereupon prepared a paper for consideration of the Cabinet Committee on Political Affair (CCPA) seeking approval for:

- Taking necessary steps to set up a Coast Guard organization.
- Appointing an Officer on Special Duty (OSD) in the Ministry of Defence in the rank of Vice Admiral with a nucleus Headquarters and appropriate staff to prepare a detailed plan for the Coast Guard Organization.
- Creation of an interim Coast Guard Force with two frigates seconded by the Navy and transferring of five patrol vessels from the Ministry of Home Affairs.

On 07 January 1977, the Cabinet approved the proposal for the setting up an interim Coast Guard Organization within the Navy to undertake specified Coast Guard tasks. The CCPA directed that the budgetary provision for the Coast Guard should be under a separate head in the estimates of the Department of Revenue and Banking. Further, it had also directed that a detailed plan for the development of the Coast Guard should be drawn up.

With the increasing awareness of the economic benefits to be gained from the sea and sea beds, certain Coastal States had claimed jurisdiction over the vast areas of sea around them. The Third conference of the UNCLOS resolved the inadequacies and evolved a regime for the international sea bed area. In conformity with the existing trend the world over, the Government of India enacted the 'Maritime Zones Act' on 25 August 1976.

This Act came into force on 15 January 1977, bringing the entire Exclusive Economic Zone (EEZ), an area of 2.1 million square kilometres within our national jurisdiction. The policing of this vast sea area and to enforce the national laws and protecting the national interests would be a mammoth task and call for a dedicated organization. On 07 January 1977, following the Cabinet's decision the interim Coast Guard Organization came into being under Naval Headquarters on 01 February 1977.

The force consisting of two frigates (Navy Ships Kirpan and Kuthar) seconded from the Indian Navy and five patrol boats (Pamban, Puri, Pulicat, Panaji and Panvel) transferred from the Home Ministry. These assets were deployed for the discharge of the Coast Guard duties along the coasts and around the Island territories. The aim was to maintain surveillance of our sea area and to assess the extent of maritime activity in our maritime zones with a limited force.

The overall plan for the Coast Guard Service was prepared by the Officer on Special Duty (OSD), Vice Admiral VA Kamath as required by the terms of reference in three parts and submitted on 05 July 1978 for the approval of the Cabinet Committee on Political Affair (CCPA).

The Plans included:

- Part I dealing with the Main Plan supported by the detailed appendices and Part II covered the following:
- A study of the various maritime agencies in India and identification of such activities, which may be dovetailed to avoid duplication of effort and ensure an integrated approach.
- Organization and assigning roles for the Coast Guard.
- Terms and conditions of the service.
- Legal aspects of raising the new Service.
- Identification of areas in which the Coast Guard would have to rely on the Indian Navy and other Central Govt agencies.
- Budget.
- Part III dealing with the development plan for the Coast Guard, a six-year roll-on plan, for the period 1978-84.

The process, which began nearly a decade ago, had crystallized with the formation of the Coast Guard Service by passing an Act in the Parliament on 18 August 1978 and brought into force on 19 August 1978.

Beginning in 1978 with two old frigates seconded by the Navy and five small patrol vessels, the ICG expanded over the following two decades to attain a force level of 52 ships and craft and 35 aircraft and helicopters. An Air Wing was formed in 1982 with Indian Navy assistance to aid the surface fleet.

The first helicopter Squadron was formally commissioned in May 1982 and the first fixed-wing unit was activated in 1982. One of the Coast Guard's greatest ever tests began on 26 December 2005, when an earthquake off Indonesia triggered a giant Tsunami wave which caused massive destruction along the coastlines of the Indian Ocean.

Coast Guard operates fixed wing aircraft from shore Air Stations for surveillance of the Exclusive Economic Zone. In addition, helicopters are embarked on Coast Guard Offshore Patrol Vessels to provide local surveillance and perform Search and Rescue missions at sea. Operating these aircraft at sea is a challenging task and will bring your special skills to the fore. As an Officer of the Pilot/Navigator Branch, you will have opportunity to serve both in the Shore Air-Stations along the coasts of India, as well as embark ships.

Coast Guard personnel immediately began relief operations in the remote Andaman Islands from Port Blair, and in the regions of Chennai and Mumbai on the mainland. A Coast Guard Dornier 228 (CG 753) was also the first aircraft to deliver medicines and essential supplies to the Maldives within 24 hours of the tragedy. A total of 230 sorties were flown by aircraft and helicopters in the period up to 21 January 2006.

Key Dates in History

September 1974	Rustamji Committee set up to study creation of a coast guard service
31 July 1975	Rustamji Committee strongly recommends creation of the Coast Guard
25 August 1976	The Maritime Zones of India Act passed
01 February 1977	Interim Indian Coast Guard organization created by the Navy
18 August 1978	Coast Guard Act passed in Parliament
19 August 1978	Coast Guard Act comes into force - ICG formally established
22 May 1982	First air squadron (CGAS 800) commissioned with helicopters
June 1984	First trainee Coast Guard aviators qualify for their wings
7 July 1986	First two Do 228s handed over in Germany
18 March 2002	First Dhruv helicopter delivered

Present Scenario

Personnel Strength: The Coast Guard has strength of approximately 1000 officers and 5200 enrolled personnel and 706 civilians. The force is led by a Director General and a Deputy Director General. Vice Admiral

Rustom Faramroze Contractor is the present Director General of the Coast Guard.

Bases: The Indian Coast Guard's Central Headquarter is located in New Delhi, capital of India.

It has three regional command headquarters located at Mumbai, Chennai and Port Blair in the Andaman & Nicobar Islands.

West Coast District Headquarters are located at Porbandar, Mumbai, Mangalore, Kochi and Goa.

The District Headquarters at Porbander includes coast guard stations at Jakhau, Vadinar and Okha and an air station at Porbandar itself.

The District Headquarters at Kochi includes coast guard stations at Kavaratti and Vizhinjam.

The District Headquarters at Goa includes an coast guard air enclave at Daman.

East Coast District Headquarterss are located at Chennai, Vizag, Paradip, Haldia and Kolkata.

The District Headquarters at Chennai includes coast guard stations at Tuticorin and Mandapam.

Port Blair District Headquarters are located at Diglipur and Campbell Bay.

There are six Coast Guard stations: Jakahu, Okha and Vadinar in Region West; and Tuticorin and Mandapam in Region East, under their respective district commands.

Air Bases: The Indian Coast Guard Air Wing currently operates from two main air bases, and a number of air enclaves along India's coast. The need for a full fledged Air wing for Indian Coast Guard was felt right from the time of its inception. The first ICG aviation unit to be commissioned was 800 SQN on 22 May 1982 with two Chetak helicopters at Goa.

The first fixed wing squadron of Indian Coast Guard (ICG) was commissioned with 02 Fokker Friendship (F-27) aircraft on 30 Jul 1983. These aircraft were taken on lease from Indian Airlines. These aircraft did a yeomen service to ICG through their tireless operation from Dumdum Airport in maritime surveillance and SAR roles covering the entire Exclusive Economic Zone (EEZ).

At present the air arm of Indian Coast Guard covers Arabian Sea & Bay of Bengal with an inventory of seventeen Chetak helicopters, twenty four Dornier aircraft, three ALH (Advanced Light Helicopter).

The Air Wing of Coast Guard is operated from two air stations and six air enclaves.

- Indian Coast Guard Air Station (ICGAS), Chennai
- Indian Coast Guard Air Station (ICGAS), Daman
- Indian Coast Guard Air Enclave (ICGAE), Kolkata
- Indian Coast Guard Air Enclave (CGAE), Port Blair
- Indian Coast Guard Air Enclave (CGAE), Kochi
- Indian Coast Guard Air Enclave (CGAE), Goa
- Indian Coast Guard Air Enclave (CGAE), Goa
- Indian Coast Guard Air Enclave (CGAE), Port Blair
- INS Kunjali, Mumbai

Organizational Structure

Organizational setup of Indian Coast Guard from top to bottom is:

- Director General
- Inspector General
- Deputy Inspector General
- Commandant
- Assistant Commandant
- Yantriks

  Yantrik
  Pradhan Yantrik
  Sahayak Engineer
  Uttam Sahayak Engineer
  Pradhan Sahayak Engineer

- Naviks

  Navik
  Uttam Navik
  Pradhan Navik
  Adhikari
  Uttam Adhikari
  Pradhan Adhikari

Chiefs of Indian Coast guard

- Vice Admiral V. A. Kamath (19 Aug 1978 to 31 Mar 1980)
- Vice Admiral Swaraj Prakash (01 Apr 1980 to 31 Mar 1982)
- Vice Admiral M. R. Schunkar (01 Apr 1982 to 31 Mar 1984)
- Vice Admiral S. Jain (19 Jun 1984 to 14 Feb 1985)
- Vice Admiral I. J. S. Khurana (15 Feb 1985 to 30 Jun 1987)
- Vice Admiral H. Johnson (10 Jul 1987 to 27 Jun 1990)
- Vice Admiral K. K. Kohli (05 Oct 1992 to 03 Jan 1995)
- Vice Admiral P. J. Jacob (04 Jan 1995 to 17 Nov 1996)
- Vice Admiral R. N. Ganesh (18 Nov 1996 to 04 Mar 1999)
- Vice Admiral C. DeSilva (05 Mar 1999 to 06 Mar 2001)
- Director General Rameshwar Singh (07 Mar 2001 to 29 Sep 2001)
- Vice Admiral O. P. Bansal (30 Sep 2001 to 12 Jan 2003)
- Vice Admiral Sureesh Mehta (13 Jan 2003 to 19 Aug 2004)
- Vice Admiral A. K. Singh (20 Aug 2004 to 24 Feb 2006)
- Director General Dr. P. Paleri (28 Feb 2006 to 31 Aug 2006)
- Vice Admiral R. F. Contractor (from 31 Aug 2006)

Duties and Functions

Motto: Indian Coast guard Motto is ***"Vayam Rakshaamah"*** meaning **"We Protect"**.

Maxim: It shall be the duty of the Coast Guard to protect by such measures, as it thinks fit the maritime and other national interests of India in the maritime zones of India.

- Ensuring the safety and protection of artificial islands, offshore terminals, installations and other structures and devices in any maritime zone.
- Providing protection to fishermen including assistance to them at sea while in distress.
- Taking such measures as are necessary to preserve and protect the maritime environment and to prevent and control marine pollution.
- Assisting the customs and other authorities in anti-smuggling operations.

- Enforcing the provisions of such enactment as are for the time being in force in the maritime zones and.
- Such other matters, including measures for the safety of life and property at sea and collection of scientific data as may be prescribed.
- The Coast Guard shall perform its functions under appropiate section in accordance with, and subject to such rules as may be prescribed and such rules may, in particular, make provisions for ensuring that the Coast Guard functions in close liaison with Union agencies, institutions and authorities so as to avoid duplication of effort.

Protection of Indian Interests in Indian Maritime Zone: History has taught india two bitter lessons: firstly, that neglect of maritime power can culminate in a cession of sovereignty, and secondly, that it takes decades to revert to being a considerable maritime power after a period of neglect and decline.

The implications of the end of the Cold War are now more apparent. An obituary for war would be premature, although the situation on the macro-level is moving towards reconciliation. At micro-level, however, ethnic strife, conflict and tensions have escalated. Low intensity conflict and crises are adversely affecting development and liberation processes in many states. Threats to internal security and sub-nationalism have preoccupied most of the governments, at least in the Asian region.

Alongside the end of Cold War, the historic treaty on laws of the seas has also revived latent maritime disputes and confrontation. While some neighbouring states have adopted a confrontational attitude over maritime zone delimitation, there is enough scope within the United Nations Convention on the Law of the Sea (UNCLOS) to settle disputes amicably through negotiation and arbitration. India has resolved maritime zone delimitations with all its neighbours, except Pakistan and Bangladesh.

Exploitation of oil, gas and offshore minerals, fishing, harnessing of thermal, wave and tidal energy, creation of artificial space in offshore areas are some spheres where interests are growing. Resources in the exclusive economic zone (EEZ) can be considered as an extension of those on land and therefore need to be viewed with the same security outlook.

Sub-continental India has a coastline of 6 300 kilometres with the island territories of Lakshadweep and Andaman, and Nicobar islands adding another 1 200 kilometres. This coastline harbours eleven major, twenty intermediate and 144 minor ports. When the new Law of the Sea are applied to the country's coastline, it gives India a staggering 2, 2 million square kilometres of EEZ.

India's natural outlet is towards the sea, through which 95 per cent of its overseas trade passes. The country's sea lanes are economically important and serve as vital seaborne trade routes through the Indian Ocean. India's other maritime interests include high value assets in the form of offshore oil and the vast potential of minerals and seabed resources in the waters surrounding it. In addition, India has fishing interests in its EEZ, and the local shipbuilding industry has seen resurgence in recent years largely due to the Indian urge for self-reliance.

The growth of the Indian Coast Guard has mainly been commensurate with the country's expanding maritime interests, and should be viewed in that light. The Indian Coast Guard has come a long way since its conception, when it inherited a modest collection of few boats. Rightly recognising the vital role the Coast Guard would play in the maritime defence of the country, the development of the Coast Guard started slowly and progressed gradually over the years.

The Indian Coast Guard of today is a three-dimensional combat force which is capable of performing multifarious tasks. The teeth of the Coast Guard are the ships and aircrafts. Over the last three decades, the Indian Coast Guard has established a capable in-house design organization. As for the future, India has an on-going programme for the construction of ships to meet the force level requirements of the Coast Guard. Keeping the considerable interests of the country and the prevailing environment in the Indian Ocean region in view, the requirement for a strong Coast Guard is evident. What is equally important is that this need is recognized by the Government and people.

The classic constituents of sea power have remained unchanged in the last century - naval power, technology, port and maritime infrastructure, political will, seafaring population and economic strength have only gained significance with time.

Sea power is vital to the growth of commerce. With increasing transnational trade, shipping assumes considerable significance. Protection of home shipping and cargo fosters economic growth. In India, for example, Indian hulls carry 25 per cent of the outbound cargo, a figure which is likely to increase to forty per cent by the turn of the century.

Associated with trade, is the development of ports and maritime infrastructure. These can neither be neglected nor left unprotected.

The policing role entails the protection of resources, enforcing national maritime laws relating to merchant shipping, fishing, fiscal, marine environment, contraband control, drug running and immigration. In recognition of the need to police long coastal lines and large EEZs, India has created Coast Guard services to manage and fulfil these functions. There are certain advantages, however, to having a Coast Guard which concentrates its energies on law enforcement in the EEZ, leaving the navy to hone its war-fighting skills.

Anti smuggling activities: A major mission of the Coast Guard is to prevent and detect the smuggling of contraband and prohibited articles, the import and export of which are controlled under the laws of India, for the purpose of protecting the community and environment, maintaining public health and fulfilling international obligations. Items being smuggled include dutiable commodities, narcotics, firearms, strategic goods, infringing copies, goods bearing forged trademarks and goods with false origin labels. In the fight against smuggling activities, the Coast Guard has strived to maintain a proper balance between control and trade facilitation to ensure speedy flow of legitimate cargoes at the entry and exit points.

The Coast Guard is the leading agency for maritime smuggling interdiction, making it a key player in combating smuggling to the India. The Coast Guard's mission is to reduce the supply of smuggled items as proximate to the source as possible, by denying smugglers the use of maritime routes in the transit zone.

Anti Piracy Activities: Piracy is a robbery committed at sea, or sometimes on the shore, without a commission from a sovereign nation. Seaborne piracy against transport vessels remains a significant issue with estimated worldwide losses of US $13 to $16 billion per year, particularly in the waters between the Pacific and Indian Oceans, off the Somali coast, and also in the Strait of Malacca and Singapore, which are used by over 50, 000 commercial ships a year.

Till the 1980s, piracy was generally considered history and restricted to the silver screen but the 1990s has seen resurgence in maritime piracy. Clearly, various political, economic and military reasons are responsible for the rise of crime on the high seas. The cold war cease-fire resulting in a shrinking Soviet navy and the limited US naval presence may have also contributed to encouraging piracy. Likewise the handover of Hong

Kong to the People's Republic of China led to the exit of the British Royal Navy.

Similarly the recent Southeast Asian economic crisis has also depressed defence budgets and thereby scaled down naval activity like patrolling by regional navies. This move has also increased piracy in recent times in these waters.

The most horrifying aspect of maritime piracy is the associated violence. There is a typical pattern, which has emerged over the years with the crew traumatised, hurt, injured, left adrift or even killed. The international shipping community is growing more pessimistic over the ability of states to suppress piracy. In the first quarter of 1999, the International Maritime Bureau reported more than 70 attacks, most of which occurred in waters off Indonesia.

From a mere 43 reported attacks of violence to crew in 1991, the figure rose sharply to 290 in 1996. In 1995 and 1996 there were 26 reported cases of killings each year. Invariably a ship's crew are taken hostage, assaulted or even killed and their belongings normally stolen. Often the entire ship and its cargo are sold illegally. Like hijacking, piracy is an international crime, which affects not only the passengers, crew and ship-owners but also threatens the shipping community.

Modern pirates can be successful because a large amount of international commerce occurs via shipping. For commercial reasons, many cargo ships move through narrow bodies of water making them vulnerable to be overtaken and boarded by small motorboats. As usage increases, many of these ships have to lower cruising speeds to allow for navigation and traffic control, making them prime targets for piracy. Small ships are also capable of disguising themselves as fishing vessels or cargo vessels when not carrying out piracy in order to avoid or deceive inspectors.

In some cases, modern pirates are not interested in the cargo and are mainly interested in taking the personal belongings of the crew and the contents of the ship's safe, which might contain large amounts of cash needed for payroll and port fees. In other cases, the pirates force the crew off the ship and then sail it to a port to be repainted and given a new identity through false papers often purchased from corrupt or complicit officials.

Many nations forbid ships to enter their territorial waters or ports if the crew of the ships are armed in an effort to restrict possible piracy.

Shipping companies sometimes hire private security guards.Modern pirates also use a great deal of technology. It has been reported that crimes of piracy have involved the use of mobile phones, modern speedboats, assault rifles, shotguns, pistols, mounted machine guns, and even RPGs and grenade launchers. However, more primitive weapons such as knives, batons, or boat-hooks are also often used.

Convention on the high seas held at Geneva, on 29 April 1958 proclaimed the modern international law on piracy. The convention has nine out of 29 operative articles which deal specifically with piracy and its control. Article 15 of the convention defines piracy as an illegal act of depredation, committed for private ends by the crew or the passenger of a private ship or a private aircraft and directed on the high seas against another ship or aircraft. A more authoritative codification of the international law on piracy is, however contained in Article 101 of the 1982 United Nations Convention on the Law of the Sea (UNCLOS).

The 1982 UNCLOS definition remains unchanged from the earlier 1958 Geneva Convention on the High Seas. This narrow definition restricts it to unlawful acts committed by a private ship against another ship for private ends. However, a broader view postulates that acts committed for other than private ends can constitute piracy. Explanations of the jurisdiction over the place and persons who can apprehend a pirate or property in control of the pirates are highlighted in Article 105 and 107 of 1982 UNCLOS. In the absence of an international tribunal to punish piracy, it has become imperative for individual nations to try and punish the offence. Purely because pirates in the international sense are enemies of al hotis humani genesis. So pirates merit to be treated as criminals regardless of their nationality. Interestingly the 1982 UNCLOS also considers piracy committed by a warship, government vessel or an aircraft whose crew has mutinied and seized control, as illegal and to be treated as an act of piracy.

Since no state can exercise its writ on the high seas, 1982 UNCLOS Article 100 urges all countries to cooperate and collectively curb piracy outside their maritime jurisdiction. Article 105 notes that the courts of the seizing state may decide on the penalties and determine the action to be taken with regard to the ships, aircraft or property captured from the pirates. Despite this proviso, it seems to be a general principle of law that pirata non mutual dominium, irrespective of the rules of municipal law about acquisition in good faith or stolen property.

It is traditional for the captor to be rewarded for saving private property. The International Maritime Bureau defines piracy as 'an act of boarding any vessel with the intention to commit theft or any other crime and with the intent or capability to use force in the furtherance of that act. It is a wider definition and allows the International Maritime Bureau to undertake a detailed analysis of all acts of violence and theft against the seafaring community at sea and not restricted to the high sea only which is the classical United Nation's definition. This is like casting the net wider.

The UNCLOS 1982 covers piracy under Articles 100 to 105. It also confers right of government vessels to search and seize vessels engaged in acts of piracy. The Indian Navy enjoys a unique regulation contained in the Navy Act 1957. This Act was passed by the Indian parliament and defines the term 'pirate' in Section 3 Chapter I of the Act as: 'Enemy includes all armed rebels, armed mutineers, armed rioters and pirates and any person in arms against whom it is the duty of any person to act'.

Further, section 34 states: 'If the commanding officer of a naval vessel fails to pursue the enemy, whom it is his duty to pursue, then the punishment prescribed for him may range from imprisonment extending upto 7 years or if such act is committed to assist the enemy, he may even be punished with death'.

The Regulations for the Navy Part I derived from the Navy Act 1957 clearly states: "If any armed vessel, not having commission as a warship from a recognized government, whether de facto or de jure, should commit piratical acts and outrages against the vessels or goods of India's citizens or of the subjects of any other foreign power in amity with India, and if credible information should be received thereof, such armed vessel shall be seized and detained by any of Indian naval ships falling in with her, and sent to the nearest Indian port where there is a court of competent jurisdiction for the trial of offences committed on the high seas, together with the necessary witnesses to prove the act or acts and with her master and crew in safe custody, in order that they may be dealt with according to law'. The above regulations provide clear guidelines to Indian naval vessels while dealing with acts of piracy.

Among their several missions, the Indian navy and coast guard are responsible for maintaining maritime order in the Indian EEZ. They are well equipped in terms of surface ships and maritime aircraft to undertake patrolling and surveillance of the sea areas. The naval forces also include special helicopters for deployment of quick reaction forces, marine commandos, diving teams and damage control units. The Indian Coast Guard has grown over the years and plays a dominant role in policing

Indian waters with patrol vessels, interceptor boats and aircraft. In addition marine customs and police forces play an important role in handling criminal acts in and off Indian ports.

The maritime forces are based at various naval and coast guard stations and ports along the east and the west coast of India. Substantial forces are also deployed in the Andaman and Nicobar islands and the Lakshdweep group of islands. The control of naval forces is exercised by the Naval Headquarters through the Flag Officers Commanding-in-Chief based at Mumbai, Kochi and Vishakhapatnam.

Similarly, the Coast Guard headquarters at New Delhi exercises control over coast guard forces through Commander, Coast Guard Region based at Mumbai, Chennai, and Port Blair. Besides, there are Maritime Operation Centre (MOC) and Maritime Regional Coordination Centres (MRCC) located at Mumbai, Kochi, Vishakhapatnam and Port Blair.

These agencies maintain a constant communication network with maritime forces as also maritime centres located in neighbouring countries including the piracy reporting centre at Kuala Lumpur. India is also the coordinator of NAVAREA VIII for broadcasting weather reports, safety messages and other information relating to safety of mariners at sea.

The Indian maritime forces observe strict rules of engagement in accordance with international laws, treaties and conventions. These broadly dictate guidelines for procedures to be followed when investigating suspected ships. These rules are:

- The visit and search to be done with tact and consideration.
- True character is to be established by first examining papers and if there is a doubt the crew may be questioned and cargo examined.
- If the vessel flees or does not cooperate, she may be pursued and brought to by force, if necessary. A graduated increase in force is to be used till the vessel surrenders. Initial warnings are to be given on the radio and if there is no response, gun shots may be fired across the bows of the ship. The next phase involves firing into the ship to cripple the vessel by aiming at steering position. All efforts must be made to prevent loss of life.
- The Commanding Officer is the best judge at the scene of action to decide the quantum of force to be applied. When in

doubt, he is to consult his superiors keeping in mind the situation.

Search and Rescue Operations (SAR): Maritime search and rescue entails searching for persons, ships or other craft that are feared to be in distress or imminent danger, and rescuing or helping them. It is one of the operational tasks covered under the mission statement "marine safety."

The mission statement reads: "Prevent death, injuries, fatalities and property loss associated with maritime activities at sea, and reach out to those in distress and traumatic situations at all times in all weather conditions and ensure safety and security from natural or human induced disaster. "

The Coast Guard has prepared a National Maritime Search and Rescue Manual. The Coast Guard is the coordinating authority in a mission of search and rescue which is terrain-specific, not victim specific. The terrain comprises a whopping 4.6 million sq km in the maritime domain around India. The mission is carried out with the help of three maritime rescue coordination centres (MRCC) based at Mumbai, Chennai and Port Blair.

There are also rescue sub-centres functioning from Coast Guard district headquarters at Porbandar, Marmagoa, New Mangalore, Kochi, Vishakhapatnam, Paradeep, Haldia, Diglipur and Campbell Bay. These centres function round the clock. Communication for search and rescue is provided through fixed communication networks such as GMDSS (global maritime distress safety system), ATS (air traffic services) channels, DSC (digital selective calling) and through INMARSAT (the international maritime satellite earth station).

The Coast Guard has been operating the ship reporting system INDSAR (Indian M-SAR computerised ship reporting system) since 01 February 2003. It is a voluntary toll-free reporting system that will assist the MRCCs to divert the most suitable ship to the scene of distress, and also keep track of a ship that is overdue or may need urgent assistance. Participation in INDSAR is voluntary and free of cost. In addition to INDSAR, the Coast Guard plans to introduce ISLEREP, a system that may allow communication with ships within 25 miles of island territories. It is a VHF radio network system and seeks to provide additional navigational safety for ships as they pass through or close to the islands.

Preserving Maritime Environment: Environment security is one of the elements of national security. The elements are not stand-alone entities; they are mutually inclusive. They are constantly evolving variables with terrain specific characteristics. In a living planet, environment means the aggregate of all-external conditions and influences affecting the life and development of organisms. In the recent past, attention of the world has been focusing on major environmental degradation issues like deforestation, acid rain, depletion of the protective ozone layer, ocean pollution, and global warming among others. The seriousness of these debates for anybody will be understood from the fact that environmental damage can permeate through national confines.

Environmental damage due to war and military preparations, and using environment as a weapon of war are not strange issues. It has an ancient beginning when the Romans destroyed the fields of Carthage by spreading them with salt. Damages caused in Vietnam during the prolonged war, experiments in climate control as a weapon of war during the Cold War period and Environmental damage due to war and military preparations, and using environment as a weapon of war are not strange issues. It has an ancient beginning when the Romans destroyed the fields of Carthage by spreading them with salt. Damages caused in Vietnam during the prolonged war, experiments in climate control as a weapon of war during the Cold War period and intentional discharge of oil into the Persian Gulf during the Gulf War are examples. Such incidents point out that we cannot discount intentional spills in the marine environment. It could come up as an act of war or militancy, or just for economic reasons. The cautious interest in environmental damage and its effects to national security also comes from the fear of a prolonged nuclear winter that the world may face in the aftermath of a nuclear war. In a large-scale nuclear war, the resulting smoke and dust can radically alter the climate conditions of the earth.

For the Indian Coast Guard, marine environment security is a wholesome concept. It is a statutory function defined in the Coast Guard Act, 1978. The Coast Guard identifies marine environment security through four activities: Protection of marine environment, Preservation of marine environment, Prevention of marine pollution, and Control of marine pollution.

This is termed as the P3C factors of environment security. It is not related to a single activity like climate change. It involves any activity that will damage the marine environment. For example, it could be associated with red tide caused by blooming algae that can asphyxiate the fish population. It covers a wide range of concerns. Ocean by itself is a unique terrain. It is multi- dimensicnal. It has the surface, the ocean layer, the interfacial zones with air and land, and finally the depth— the large abyss of treasure. It is vital to a maritime nation. It is the only geographical terrain that provides the advantage of wealth and absolute stealth at the same time. Taking into consideration all the factors that govern the maritime security, we had defined the concept in a research thesis as the all-encompassing complementary faction of national security of a maritime nation from an ocean specific terrain assessment applicable to that nation. The essence of the ocean to humankind has been considered widely by a generic term, ocean wealth that under the concept of geoproperty can be amplified as ocean property to include all the variables that contribute to maritime security.

The Coast Guard is the coordinating authority for the P3C aspects of marine environment security according to the Act. The marine environment security, therefore, is one of its statutory duties. Since its formal inception in 1978, the Coast Guard has come a long way in marine environment security, especially in oil spill response management. But it needs to evolve further and develop its capabilities to envelop the entire P3C aspects. Being the national coordinator in oil spill response, it has a variety of responsibilities under the National Oil Spill Disaster Contingency Plan (NOS-DCP). It is the coordinator for oil spill response in the entire maritime zones of India with specific allocation for direct response functions in the maritime zones outside the port limits and notified areas around offshore oil facilities. This is a dual responsibility in which it has to develop its response capabilities and the prowess for coordination through various resource agencies and governmental set up.

The responsibility under the P3C concept is much larger. It covers total marine environment security. The Coast Guard needs to develop an edge towards this objective in its doctrinal approach to the problem. Technology, especially space applications will be a major contributing factor. India is an active partner in the South Asian Seas Programme of the United Nations through which it has been involved in developing a regional contingency plan for South Asia for combating oil and chemical spills at sea. The nodal agency is the Department of Ocean Development. The Coast Guard is a party to the plan. Once established, it is expected that there will be bilateral cooperation between the South Asian maritime states in oil spill response in the area. The Coast Guard needs to be prepared for it.

The Coast Guard is the national agency for ensuring marine environment security in India. It involves protection and preservation of the environment and prevention and control of pollution. As an Armed

Force of the Union it has the discipline, determination, and drive for it. It needs to develop its capabilities, expertise, and interactive prowess towards this object. It will be able to do so with a doctrinal approach well supported by the government. Here the emphasis is varied; technology, law, and funding are the key factors. In a doctrinal approach environment security at the national level should be seen separately with marine environment security as part of it.

Evolution of marine environment technology is vital to this doctrine. The doctrinal approach can identify the domains through which the goal of environment security can be achieved. Oil spill management is complementary to this goal in such an approach. It is vital to wealth generation and protection in the overall scenario.

Combating Oil Spills: An oil spill is the release of a liquid petroleum hydrocarbon into the environment due to human activity, and is a form of pollution. The term often refers to marine oil spills, where oil is released into the ocean or coastal waters. The oil may be a variety of materials, including crude oil, refined petroleum products (such as gasoline or diesel fuel) or by-products, ships' bunkers, oily refuse or oil mixed in waste. Spills take months or even years to clean up.

The oil penetrates and opens up the structure of the plumage of birds, reducing its insulating ability, and so making the birds more vulnerable to temperature fluctuations and much less buoyant in the water. It also impairs birds' flight abilities, making it difficult or impossible to forage and escape from predators. As they attempt to preen, birds typically ingest oil that coats their feathers, causing kidney damage, altered liver function, and digestive tract irritation. This and the limited foraging ability quickly causes dehydration and metabolic imbalances. Most birds affected by an oil spill die unless there is human intervention.

Marine mammals exposed to oil spills are affected in similar ways as seabirds. Oil coats the fur of Sea otters and seals, reducing its insulation abilities and leading to body temperature fluctuations and hypothermia. Ingestion of the oil causes dehydration and impaired digestion.

Indian Coast Guard have various plans to combat oil spills such as National Oil Spill Disaster Contingency Plan. Various methods used by it to clean oil spills are:

- Use of microorganisms or biological agents to break down or remove oil

- Controlled burning can effectively reduce the amount of oil in water, if done properly. But it can only be done in low wind and can cause air pollution.
- Dispersants act as detergents, clustering around oil globules and allowing them to be carried away in the water. This improves the surface aesthetically, and mobilizes the oil. Smaller oil droplets, scattered by currents, may cause less harm and may degrade more easily. But the dispersed oil droplets infiltrate into deeper water and can lethally contaminate coral. Recent research indicates that some dispersants are toxic to corals.
- In some cases, natural attenuation of oil may be most appropriate, due to the invasive nature of facilitated methods of remediation, particularly in ecologically sensitive areas.
- Dredging for oils dispersed with detergents and other oils denser than water.
- Skimming
- Solidifying

The biggest of this kind of operation was operation Safai in which the largest threat from an oil-spill faced by India was successfully combated. The collision between two super tankers at the entrance to the straits of Malacca on January 21, 1993 spread oil which ultimately extended to a distance of 90 nautical miles and covered an area of 8000 sq nautical miles. The slick reached as close as 10 nautical miles to the Nicobar Island and, but for the efforts of the Coast Guard, the ecological and environment damage to Nicobar group of Island would have been catastrophic. The professional skill and competence displayed by the men of the service drew appreciation of all.

Welfare activities: The Coast Guard introduced community interaction programmes in August 1999 specifically to interact with coastal communities including fishers. These programmes have been only partially successful, because of the limitations imposed on the Coast Guard by other mandated duties.

The interaction with fishers aims at inducing safety awareness among them, warning them when weather conditions deteriorate, making friendly contacts related to public safety, and providing distress relief services including medical relief. These programmes have been appreciated by the community in various coastal states and islands. Though the Coast

Guard has been able to strike a chord with the fisheries community on safety matters, much more needs to be done. Fishers in India are either traditional or follow a traditional safety mindset even when they operate larger vessels. Mechanization ensures speed through engines or outboard motors in place of traditional oars which necessitated longer stay at sea, thereby increasing the probability of distress. On other aspects of safety – inspection of vessels, communication equipment, weather information through radio, life saving appliances, safety training, organized search and rescue efforts, coordination with the Coast Guard is good.

A more proactive approach to safety by the Coast Guard, by fisheries administrations and by fisher communities will improve safety at sea. To sum up, the Coast Guard plays a definite role in safety of life and property of fishers in India. The limitations lie in the disorganized state of fishers in India with respect to safety as low awareness, poor compliance with safety procedures and also in the modest personnel size of the Indian Coast Guard relative to the tasks. But the Coast Guard has the will and determination to effectively carry out its missions, including that of enhancing the safety of fishers.

Acts, Rules & Regulations

Section 1 - 3: This is Preliminary section. It includes:

- Section 1: Short title and commencement
- Section 2: Definitions
- Section 3: Persons subject to this Act

Section 4 – 13: Deals with Constitution of the Coast Guard and Conditions of Service of the Members of the Coast Guard. It includes:

- Section 4: Constitution of the Coast Guard
- Section 5: Control, direction etc
- Section 6: Enrolment
- Section 7: Liability for service outside India
- Section 8: Oath of allegiance
- Section 9: Resignation and withdrawal from the post
- Section 10: Tenure of service under the Act
- Section 11: Dismissal or removal by Central Government and by other officers
- Section 12: Certificate of termination of service
- Section 13: Restrictions respecting right to form association, freedom of speech, etc.

Section 14: Deals with Duties and functions of Coast Guard

Section 15 - 52: Deals with various types of offences.

- Section15: Correspondence, etc with offenders
- Section 16: Deserting post and neglect of duty
- Section 17: Mutiny
- Section 18: Persons on board ship or aircraft seducing Coast Guard personnel from allegiance
- Section 19: Striking or threatening superior officers
- Section 20: Disobedience to superior officer
- Section 21: Ill-treating subordinates
- Section 22: Quarrelling, fighting and disorderly behaviour
- Section 23: Certain forms of disgraceful conduct
- Section 24: Drunkenness
- Section 25: Desertion and aiding desertion
- Section 26: Breaking out of ship and absence without leave
- Section 27: Losing ship or aircraft
- Section 28: Dangerous unauthorised flying
- Section 29: Inaccurate certificate
- Section 30: Low flying and annoyance by flying
- Section 31: Disobedience of lawful command of captain of an aircraft
- Section 32: False accusations
- Section 33: Falsifying official documents and false declarations
- Section 34: Offences in respect of property
- Section 35: Damage to property
- Section 36: Taking unauthorised goods on board
- Section 37: Offences in respect of papers relating to vessel, craft or aircraft taken into custody
- Section 38: Offences in respect of vessel, craft or aircraft taken into custody
- Section 39: Unlawful taking of ransom
- Section 40: Offences relating to Coast Guard Courts
- Section 41: Escape from custody
- Section 42: Violation of the Act, rules and orders
- Section 43: False answers on enrolment

- Section 44: Offences against good order and discipline
- Section 45: Attempt
- Section 46: Abetment of offences that have been committed
- Section 47: Abetment of offence punishable with death and not committed
- Section 48: Abetment of offences punishable with imprisonment and not committed
- Section 49: Civil offences
- Section 50: Civil offences not triable by a Coast Guard Court
- Section 51: Period of limitation for trial of offences under the Act
- Section 52: Trial, etc of a person who ceases to be subject to the Act

Section 53 - 58: Deals with various types of punishments.

- Section 53: Punishments awardable by Coast Guard Courts
- Section 54: Alternative punishments awardable by Coast Guard Courts
- Section 55: Combination of punishments
- Section 56: Punishments otherwise than by Coast Guard Courts
- Section 57: Minor punishments
- Section 57A: Punishment for officers below the rank of Commandant
- Section 58: Provisions as to award of punishments

Section 59 - 63: Deals with Proceedings before Arrest and Trial.

- Section 59: Custody of offenders
- Section 60: Duty of Commanding Officer in regard to detention
- Section 61: Arrest by Civil authorities
- Section 62: Capture of deserters
- Section 63: Coast Guard police officers

Section 64 - 72: Deals with Coast Guard Courts

- Section 64: Power to convene a Coast Guard Court
- Section 65: Composition of Coast Guard Courts
- Section 66:Dissolution of a Coast Guard Court

- Section 67: Powers of a Coast Guard Court
- Section 68: Prohibition of second trial
- Section 69: Application of Act during term of sentence
- Section 70: Place of trial
- Section 71: Choice between criminal court and Coast Guard Court
- Section 72: Power of criminal court to require delivery of an offender

Section 73 - 95: Deals with Procedure of Coast Guard Courts

- Section 73:Law Officer
- Section 74: Challenges
- Section 75: Oaths of members, Law Officer and witness
- Section 76: Voting by members
- Section 77: General rule as to evidence
- Section 78: Judicial notice
- Section 79: Summoning of witnesses
- Section 80: Documents exempted from production
- Section 81: Commissions for examination of witnesses
- Section 82: Examination of witness on commission
- Section 83: Alternative findings
- Section 84: Presumption as to signatures
- Section 85: Enrolment paper
- Section 86: Presumption as to certain documents
- Section 87: Evidence of previous convictions and general character
- Section 88: Lunacy of accused
- Section 89: Subsequent fitness of lunatic accused for trial
- Section 90: Transmission to Central Government of orders under section 89
- Section 91: Release of lunatic accused
- Section 92:Delivery of lunatic accused to relatives
- Section 93: Order for custody and disposal of property pending trial
- Section 94: Order for disposal of property regarding which offence is committed
- Section 95: Powers of Coast Guard Court in relation to proceedings under this Act

Section 96 - 114: Execution and Suspension of Sentences

- Section 96: Form of sentence of death
- Section 97: Interim custody until execution of sentence of death
- Section 98: Execution of sentence of death
- Section 99:Commencement of sentence of imprisonment or detention
- Section 100:Execution of sentence of imprisonment
- Section 101: Temporary custody of offender
- Section 102: Conveyance of prisoner from place to place
- Section 103:Communication of certain orders to prison officers
- Section 104: Execution of sentence of fine
- Section 105: Informality or error in the order or warrant
- Section 106: Imprisonment or detention of offender already under sentence
- Section 107: Suspension of sentence of imprisonment or detention
- Section 108: Release on suspension
- Section 109: Computation of period of suspension
- Section 110: Order after suspension
- Section 111: Reconsideration of case after suspension
- Section 112: Fresh sentence after suspension
- Section 113: Scope of power of suspension
- Section 114: Effect of suspension and remission on dismissal

Section 115 - 116: Chief Law Officer and Law Officers

- Section 115: Appointment of Chief Law Officer and Law Officers
- Section 116: Functions of Chief Law Officer

Section 117 -118: Judicial Review of Proceedings of Courts

- Section 117: Judicial review by the Chief Law Officer
- Section 118: Consideration by the Director General

Section 119 - 120: Modification of Findings and Sentences, Pardons, Commutation and Remission of Sentences

- Section 119: Petitions to Central Government or Director General against findings and sentences

- Section 120: Powers of Central Government and Director General in respect of findings and sentences

Section 121 – 123: Miscellaneous

- Section 121: Powers and duties conferable and imposable on members of the Coast Guard
- Section 122: Protection for acts of members of the Coast Guard
- Section 123: Power to make Rules

Weapons and Equipments

The Coast Guard, in 1978 began with two old frigates seconded by the Navy and five small patrol vessels from MHA. Over the past two decades, it has attained a force level of 65 ships and craft and 44 aircraft and helicopters as follows:

Advance Offshore Patrol Vessels	04
Offshore Patrol Vessels	09
Fast Patrol Vessels	10
Inshore Patrol Vessel	13
Seaward Defence Boats	02
Hovercraft	06
Interceptor Boats	12
Interceptors (Vadyar Class)	08
Interceptors (Bristol Class)	01
Dornier Aircraft	24
Chetak Helicopter	17
Advance Light Helicopter	03

Coast Guard weaponry includes FN 35 and Glock 17.9 mm pistols, Heckler & Koch MP5 sub-machine guns, INSAS 5.56 mm assault rifles. INSAS 5.56 mm light machine guns, AGS-17 Plamya 30 mm automatic grenade launcher and Igla-19K310/ SA-16 Gimlet portable Surface to Air Missile and 30 mm gun. Type 81 Assault rifles, AKM rifles, INSAS 5. 56 MM Assault rifle, G3A3 Battle rifle, MP5 Submachine-gun ; Uzi submachinegun, M9 pistol ; RPG 7 Rocket-propelled grenade launchers ; and M67 hand-grenades. CRPF also uses landmine detectors ; Light Machine-Guns and Heavy-Machine-Guns.

Recruitment

Officers: The recruitment of officers into the Coast Guard is carried out twice in a year to match with the dates of commencement of basic training at Naval Academy. The applications for the post of Assistant Commandant is advertised through National Dailies, Employment Exchange and Coast Guard Website. The preliminary selections of the candidates is conducted at Delhi, Mumbai, Chennai and Kolkatta by conduct of Mental Ability Test and an Interview.

These shortlisted candidates are invited to face Coast Guard Selection Board at Noida. The selection procedure followed at CGSB is a three pronged system, where in candidates are assessed for officer like qualities by three different techniques. The system is similar to the one followed by Army, Navy and Air force. Those who are recommended by the Board and found medically fit are offered the appointment as per merit viz-a-viz number of vacancies.

The enrolment of the selected candidates for the post of Assistant Commandant is carried out at Indian Coast Guard Station Delhi. These officers are also given a 10 days short course on personality development prior sending them to Naval Academy for basic training.

The qualifications required to become an officer in the Coast Guard are: 10+2+degree with Physics or Mathematics in order to join under General Duty; 10+2 and a commercial pilot license or BSc degree with Physics and Maths to join under Pilot/Navigator; a degree in Naval Architecture/ Mechanical/ Electrical/ Electronics/ Marine/ Design Engineering for the Technical branches.

Other Ranks: Recruitment to the OR is done bi-annually. Candidates can join one of three branches: Yantriks, Naviks (General Duty) or Navik (Domestic Branch).

Entry to the Naviks is done through a Mental Ability Test, entrance test and an interview. Qualified candidates undergo a medical examination and those who pass are selected on the basis of merit. Yantrik candidates undergo a written test, followed by an interview, followed by a medical examination.

The qualifications required are: Matriculate Diploma in Mechanical/ Electrical/ Electronic / Aeronautical engineering for a Yantrik; Class X or equivalent for Naviks (GD) and Class VIII pass for Naviks (DB). All candidates must be within the age of 17-22 years (with five year relaxations for SC candidates and three year relaxation for OBC candidates).

Training: The training needs of the Indian Coast Guard are taken care of by Indian Navy. The Coast Guard Officers are trained at Naval Training establishments along with Naval Officers. On completion of basic training of 72 weeks at naval Training establishments / ships, these officers are subjected to Coast Guard specific training for 8 weeks at Coast Guard Training Centre, Kochi.

Further training is performance based. Those who perform meritoriously during basic training are selected for advance / specialized training at specific Naval training establishments. The disciplines in which advanced and specialized training is given are Navigation and Direction, Communication, Gunnery, Logistic, Metrology and Information Technology.

The Technical entry officers, on completion of specialized training in electrical and mechanical branches are selected for advance training at Indian Institute of Technology, Mumbai / Indian Institute of Armament Technology, Pune, based on their performance.

The deserving officers are also given opportunity for specialised training Abroad with reputed organization such as US Coast Guard, Japan Coast Guard etc. The field in which such training is given are Marine Pollution Control, Search & Rescue, Crisis Management, Entry Level Port Ops GMRP3, International Maritime Officer, Boarding Officers course etc. Coast Guard officers are also trained in inter service Training establishments such as Defence Services Staff College (Wellington), College of Defence Management (Secunderabad) and National Defence College (New Delhi).

The requirement of Air arm of Coast Guard is met by Indian Air Force. The basic flying training of Coast Guard pilots is held at Basic Flying training School (Allahabad) with Indian Air Force. Further, the advance training course at Air Force Station Tambaram, Chennai is also taken care by Indian Air Force.

Famous Operations

Operation for Saving Olive Ridley Turtles: On 03 May 1985 an Indian Coast Guard Ship whilst on patrol observed an unusual movement of a floating object west of Murmagao Head. The Ship reduced her speed and manoeuvred to get close to the floating object to investigate. On stopping it was observed that two live sea turtles were entangled in the fishing nets. The ship recovered the turtles onboard and the nets were cut immediately with utmost care so as to avoid injury to the turtles. The turtles were thereafter released into the sea. Operation *Olive,* launched by Coast Guard, is an annual feature. It has helped in the protection of the endangered *Olive Ridley* turtles from being poached off the Gahrimatha coast in Orissa. A regular patrol by Coast Guard keeps fishermen at bay from fishing the endangered species.

Capture of Pirated Ship Alondra Rainbow: It is the MV Alondra Rainbow case that gives merits to Coast Guard. The standoff between the hijacked MV Alondra Rainbow, a 7, 000 ton Panama registered vessel, belonging to Japanese owners and Indian coast guard ships in November 1999, and its final capture was regarded as a great success for maritime community to counter sea piracy. The vessel was en route from Kuala Tanjung, Indonesia to Milke, Japan. The Piracy Reporting Centre (PRC) of the International Maritime Bureau (IMB) had announced through a worldwide broadcast that pirates had captured the vessel. According to the PRC, the crew of the vessel were found safe in Thailand and the vessel was expected to turn up in any Indian port to discharge cargo. What followed was a drama on the high seas leading to the arrest of pirates who came up for trial in Mumbai.

SAR Support to Maldives Coast Guard: On 10 July 2004 Maritime Rescue Coordination Centre(MRCC), Mumbai received a distress message from Maldives Coast Guard regarding a missing fishing boat with four persons onboard. According to the information the fishing boat named Mush Tharee was on passage from Naifaru island to Kaashidhoo island in the Maldivian group of islands and was last sighted on 09 July 04 at 1030 hrs. The reported position of the boat was 150 nautical miles outside Indian Search and Rescue Region (ISRR). The concerted efforts of Indian Coast Guard resulted in sighting of vessel by a merchant vessel named MV Bonthi on 12 July at 1417 hrs (IST) in position 270 miles South West of Trivandrum. All the crew have been reported to be in healthy condition. Coast Guard, Maldives thanked Indian Coast Guard for prompt assistance and cooperation. Indian Coast Guard has supported and cooperated with Maldives Coast Guard on many occasions in the past also.

Search and Rescue of Sri Lankan Fishermen: On 30 June, Maritime Rescue Coordination Centre (MRCC), Chennai received a telephonic message regarding a distress incident from MV SBS Nimbus, (C/S VQPJ5) operating in Kaveri Basin off the coast of Andhra Pradesh. According to the information, the vessel had sighted a fishing boat adrift at 1306 hrs on 30 June in position 115 Nautical Miles South West off Kakinada.

The fishing boat was identified as FV AYOSA BABBY (NM 278) with five crew of Sri Lankan nationality onboard. The crew were reported to be in dehydrated state as the fishing boat was adrift since last 20 days due to defect in her main propulsion machinery and there was no food onboard for last five days. MRCC, Chennai assumed Coordination for SAR and directed MV SBS Nimbus to provide food & water to the fatigued crew. Since Kakinada Port was identified as the nearest harbour from the position of the distress, MV SBS Nimbus was directed to tow the fishing boat there. A Coast Guard Dornier Aircraft was also launched simultaneously from Chennai PM 30 June.

Rescue of MV Genius Star VI Crew: Indian Coast Guard Maritime Rescue Coordination Centre, Chennai received a distress alert from a merchant ship MV Genius Star VI on 13 Apr 04 at about 0400 hrs. The vessel was in position about 160 nautical miles South East of Sagar Island and was listing dangerously. The vessel was 96 metres long with 17 crew onboard (16 Chinese and one Taiwanese). In response to the alert received a CG Dornier aircraft was tasked in the area along with two CG ships ICGS Razia Sultana and ICGS Varaha. In addition, three merchant ships viz., MV Lok Maheshwari, MV Julian and MV Tonghai in the vicinity of the incident site were also diverted to render assistance. At about 1200 hrs the ICG Dornier on task reported sinking of the ill-fated vessel and sighting of the crew onboard two lifeboats and one life raft. Out of the total 17 crew 15 were rescued in a well-coordinated SAR operation involving two Coast Guard ships, one Dornier and two merchant ships viz., MV Julian and MV Tanghai.

Interrogation of the rescued crew revealed that out of the three life boats lowered prior sinking, one life boat capsized owing to heavy listing of the ship and rough sea condition. It was further learnt that the ship sank due to uncontrolled flooding in the aft engine room. The successful saving of the 15 Chinese crew of the ill-fated vessel out of a total of 17 onboard, has been lauded by the Chinese and Indian Press. The efforts of Indian Coast Guard have also been appreciated by the Chinese Ambassador in India. Safina-Ul-Badria Coast Guard Maritime Rescue Sub Centre, New Mangalore received a telephonic call at about 1130 hrs on 31 March 2004 regarding the vessel "Safina-Ul-Badria" in distress, in position 17 Miles South West of New Mangalore.

ICGS Sarojini Naidu was sailed immediately with all damage control items onboard. On arrival it was observed that the aft portion of the vessel Safina-Ul-Badria was already submerged due to flooding of the compartments.

The vessel was precariously balanced with the forward part projecting out of water. The six in number crew abandoned the vessel and were rescued by CGS Sarojini Naidu. The vessel Safina-Ul-Badria later sank in the same position at 1356 hrs.

Rescue of Malaysian Tug Crew: Coast Guard Maritime Rescue & Coordination Centre (MRCC) Port Blair received a message on 31 March 2004 from Maritime Rescue Coordination Centre (MRCC) Malaysia that a Malaysian vessel "TB Mayang Sari", has sunk in position 50 nautical miles (East of Nancowry island in the Andaman group of islands) at about 0700 hrs. All eleven in number crew (all Indonesian) of the ill-fated vessel had abandoned the vessel and were reported to be afloat in a liferaft. MRCC, Port Blair immediately diverted a Coast Guard vessel, ICGS Gangadevi, which was at sea on EEZ patrol, for search and rescue operation.

Simultaneously, a Coast Guard Dornier aircraft was also launched from Port Blair at 1130 hrs in SAR configuration with droppable liferafts. ICGS Gangadevi arrived in area at 1300 hrs and rescued all the 11 crew members. After providing with first aid and completion of detailed joint interrogation by the various authorities, the rescued crew was handed over to local authorities.

Rescue of MSV Jal Jyoti Crew: Indian Coast Guard Maritime Rescue Coordination Sub-Sub Centre, Okha received an information at 1115 hrs on 20 February 2004 from authority of Mandavi Port, Gujarat that MSV Jal Jyoti has sunk in position about 22 nautical miles North West of Okha at 2330 hrs on 19 February 2004. Ten in number crew of the vessel had abandoned the vessel and were adrift at sea in a life raft.

Within 15 minutes of receipt of the distress message, a hovercraft H-184 was sailed from Okha and another Coast Guard vessel C-141 which was operating along IMBL was also diverted for Search and Rescue. H-184 arrived at the distress position at 1215 hrs and began carrying out a planned search pattern based on the life raft's most probable position due to wind and current. At about 1500 hrs the crew of MSV Jal Jyoti were located. The crew were thereafter taken to Okha for medical assistance.

Rescue of French Tourist: Maritime Rescue Coordination Centre, Port Blair received a distress message at 1425 hrs on 31 January 2004 regarding a French tourist suffering from decompression sickness and was stated to be in serious condition. The tourist Mr Guillon was diving off Barren Island in Andaman and Nicobar group of islands when he suffered from decompression sickness and MRCC (Port Blair) was requested for saving his life through immediate evacuation. Maritime Rescue Coordination Centre carried out a quick assessment of the situation considering various factor like sunset time, distance and condition of the casualty.

Thereafter, a Indian Coast Guard helicopter, CG 804 was launched at 1518 hrs from Port Blair. Simultaneously a Dornier aircraft, CG 770 was also launched to act as a communication link and a CG ship was kept standby for SAR cover. The patient was airlifted by helicopter and brought to Port Blair, where he was admitted at GB Pant hospital in a serious condition. The patient recuperated and was thereafter transferred to Thailand for further medication on own request using private ambulance aircraft.

Anti-piracy Attempt off Kerala Coast: On 27 July 2004 MRCC Mumbai received information regarding piratical attack on MV Sea Diamond III approximately 18 nautical miles west of Quilon. The vessel was towing a barge, Kirty II, when pirates from 12 fishing vessels boarded the barge and stole its emergency towing rope. Communication was established with Master of MV Sea Diamond III by CGS Durgabai Deshmukh to ascertain details. Random checks of the fishing boats in the vicinity were conducted to establish the theft.

Tsunami Relief Operations: Coast guard did a veru commendable job during Tsunami relisf operations in India, Maldives, Colombo and Male.

India: The Indian Coast Guard(ICG) had launched massive distress relief operations off the Eastern and South Western coasts of India and Andaman & Nicobar group of Islands w. e. f. from 26 December 2004. The Ships and Aircraft carried out extensive coastal surveillance effort over the effected areas. ICG carried out relief operations in Sri Lanka and Maldives also.

ICG ships and aircraft successfully evacuated thousands of personnel from the effected areas, and rescued dozens from the sea. A total of 23 ICG ships were deployed for the relief operations, 230 sorties were flown by aircraft and helicopters, 365 tons of relief material were distributed and medical relief was provided to over 2850 personnel.

Maldives: The ship had disembarked 86 tonnes of relief material at Male for southern group of islands. Her Helicopter and ship's company had been extensively used for helping the needy ashore including repair of diesel generators and supply of medicines, drinking water and medical relief by the ships medical team.

The ship's relief team comprising technical and medical personnel were disembarked by local boats on 06 January 2005 for carrying out emergency relief and medical care in folowing islands:

- Kudahuvadhoo
- Vanee
- Ribudhoo
- Hulhudheli

The medical team of ICGS Sagar alongwith a International Red Cross team has evacuated seriously ill patients from Vanee island and provided life saving drugs to them. The technical team of the ship has also restored power supply in Hulhudheli and Ribudhoo islands by rectification of power distribution boxes.

Relief teams of ICGS Sagar had visited all the inhabited islands of Maldvies by 06 January 2005. The ship returned to Mumbai on 14 January 2005.

Colombo: ICGS Samar sailed from Kochi 01 Jan. 2005 and distributed relief material at Colombo on 02 January 2005. The ship returned to Kochi for a second run on 05 January 2005 and recommenced relief operations at Colombo wef 17 January 2005. The ship disembarked 101 tons of relief material on 18 January 2005. On 20 January 2005, the ship de-inducted 77 Army personnel of 402 Field Ambulance along with their equipment from Colombo and returned Kochi 21 January 2005.

Male: ICGS Vigraha Sailed from Kochi on 09 Jan. 2005 to arrive Male 10 January 2005 and commenced relief operations. The ship was engaged in disembarkation of relief material in the Southern Group of Maldives Atoll. The ship departed Male on 21 January 2005 and returned Kochi on 23 January 2005 on completion of deployment.

Medical Evacuation from MV Annapurna: On 12 Apr. 2007 at about 1630 hours the Maritime Rescue Coordination Centre, (MRCC), Port Blair received a request from MV Annapurna in position about 11 nautical miles North-East of Narcondum Island (A & N Island) for immediate medical evacuation of one crew who has severed right hand finger while working on board.

On receipt of the information, the ICGS Akka Devi on patrol in the area was diverted to evacuate the injured crew to Diglipur. ICGS Akka Devi established communication with the vessel at 1705 hours on 12 Apr 07 and evacuated the injured crew at 1915 hours on 12 Apr 07 in position

54 nautical miles North-East of Diglipur Island. The injured crew was administered first aid and thereafter handed over at Diglipur AM 13 Apr 07 to the District Medical Officer, Diglipur.

Medical Evacuation from Dredger Prof. Gorjunov: On 15 Apr. 2007 at about 0040 hours the Maritime Rescue Coordination Centre, (MRCC), Chennai received a request from the Master of Dredger Prof Gorjunov in position about 15 nautical miles South East of Point Calimere (Tamil Nadu) for immediate medical evacuation of one crew, who had dislocated his shoulder. On receipt of the information, the ICGS Jijabai on patrol in the area was diverted to evacuate the injured crew. At about 0745 hours one 15 Apr. 2007, ICGS Jijabai arrived in the area. The Patient was transferred to ICGS Jijabai and brought to Indian Coast Guard Station Mandapam (Tamil Nadu). The patient was handed over to DCI representative in Rameshwaram and admitted in Pioneer Hospital, Ramnad.

Awards

President Tatrakshak Medal(Gallantry)	02
Tatrakshak Medal (Gallantry)	44
President Tatrakshak Medal (Meritorious)	15
Tatrakshak Medal (Meritorious)	78

Modernization

India has a 7, 516 km coastline, 1197 islands and an Exclusive Economic Zone (EEZ) spanning 2.02 million sq km, which is expected to go up to almost 3 million sq km after the delimitation of the continental shelf. The Coast Guard has also seen a sharp increase in piracy on the high seas, smuggling contrabands, search-and-rescue operations and to prevent 'possible' covert transfers of weapons of mass destruction and thus additional personnel & equipment will be needed to effectively carry out its duties. Rajat Pandit reports that the Coast Guard envisions having 169 vessels, including 12 hovercraft, and 99 aircraft as per the 2002 - 2012 Perspective Plan.

Overall, the Coast Guard has projected force-levels of 268 vessels (including 173 small patrol craft), 113 aircraft, 18 Nishant UAVs (unmanned aerial vehicles) and Aerostat & OTH (over-the-horizon) radars by 2017, which is just a little over a decade away. Included in these force levels are 60 helicopters, 35 Do-228 aircraft for coastal surveillance (an increase from the 24 aircraft currently in service), 11 medium-range reconnaissance aircraft, more than 40 interceptor boats and six deep-sea patrol vessels. Rajat Pandit also reports that the present Coast Guard manpower strength will need to be increased to around 15, 000 officers & personnel.

Government has placed acquisition orders for five fast patrol vessels, two advanced offshore patrol vessels, three pollution control vessels, five inshore patrol vessels and 11 interceptor boats. The Coast Guard realizes that ship traffic in the Gulf of Mannar and Palk Bay is expected to grow immensely, with the Sethusamudram (pronounced as Saythu-Samu-Dhram) ship canal project, currently being built near Rameshwaram in Tamil Nadu as a shorter maritime route between India's eastern and western coasts. The force is also gradually taking over the activities related to Operation Tasha and Operation Swan, currently conducted by the Indian Navy. Operation Tasha involves patrolling conducted in the Palk Bay, along the Tamil Nadu coast, mainly due to terrorist activities and the influx of refugees. Operation Swan began after the 1993 Mumbai serial blasts, to enhance coastal security and patrolling on the west coast against suspicious movement of hostile ships.

The ageing platforms and systems of the Indian Coast Guard will soon be replaced and the government is working out a suitable schedule for their replacement through the forthcoming annual acquisition plans like faster pace of modernization of the Coast Guard in view of the emerging seaward threat.

India gained international stature and became an economic powerhouse, the Coast Guard's responsibilities were bound to increase. Infiltration from land borders was becoming increasingly difficult for terrorists, thanks to constant vigil by security forces and the changing environment in Jammu & Kashmir the sea route was becoming another option for these elements.

As the pressure on terrorists on land increases, this threat is more likely than ever to come from the sea. Government is aware of the need for acquiring new aircraft and surveillance equipment for the Coast Guard for it to perform its multifarious role effectively. Enforcement of maritime laws is another domain that is becoming increasingly important due to rising threat of terrorism from the sea. To meet such varied challenges, up-gradation and modernization of aviation assets is necessary.

73 coastal state police stations will soon be set up for better vigil along the country's vast coastline. Pollution Control Vessels would be procured.

Miscellaneous

BUVIK (Bureau of Naviks): The Bureau of Naviks is an independent unit directly responsible to Director General Coast Guard for its functioning. The Bureau being located in Mumbai is under the administrative control of The Commander, Coast Guard Region (West), Mumbai. Bureau of Naviks as Record Office began its functioning in the premises of Coast Guard Regional Headquarters (West) at Worli, Mumbai in 1981. Later on this office was shifted to CABS building at Mankhurd on 01 Dec 1982 and was named as Bureau of Naviks (BUVIK). Bureau celebrates its anniversary on 01 December.

The aim of this Bureau is to position the manpower of right type and in right numbers to the various Coast Guard ships/establishments within the existing resources to ensure highest degree of operational readiness and efficiency all the time.

The role of this bureau is the Development and Management of the Enrolled personnel of Indian Coast Guard right from their inception till discharge/ retirement from service and to advice Coast Guard Headquarters in formulation of rules and policies for optimum growth of men and service.

The Officer-in-Charge, Bureau of Naviks (BUVIK) is directly responsible for implementation of the policies of Coast Guard Headquarters in respect of training, promotion, transfer, release and pension of CG Enrolled Personnel. Bureau is concerned with all aspects of EPs career in the service right after their recruitment till their retirement/ discharge from service and also with cases relating to post retirement benefits. The role profile covers the following aspects:

- Transfers of Personnel.
- Deputing personnel for various training.
- Preparation of panel for Higher Rank Boards.
- Processing of cases relating to change of branch, NOC for applying jobs outside Coast Guard and NOC for Passports.
- Computerisation of records of serving and retired CG Personnel.
- Maintenance of Database.
- Maintenance of statistical data.
- Preparation/Revision of Manning Plan of EPs.
- Verification of Service Book, Educational and Caste certificate.

- Keeping track of Medical Records and ensuring timely completion of Re-categorisation Medical Board.
- Preparation of panel for DPC twice in a year.
- To assist Coast Guard Headquarters in formulation of rules and policies for the growth of men and service.
- Maintenance of records in respect of EPs viz courses/training, annual assessment, DO's remarks, GCBs, award of medal and particulars of NOK/ family.
- Verification of SBs/leave accounts, Verification of educational qualifications/character and antecedents/ caste etc.
- Medical Records.
- Early settlement of pension gratuity and other claims as may be admissible on retirement/ release/discharge.

REFERENCES

Can India Overtake China?: Foreign Policy, July–Aug. 2003.

The Role of Perception in Naval Diplomacy: Naval War College Review, Sep.–Oct. 1974.

World Military Aircraft Inventory: Aerospace Source Book 2007, Aviation Week & Space Technology, Jan. 15, 2007.

Asia Times, Aug. 20, 2004.

AVIA Newsletter.

Baldev Raj Nayar and T. V. Paul, India in the World Order: Searching for Major-Power Status, Cambridge, U.K.: Cambridge Univ. Press, 2003.

C. Raja Mohan, Crossing the Rubicon: The Shaping of India's New Foreign Policy, New Delhi: Viking, 2003.

Clyde Prestowitz et al: The Great Reverse.

Daily Pioneer, Mar. 15, 2004

Deccan Herald, Mar. 13, 2004

Deep Waters: Life in the Coast Guard.

Dte General, Indian Coast Guard, New Delhi

Employment News.

Hindustan Times, Feb. 09, 2004.

Hindustan Times, Mar. 04, 2004.

India and China: A Special Economic Analysis," Morgan Stanley Equity Research.

India Express, Mar. 12, 2004.

Indian Express, Feb. 13, 2004.

International Order and the Future of World Politics, by T. V. Paul and John A. Hall, Naval War College Review, Autumn 2000.

Ministry of Defence.

New India Press, Mar. 15, 2004.

Stephen P. Cohen,"Situating India," in India: Emerging Power, Washington, D.C.: Brookings Institution Press, 2001.

Stephen Peter Rosen,"Strategic Traditions for the Asia-Pacific Region," Naval War College Review, 2001.

Telegraph India, Apr. 02, 2004.

Telegraph India, Mar. 19, 2004.

Thales News, Feb. 2002.

The Hindu, Mar. 01, 2004.

The Hindu, Mar. 10, 2004.

The Telegraph, Mar. 02, 2004.

The Week, Mar. 28, 2004 .

Times of India, Mar. 06, 2004.

Times of India, Mar. 17, 2004.

Times of India, Mar. 23, 2004.

Yale Global, Sept. 2004.

PART – III
PARAMILITARY FORCES UNDER MINISTRY OF HOME AFFAIRS

4

Assam Rifles

"Friends of the Hill People"

Introduction

Since Independence, some of the North-Eastern States became an arena for secessionist and insurgent activities. Maintenance of law and order, countering insurgency and reassuring the people of the region became an important tasks for the security forces.

These tasks initially fell on the Assam Rifles and when the Army eventually assumed control, the latter relied heavily on the experience and competence of the former. With the problems still continuing unresolved, the Assam Rifles, in conjunction with the Army, continues to remain deployed in remote and under-developed areas, braving hostile terrain, extreme climates and effectively combating insurgency. Through its long deployment in the tribal belt, the Assam Rifles have developed ethos primarily based on friendship with the peoples of the region.

The Assam Rifles have traditionally participated in all developmental activities of the region and have helped in bringing the people of this remote and under-developed region into the national main stream. The AR along with the Church, have managed to transform pre-historic animalistic societies of the northeast from the stone-age to space-age in three or four generations. Their humane and tactful handling of the inhabitants of there far-flung regions and tribal areas; be it during the initial era of pacification, or in the immediate post-Independence period of political turmoil, instability, ethnic tribal aspirations and resultant disturbed conditions; the AR troops have managed to win the hearts and minds of the populace in a good natured and large-hearted manner. It is, therefore, not for nothing, that the famous anthropologist and naturalist, Verrier Elwin who was an adviser on Tribal Affairs to North-East Frontier Agency has bestowed on them a singularly significant sobriquet of sorts: "The Friends of the Hill People" This is what he has said of them in tribute

"The custodians of law and order, pioneers of every advance into the interiors, the guardians of our borders and, above all, the friends of the hill people. Modestly, without fuss, they have faced every possible hardship and difficulty, and thousands of villagers in the wildest areas think of them with affection and gratitude. May they long continue to provide the foundations of security and order in our border areas".

The AR operations are characterised by their total lack of any unfavourable post-operation fall-out whatsoever. They rely heavily on real-time intelligence and very swift reactions against pinpointed targets and specific individuals. They are loath to the ham-handed ways of the other forces, including the army, which only go to firm up the resolve of the dissidents and those gone astray, apart from antagonising the general public. They are past masters at roughing it out, and of course, very adept at improvisation, make do and living off the land with good grace.

They know the border areas of their deployment like the palms of their hands. Experts in water crossing expedients, braving the elements and long cross-country marches on a self contained basis, they lend themselves excellently to their role as "the sentinels of the northeast" as Major General DK Palit, VrC, FRGS (Retd) refers to them in his definitive regimental history of this remarkable Force. The AR units communicate on a very reliable, quick-response, secure and efficient static radio grid.

Their MT drivers are experts in winding up and down narrow hill tracks in all kinds of weather conditions. It speaks volumes of their savvy in daily technical chores that, despite the step-motherly treatment meted out to them, they manage to keep the large vehicle fleet in a good roadworthy condition. These soldiers are quite skilled at elementary civil engineering tasks like construction of living quarters and road building including bridging. The troops are very mature, hardy, weather beaten, courageous, and know how to get on with the job at hand. They have the added advantage of conversing in the local lingo - a definite asset in a counter insurgency environment.

This capability of the AR is further augmented by the presence of the locally recruited lads in units. Properly handled, these boys are real treasures in different situations such as in disturbed areas. Contrary to a misconception, the AR ethos is, in fact, one of accountability and honesty; sincerity and sagacity; the 'do or die' kind. Despite all these substantial positive attributes, it generally takes committed and sympathetic leadership to bring out the best in the men. They cannot be taken for granted for they can see through commanders in no time. Army officers have generally earned a good reputation for themselves. Names like Sushil Kumar, Father Lazarus, OP Bhandari, Sidhiman Rai, Kukreti, Jas Ram, RS Dayal and Krishan Pal are legends. One or two of these officers are even revered as demi-Gods. At present the Force is deployed primarily in the northeast.

It is helping out the civil administration in the maintenance of law and order, assisting the army in counter insurgency duties, and the general welfare of the locals and development of the inaccessible areas. It has proved itself as more than a match at least, if definitely not a rival for vying for honours and awards of army units engaged in counter insurgency and border surveillance roles. It can, therefore, be safely argued that, there exists a strong case for independent and more substantial role for this extraordinary Force, in the realm of the strategic defence of the Nation. For example, to start with, the DG AR could be entrusted with operational duties as well. He could be directly responsible to the Army's Eastern Command for CI Ops in the northeast particularly in the troubled states of Nagaland, Mizoram, Tripura, Manipur, and Arunachal. Army formations should be pulled out from these areas, because they hardly provide any tangible benefits in a CI environment when the AR is placed under their command.

Assam rifles also has the role of maintaining law and order in the tribal areas of Assam; a role that is now being abrogated to the police forces of the States and Union Territories that have emerged in northeastern India. The AR traces its genesis back to 1835, when it was raised as a semi-military force known as the Cachar Levy with a complement of only 750 personnel. The role of this Force, as it was then conceived, was to maintain law and order in the Lushai Hills, and more generally to safeguard British interests; like tea gardens and other developmental work in relation to the opening up of the Assam area from the depredations of the head-hunting tribes which found great outdoor relief in raiding neighbouring settlements just for adventure and the fun of it.

The Force was extensively used for extending administrative control over remote tribal areas in very difficult conditions with only rudimentary administrative back-up and at nominal pecuniary cost; however, it bore all odds with exemplary fortitude and stoicism - characteristics which still underlie the ethos of the Force to date. Small townships, such as Aizawl, Lungleh, Kohima, Mokokchung, Tuensang, Haflong, Cherrapunji and Tura gradually mushroomed around its outposts. These are bustling population centres now. Variously designated and reorganized from time to time, as the Assam Frontier Police (1883), the Assam Military Police (1891) and Eastern Bengal and Assam Military Police (1913), it came to be known by its present name of the Assam Rifles in 1917 in recognition of its contribution to the war effort during the Great War.

History

Need: From the time of Independence, India's North-Eastern States had became a ground for proponents of insurgent activities. Preserving law and order, counterinsurgency and providing safety to the people of the area became a significant job for the security forces.

These jobs primarily became the responsibility of the Assam Rifles and when the Army eventually assumed control, the latter relied heavily on the experience and competence of the former. With the problems still continuing unresolved, the Assam Rifles continues to remain deployed in remote and under-developed areas, braving hostile terrain, extreme climates and effectively combating insurgency.

It was only after independence that the force really gained in stature as a strategic asset in the defence of North-Eastern India. The Force is a happy blend of both military and civil and its officers have distinguished themselves in both fields. Today its 24 battalions are deployed in Counter Insurgency Operations in North-East Region and seven on border guard duties.

Origin: Before the advent of the British there did not seem to be any organized police force in Assam, either under the Ahom Kings or earlier.The army as well as the various officers of the kingdom were responsible for the maintenance of peace and safeguarding the lives and properties of the people. On taking over the administration of Assam, the British also did not immediately introduce any revolutionary changes in this respect and the army was employed in the task of maintaining law and order. Army out posts were also set up at different places for this purpose.

The high expenditure involved in maintaining a large body of troops at a time when the country had just settled down, compelled the government of the time to undertake a review of the situation and a policy of gradual reduction of the forces was adopted. By 1839-40 the number of troops in Assam was reduced to four regiments only. Along with the reduction of troops, steps were taken to increase the armed component of the Civil Police in the province. The necessity of raising a separate force under the civil government apart from the armed civil Police was also felt and the first unit of this new organization was formed in the year 1835 by one Mr. Grange who was the Head of the civil administration of Nowgong District at that time.

Till the advent of the British the police force was not a separate and distinct organization entrusted with specific functions. The British created it to serve its colonial interests, and hence, it was loyal to the British Government. But after independence, it has undergone a dramatic change and today its loyalty is not merely to the Government, but also to the Sate, the Constitution and to the laws of the land.

There is no evidence of there being a regular police force in the state of Assam till the British took over after the Yandabu treaty of 1826. At the fag end of the Ahom rule and during the reign of Kamaleswar Singha (1795 -1811), an armed force on the British model was raised to serve the dual functions of maintenance of law and order and border defence. It was, however, not a regular and fully organized police force in the real sense of the term. After 1862, the British deployed regular troops in several parts of Assam to consolidate its occupation and a police establishment consisting of one Darogah, one Jamadhar and a number of constables was maintained at each district headquarters.The most important development in this process was the raising of the "Cachar Levy" in 1835 by the Civil Service Officer, in-charge of Nowgong district, Mr. Grange, to guard new settlements and tea estates. It consisted of 750 officers and men of different ranks, viz., Inspectors, Head Constables and Constables. Three years later, a similar body, called "Jorhat Militia", was formed to protect the border areas against frequent border transgressions. It was also known as the "Shan" militia, as the recruits were mostly from the Shan community. Eventually it was merged with the "Cachar Levy", which was subsequently renamed as "Frontier Police" in 1883 and then as "Assam Military Police" in 1891 and then again as "Assam Rifles" in 1920. The duties of the levy included the guarding of the Eastern Frontier of Assam from the Brahmaputra River to Cachar. The levy was a force of a semi-military nature. The men were poorly paid and the duties were arduous and often involving fighting. It is important to note that at the initial stage most of the recruits were from Bengal, as the local Assamese were not interested in joining the low-paid police service.

In 1870 the existing elements were merged into three Assam Military Police battalions in the Lushai Hills (later 1st battalion), Lakhimpur (2nd battalion) and Naga Hills (3rd battalion). A fourth battalion was formed 1915 in Imphal.

During the World War I, Assam Military Police troopers were part of the Indian forces that fought for Britain in Europe and Middle East. The name Assam Rifles was assigned in 1917 as recognition of their part in the war. After the war they served in Northern India against rebellions and riots.

The Second World War saw the Assam Rifles under-taking multifarious roles. The Assam Rifles were tasked to organize a resistance group on the Indo-Burmese border to counter the Japanese invasion and to disrupt their lines of communication. The whole concept was contained in Plan Number V, and the Resistance Force so formed and organized, came to be known as 'Victor Force'. The Assam Rifles, which formed the nucleus of this Force, covered itself with glory with the exemplary performance of its platoons. They fought gallant independent actions far into Burmese territory behind the enemy lines and later fought doggedly in the defence boxes established along the line from Kohima to Ukhrul. No less spectacular was the operation carried out by the 1st Battalion as a part of the Lushai Brigade, who ventured ahead to resist the Japanese in the Chin Hills. As part of the V Force, a number of Assam Rifles platoons acted as covering forces both during the defensive and the offensive phases of the operations in Burma. One of the platoons of the 4th Battalion was also trained as paratroops and dropped near the Sittang River behind Japanese lines. By the time the war ended, officers and men of all the five battalions had distinguished themselves by displaying high professional excellence and great valour. The Force won as many as forty eight awards consisting of three Members of the British Empire, five Military Cross, four Order of British India, one Indian Order of Merit, thirteen Military Medals, fifteen Indian Distinguished Service Medals and seven British Empire Medals.

In 1944, Kohima in the Naga Hills of Assam, north-east India, was an important hill station on the only road between the major British supply base at Dimapur and Imphal. When the Japanese launched their U-Go offensive in March 1944, the Kohima garrison was made up from a few units of the Assam Rifles, the 1st Battalion Assam Regiment and line of communication troops. As the full strength and threat of the Japanese offensive became apparent to the British, reinforcements were hastily moved to the Imphal-Dimapur area, many by air from the Arakan.

Of these, the 161st Brigade, of the 5th Indian Division, was flown to Dimapur in late March 1944. The brigade soon advanced down the road to Kohima and began to establish defensive positions around the village. The key terrain was Garrison Hill and the wooded slopes of Kohima Ridge with key features such as Jail Hill, Field Supply Depot (FSD) Hill and Detail Issue (DIS) Hill. There was space to deploy only a single battalion – the 4th Royal West Kents, supported by the Assam Rifles and the Assam Regiment. The brigade's remaining Infantry – the 1st/1st Punjab Regiment and the 4th/7th Rajputs were deployed two miles west of Kohima at Jotsoma, with the brigade's artillery.

The first attack on Kohima was made after dark on April 4th but was unsuccessful. The 161st Brigade was rushed forward to reinforce Kohima. There was space to deploy only a single battalion – the 4th Royal West Kents, supported by the Assam Rifles and the Assam Regiment. The brigade's remaining Infantry – the 1st/1st Punjab Regiment and the 4th/7th Rajputs were deployed two miles west of Kohima at Jotsoma, with the brigade's artillery.

No sooner had the positions been established by April 5th than the advance guard of the Japanese 31st Division attacked. After the initial attack, the West Kents withdrew from exposed positions and the Japanese were able to establish themselves elsewhere on the ridge. By April 7th, however, the now hard pressed West Kents were reinforced by a company of Rajputs from Jotsoma. Further Japanese attacks began on April 8th and by the next day the defenders had been forced back to the tennis court at the Deputy Commissioner's (DC) Bungalow. At the same time, the defenders were cut off as the Japanese now also blocked the tracks to Jotsoma and the road between Jotsoma and Dimapur. Further Japanese gains at Kohima were made on April 10th and 11th.

Ferocious, hand-hand fighting erupted on April 13th as the Japanese attempted to seize the DC's bungalow and tennis court positions. The attacks were finally beaten by artillery fire from Jotsoma and the Japanese now focussed on eliminating these positions but without success. On April 14th, the newly arrived British 2nd Division and the 161st Brigade had opened the Dimapur-Kohima road. Desperate Japanese attacks were launched against FSD hill on the evening of April 16th and the positions changed hands several times before the British withdrew to Garrison Hill. A dangerous situation for the defenders, now hemmed in on three sides at Garrison Hill was relieved when on April 18th, troops of the 2nd British Division, the 161st Brigade and tanks of the 149th RAC forced the Japanese away from the road and Garrison Hill. The siege of Kohima was lifted.

On April 20th, the 6th Brigade from the 2nd Division took over at Kohima and the remnants of the garrison were sent to Dimapur and the balance of the 161st Brigade returned to Jotsoma. This small but ferocious battle was one of the decisive battles in South East Asia.

Now began the bloody task of clearing the Japanese from the Kohima area. By May 13th, many of the Japanese positions had been taken in fierce fighting. A few positions still held out including the DC's bungalow. Continued fighting eventually forced a Japanese withdrawal that began by mid-May. Further reinforcements now came in to relieve the 2nd Division and the 33rd and 161st Brigades whose Infantry had born the brunt of the fighting.

Attention now turned to lifting the siege of Imphal and clearing the Japanese from the road between Kohima and Imphal. Continued heavy and close quarter fighting resulted in the eventual opening of the road and British and Indian troops of the 2nd Division from Kohima and the 5th Division from Imphal met on 22nd June at Milestone 110. The siege of Imphal was now over.

The Kohima fighting resulted in British and Indian losses of around 4, 000 men dead, wounded and missing. The Japanese lost more then 7, 000 in the fighting around Kohima.

Between the end of World War II and Indian independence, the Assam Rifles were composed of 5 battalions that were one part of the civil police under the Assam Inspector General of Police. After independence, the Indian government assigned the Assam Rifles its own Director General.

The Assam Police Frontier regulation of 1882 provided for the maintenance of proper discipline in the force and fixed the terms and conditions of service in the Assam Frontier Police. Further changes were witnessed in 1883 when the Frontier Police was re-organized to give it a distinct military role and the defence of the entire Frontier line was placed in its hands. The Frontier Police was organized into four corps which was stationed in Cachar, Lakhimpur, Garo Hills and Naga Hills. With the exception of these four districts the duties of guarding the Jails and Treasuries were taken over by the Civil Police.

At the turn of the 20th century there was no significant increase in the strength of the civil police force. The Assam Police faced an entirely novel set of circumstances during 1942. It became clear in the early part of the year that the triumphal march of the Japanese armed forces could not be stopped and the fate of Burma was hanging in the balance. The flow of refugees from Burma which commenced towards the end of 1941 gathered momentum. With the rapid march of the war to the borders of Assam, it soon became apparent that the police force was inadequate to meet the new situation and various sanctions were asked for and received during the year for raising of forces for the protection of the railways, the guarding of aerodromes and other security duties in connection with the war. There was an increase in the Police force by nearly one half of its original strength.

During the cold weather of 1942-43 the stream of refugees from Burma began to dry up but the danger of infiltration by enemy agents increased. To combat this menace, security measures were further tightened and extra force was sanctioned. The preparation for the invasion of India by the Japanese forces created new problems of internal security which the Assam Police was called upon to tackle. The Naga Hills and Manipur became the main targets of attack by the Japanese forces and the Assam Police supplied officers and men to augment the local Police forces and helped in establishing intelligence screens in these areas. When the threat of the Japanese to the railway and other vital communications was at its height, the Police, stationed in the airfields bombed by the enemy, in the isolated pockets and in the threatened areas, remained firm. As India became Independent in 1947, there were two significant developments having a far reaching impact, (a) The British officers left the State and their positions were occupied by Indian officers. All the high positions in the police administration during the colonial era were occupied by the British and after their departure, there was a vacuum in the administration because of the absence of experienced and qualified officers. (b) There was complete separation of the Assam Rifles from the Assam Police. These two branches had been working as one unit and with the numerical growth of the Assam Police the need to separate these branches was felt to ensure greater efficiency and control.

Key Dates in the History

March 1835	Formation of Cacher Levy
June 1887	Formation of Assam Military Police
May 1917	Name Assam Rifles was assigned
April 1942	Foundation of V Force
March 1944	Battle of Kohima
August 1950	Role in Assam Earthquake
April 1959	Escorted His Holiness Dalai Lama to Safety
Dec. 1988 - Feb. 1990	Operation Pawan

Present Scenario

Personnel Strength: The Assam Rifles has strength of approximately 65, 000 troops and 46 battalions. The force is led by a Director General aided by two Inspectors General. Lt. General K. S. Yadav is the present Director General of the Assam Rifles.

Bases: The Force is commanded by an officer of the rank of Lieutenant General of the Army. The highest Headquarter of the force known as the HQ Directorate General of Assam Rifles is located at Shillong. Assam Rifles is a region specific force with its operational role in the North-East and therefore the HQ DGAR is also located in the East.

HQ Inspector General Assam Rifles comes next in chain of command after HQ DGAR. HQ IGAR is commanded by an officer of the rank of Major General from the Army. HQ IGAR in turn exercises command and control over the sector HQs. There are two HQ IGAR which are operationally deployed.

The Sector Headquarterssare commanded by Army Officers of the rank of Brigadiers from the Army. The Sector Headquarters exercises direct command and control over the Assam Rifles Battalions deployed in its area of responsibility.

The Maintenance Groups located at various location provide the requisite administrative support to the Assam Rifles formations and battalions deployed in the field. The MGAR are commanded by officers of the rank of Lt. Colonel from the Army.

The workshops are co-located with the MGAR to provide repair and recovery cover to the field formations. These workshops further provide detachments to the Sector Headquarters to provide repair and recovery cover as far forward as possible to the Battalions.

There are Forty-six Battalions of Assam Rifles.

Organizational Structure

Organizational setup of Assam Rifles from top to bottom is:

- Director General
- Inspector General
- Deputy Inspector General
- Commandant,
- Deputy Commandant
- Assistant Commandant
- Subedar Major
- Subedar
- Havildar Major
- Havildar
- Naik
- Lance Naik
- Rifleman

Chiefs of Assam Rifles

- Mr HG Bartly (17 Sep 1947 to 14 Aug 1948)
- Colonel Sidhiman Rai (15 Aug 1948 to 10 Dec 1949)
- Colonel RND Frier (16 Dec 1949 to 29 Feb 1952)
- Brigadier K Bhagwat Singh (01 Mar 1952 to 04 May 1954)
- Brigadier K S Katoch (05 May 1954 to 29 Aug 1955)
- Brigadier Harbhajan Singh (07 Sep 1955 to 30 Nov 1957)
- Maj. General AS Guraya (01 Feb 1958 to 14 Dec 1965)
- Maj. General SN Bhatia (15 Dec 1965 to 14 Feb 1968)
- Maj. General VB Tuli (15 Feb 1968 to 19 Feb 1972)
- Maj. General VB Tuli (20 May 1972 to 31 Dec 1972)
- Maj. General MG Hazari (30 Mar 1973 to 29 Feb 1976)

- Maj. General K Chiman Singh (01 Mar 1976 to 25 Jun 1979)
- Maj. General Sushil Kumar (01 Sep 1979 to 01 Dec 1981)
- Lt. General JK Puri (02 Dec 1981 to 29 Nov 1983)
- Lt. General PE Menon (30 Nov 1983 to 31 May 1987)
- Lt. General MK Lahiri (01 Jun 1987 to 21 Dec 1989)
- Lt. General RV Kulkarni (22 Feb 1990 to 09 Mar 1992)
- Lt. General VP Airy (18 Mar 1992 to 31 Mar 1993)
- Lt. General Y M Bammi (15 Jul 1993 to 30 Apr 1995)
- Lt. General TPS Rawat (19 May 1995 to 30 Apr 1998)
- Lt. General Gurpreet Singh (01 May 1998 to 18 Jan 2001)
- Lt. General GK Duggal (19 Jan 2001 to 18 Jan 2003)
- Lt. General HS Kanwar (01 Mar 2003 to 30 Apr 2004)
- Lt. General Bhopinder Singh (01 May 2004 to 30 Jun 2006)
- Lt. General Paramjit Singh (06 Jul 2006 to 31 May 2008)
- Lt General K S Yadav (01 June 2008 Till Date)

Duties and Functions

Motto: Assam Rifles' Motto is "***Friends of the Hill People***" showing their love for people of North-East India.

Maxim: To conduct counter insurgency operations in the north-east and other areas where deemed necessary, under control of the army.

- During peace and 'proxy war', ensure security of the Indo-China and Indo- Myanmar borders.
- During war, rear area security in the TBA.
- Assist army in other operational tasks during war and peace.
- Act as penultimate interventionist force of the central government in internal security situation, under the control of army; when the situation goes beyond the control of central Para-military operations.

Conducting Counterinsurgency Operations: The troops of Assam Rifles are very mature, hardy, weather beaten, courageous, and know how to get on with the job at hand. They have the added advantage of conversing in the local language - a definite asset in a counter insurgency environment. Most of the AR units are under the operational control of the army. Their battle potential is as good as that of the regular Infantry battalions. AR battalions are adept in counter insurgency operations, where their performance has been better than that of the Army/ Rashtriya Rifles.

They are especially proficient in the un-orthodox type of small-scale missions to seek and destroy/apprehend hostiles. The study of one such mission, code named Operation "Zebra", successfully launched and executed by 19 AR, was included in the curriculum of training of army Infantry battalions being inducted for counter insurgency operations. At present the Force is deployed primarily in the northeast. It is helping out the civil administration in the maintenance of law and order, assisting the army in counter insurgency duties, and the general welfare of the locals and development of the inaccessible areas.

It has proved itself as more than a match at least, if definitely not a rival for vying for honours and awards of army units engaged in counter insurgency and border surveillance roles. It can, therefore, be safely argued that, there exists a strong case for independent and more substantial role for this extraordinary Force, in the realm of the strategic defence of the Nation.

India's northeast is a geopolitically strategic region. It comprises eight states — Assam, Arunachal Pradesh, Nagaland, Manipur, Tripura, Mizoram, Meghalaya and Sikkim and is spread over a 262, 179 square kilometres area. The eight states contain a total population of 39 million. India's northeast connects with five countries-Bangladesh, Bhutan, Myanmar, China and Nepal by a 4, 500 kilometre international border; the region, however, connects to India only through a narrow and tenuous land corridor measuring merely 22 kilometres.

A fact that further jeopardizes mainland India's links with the region is the thriving militancy in most of the northeast states. The demands of the different militant groups range from autonomy within the provisions of the Indian constitution to outright secession. Such militant movements started early with India's independence in 1947. At one point, more than 120 militant groups operated in India's northeast. In recent years, the Indian government has had some success in achieving stability in the region, using tactics from negotiations to military operations to rooting out militants. Nevertheless, the region remains a potential tinderbox.

Following the induction of additional elements of regular Army, a new force was specially raised to combat terrorism in the Kashmir Valley. This force is known as Rashtriya Rifles (RR). Before Rashtriya Rifles could become fully effective, the Government decided to use Assam Rifles battalions in J&K on a trial basis. Accordingly, eight Assam Rifles battalions, namely 3, 7, 10, 18, 21, 23, 26 and 28 were inducted into J&K, and operated there under operation Rakshak for eight years, from April 1990 to January 1998.

This period proved to be a golden era for the Assam Rifles as its battalions performed commendably in J&K. Out of its various battalions operating in the state, two were awarded the coveted Chief of the Army Staff's (COAS's) Unit Citation while one was awarded the Army Commander's Unit Appreciation. The 26th Battalion of Assam Rifles was the first to get inducted into the Valley on May 25, 1990. It took part in operation Rakshak for two years. Placed under Headquarters 31 Sub Area located in Srinagar, the unit was given the initial task of road opening and convoy protection duties on Srinagar-Sonamarg road, particularly the stretch between Kangan to Captain Mark, a distance of over 60 kms. However, on September 18, 1990, on receipt of information regarding infiltration of a large group of Pakistani-trained militants in general area Talel, the battalion was tasked to carry out counter infiltration operations. Its troops, which worked day and night, tracked the militants through thick forests and ultimately engaged them at three different locations through fierce gun battles. While three terrorists were apprehended, two of them with gun shot wounds, the others managed to escape. Based on useful and accurate information extracted from the apprehended terrorists, specific operations were launched by the unit in general area Kangan, Gund, Gangagir, Reyil and Srinagar.

In these operations the unit was successful in apprehending ninety militants, retrieved the body of one terrorist killed and recovered 142 assorted weapons to include 40 mm RLs, 7.62 mm GPMGs, AK 47/56 Rifles, 9 mm pistols and a large quantity of ammunition. In a joint operation with Army, the unit also had the credit of rescuing from village Dara Shri Puran Chand, the Deputy Superintendent of J&K Armed Police, who was in militant captivity for 75 days. This battalion was awarded the coveted COAS Unit Citation apart from a 'Silver Salver' from the Governor of J&K. In addition, it earned 71 other awards including a Sena Medal to its then Commandant, Col (now Brigadier) RPS Malhan.

Seven Assam Rifles, a veteran unit, operated in J&K from April 1990 to May 1992. It initially moved to Kupwara where it was placed under 19 Infantry Division, and later it came under 28 Infantry Division. Though the unit conducted many successful operations, the most prominent one was the Dudhi Operation. Dudhi is a temporary post in

Tangdhar Sector, along the Line of Control (LoC). This post used to be occupied by Indian troops during summers, and vacated during winters due to heavy snowfall. The first encounter of the unit in this sector was on November 19, 1990 in which 16 terrorists were killed, six apprehended and 18 AK 47 rifles, three RPGs, one GPMG along with a large quantity of ammunition and warlike stores were recovered. The unit's next encounter in Dudhi took place on May 4, 1991. It was recorded to be the most successful battalion level operation ever conducted. During an engagement, which lasted over seventytwo hours, 72 terrorists were killed and one apprehended. Four RPGs, seven UMGs, 78 AK 47 rifles, large quantities of assorted ammunition and other warlike stores were also recovered.

In its 25-month stay in J&K, the battalion neutralised a total of 200 terrorists, apprehended 222 and sought the surrender of 74. It also captured an exceptionally large quantity of sophisticated arms, warlike stores and assorted ammunition, which included hand grenades, anti-tank rounds and anti-personnel mines. The battalion's achievements were outstanding by any standard. Maj Gen OP Kaushik, GOC 28 Infantry Division, under whom the battalion operated most of the time, wrote in an official letter: "The unit has performed outstandingly well in counter terrorist operations in the Valley and has been the best in successful conduct of many operations. Difficult and dangerous environments did not deter them. In fact, they are singularly responsible for eradicating the terrorist influence from Kupwara Sector". In recognition of its commendable performance, the unit received numerous awards to include two Kirti Chakra, one Shaurya Chakra, 10 Sena Medals and one Vishisht Seva Medal.The battalion also received the COAS's Unit Citation as well as a 'silver/ salver'.

Another battalion, 23 Assam Rifles, operated in J&K from July 1994 till December 1996. It performed commendably in many operations in general area Bhaderwah Tehsil of Doda district, where it was deployed. Its biggest catch was on August 11, 1996 when Ahsan Ahmed, the self styled Deputy Provincial Chief of Hizbul Mujahideen for Jammu Region, was killed while carrying an HMG and a sophisticated high power radio set. He was the highest-ranking militant killed till then. This success led to the unconditional surrender of three more armed terrorists, later to be identified as Manzoor Ahmed, a self-styled District Zonal Commander of Bhaderwah; Wasim Raja, a self-styled Section Commander of Bhaderwah and Abdul Hafiz, a local self-styled Commando. The overall achievement of the battalion in J&K included 19 terrorists killed and an equal number apprehended.

Eighteen Assam Rifles operated in the Valley from December 24, 1994 to December 1996. Initially it was deployed in Avantipur district where it performed road opening party (ROP) duties on National Highway (NH) 1-A covering the 80 km stretch from Jawahar Tunnel to Pantha Chowk. Apart from operations, the battalion also laid special emphasis on winning the hearts and the minds of the locals residents. Later, it moved to Khundru on July 18, 1997, where its three companies were placed in the counter insurgency (CI) grid while one company was employed for local protection of 21 Field Ammunition Depot, Khundru. There it was placed under the operational control of Headquarters 1 Sector, Rashtriya Rifles. The battalion also assisted in the successful conduct of State Assembly elections in its area of responsibility where over 60 per cent votes were cast. The unit also captured a large quantity of arms and ammunition and killed or apprehended many hard-core terrorists belonging to the Hizb-ul-Mujahideen.

Twentyeight Assam Rifles operated in J&K from November 1994 to January 1997. It was deployed at Ramban in Doda district, where it came under Headquarters 6 Sector Rashtriya Rifles. It was actively involved in counter-insurgency operations under the overall control of Headquarters Delta Force. It carried out various operations in the difficult and rugged terrain of Doda, and effectively contained militancy in its area of responsibility. It also facilitated uninterrupted and smooth movement of traffic along the vital highway NH1- A, and also helped in the conduct of incident-free Parliamentary elections. The best catch of the battalion was when a self-styled captain and a self-styled company commander of Harkat ul Mujahideen (HuM) group were apprehended from general area Nongam Ahdwar.

Ten Assam Rifles operated in J&K from May 1995 to January 1998. The battalion was deployed in general area Kangan and Ganderbal under Headquarters 11 Sector, Rashtriya Rifles. The battalion carried out many operations, some jointly and others independently. The best operation conducted by the battalion was on August 2, 1995 in general area of village Guripura, in which 23 Hizb-ul-Mujahideen terrorists were apprehended and 15 AK 47/56 Rifles, three Sniper rifles, 18 pistols Chinese, six grenade launchers and a substantial quantity of ammunition were also recovered. When Parliamentary elections were held during May end in 1996, the unit ensured peace in its area of responsibility, where the percentage of polling was the highest in the entire Valley.

Three Assam Rifles operated in J&K from April 27, 1997 to January 1998 and was deployed at Mamar where it came under Headquarters 11

Sector Rashtriya Rifles. Apart from counter insurgency operations, its tasks included the domination of NH 1-A. The most rewarding operation of the unit was carried out on August 10-11, 1996 at village Wurapash in Tehsil Ganderbal. In this operation, five hard-core terrorists, including four Pakistani terrorists, were killed. One of them was identified as Mudassar Jat, alias Saif, of Bhawalpur district. He was later identified as a Major belonging to the ISI, working as their commander for Srinagar district. The lone Indian terrorist killed was Farooq Ahmed Shah, a self-styled Battalion Commander of Hizb-ul-Mujahideen. On January 21, 1996, with the help of West Bengal Police, the unit also apprehended from Kolkata a confirmed terrorist named Nazir Ahmed Wani, a resident of Zukrah district.

Finally, 21 Assam Rifles was also deployed in J&K from January 1995 to March 5, 1997. It was placed under the command of 7 Sector, Rashtriya Rifles which was a part of Headquarters 28 Infantry Division, and was deployed within and around Kupwara. During its tenure of two years in J&K, the battalion was responsible for 17 terrorists killed including five foreign terrorists, apprehending 26 and receiving the surrender of six hard-core terrorists. The killed included Balram Shah, a self-styled Battalion Administrator of the Al-Burq Tanzeem and Farooq Khan, a self-styled Battalion Commander of Hizb-ul-Mujahideen. As more Rashtriya Rifles units and formations became effective in J&K, and the situation in Assam deteriorated, the Assam Rifles units were reverted to the North-Eastern states to repeat their glorious history in J&K.

Security of the Indo-China and Indo-Myanmar Borders: The force was stationed on Indo-China border in the wake of Indo China conflict of 1962 to build people's morale and inculcate a spirit of resistance in the border population against threats of subversion, infiltration and sabotage from across the border. However, the charter of duty has since been amended and it has been given the border guarding responsibilities along the Indo-Myanmar Border. The force now covers stretch of International Border. Assam Rifles, which has been assigned the task of policing the volatile Indo-Bhutan border, is likely to get a few more battalions. The proposal is part of Delhi's strategy to improve management of the country's borders. Both the borders are sensitive and frequented by militants. The Union Home Ministry is planning to assign the task of combating militants to the Assam Rifles and the CRPF, while the BSF (Border Security Force) and the SSB will be asked to focus on the frontiers. It was initially deployed in the areas near the Indo-China border, where it trained the local populace in handling arms and ammunition.

Interventionist Force in Internal Security Situations: Militants in India's northeast once enjoyed vast popular support since they, in their formative years, voiced genuine grievances of the people such as poor governance, alienation, lack of development and an apathetic attitude from the central government in New Delhi; in recent years, however, this influence has been reduced. Nevertheless, in most of the states in the northeast, anti-government militants retain significant nuisance value and often indulge in successful strikes against government interests.

Nagaland, then part of the larger state of Assam, was the first to experience militancy. Long before the British left India, Nagas considered themselves to be independent and petitioned the British to declare them as an independent country. After being snubbed by both the British and the new regime in New Delhi, Nagas, under the leadership of the Naga National Council (N.N.C.), headed by A.Z. Phizo, declared independence. In his declaration, Phizo argued that in a plebiscite held in Nagaland in May 1951, more than 99 percent of voters favoured independence. The veracity of the plebiscite remains debatable.

Subsequently, the N.N.C. split into different factions and its breakaway faction, the National Socialist Council of Nagaland (N.S.C.N.) also broke into two factions; those factions were the Isak-Muivah faction (N.S.C.N.-I.M.) and the Khaplang faction (N.S.C.N.-K.). These organizations have continued separate violent struggles for Nagaland's independence.

Similarly, Mizoram, which was a part of the state of Assam before it was granted statehood in 1987, experienced militancy after the Union government failed to respond positively to its demand for assistance during the massive Mautam famine. The Mizo National Front (M.N.F.), led by the legendary leader Laldenga, launched the movement on February 28, 1966 and demanded independence for Mizoram.

In Tripura, the smallest of the north-eastern states, migration of Hindus from the British-ruled East Bengal, which subsequently became East Pakistan and then Bangladesh, is believed to have been responsible for reducing the indigenous tribal people in the state to minority status; this development sparked a violent backlash among the indigenous people. Starting in 1970, militant groups sprang up in the state demanding the restoration of the tribal rights from the Bengali population, who are accused of dominating the political and economic affairs of Tripura state.

Migration from Bangladesh, a fact that is refuted by that country, was the source of militancy in the state of Assam as well. A movement that started demanding the deportation of the illegal migrants also witnessed the birth of the militant outfit the United Liberation Front of Asom (U.L.F.A.) in 1979. Following U.L.F.A.'s example, a number of militant groups, each claiming to represent the aspirations of different tribal communities in the state, formed. Prominent among these groups are the Bodo Liberation Tigers, the National Democratic Front of Bodoland (N.D.F.B.), the United People's Democratic Solidarity (U.P.D.S.) and the Dima Halim Daogah.

In the state of Manipur, militancy originated in protest against the forcible merger of the former Manipur Kingdom with India. In 1964, the United National Liberation Front formed with an avowed objective of ending the discrimination against Manipur, which was accorded statehood only in 1972, nearly 23 years after its merger. Subsequently, a number of militant organizations have formed with each representing the cause of different tribes, sometimes more than one outfit espousing the same cause.

Analysts indicate that most of the militant outfits in the region have been quick to transform themselves into purely terrorist entities, bereft of their original objectives and ideology. For example, U.L.F.A. in Assam, which originated as a reaction to Bangladeshi migration into the state, has found shelter in Bangladesh and, through a publication in the 1990s, has repudiated its earlier anti-Bangladeshi position. Militant outfits in Tripura, the National Liberation Front of Tripura (N.L.F.T.) and the All Tripura Tiger Force espousing the tribal cause have indulged in a number of attacks on the tribal population. Militant groups in certain states also have clashed among themselves. For example, in Nagaland, most fatalities are recorded as a result of the infighting between the two factions of the N.S.C.N., rather than from government forces.

With small arms being easily available in the region and in the neighbouring countries, capabilities of even relatively smaller groups to challenge state authority have dramatically grown over the years. As a result, militant groups have successfully transformed themselves into huge abduction and extortion rackets collecting regular contributions from the public, government servants and the business houses. With little protection available from the state government, people have often found it convenient to bribe the militant groups for peace, rather than risk death and abduction.

Security force operations using the army, state police forces and the Paramilitary Forces remain the preferred mode of official response to contain militancy. A strong military presence has been the feature of all the militancy-affected states in the region. The Union government, as a matter of policy, reimburses security-related expenditure incurred by the states. It also has an ongoing program for the modernization of the state police forces that sometimes possess weapons of lesser sophistication than the militants. Interestingly, in all of the north-eastern states, the ratio of policemen per 10, 000 people is far above the national average.

Military operations in Mizoram, where the army reportedly launched air strikes to neutralize the M.N.F. cadres, resulted in several fatalities and displacement among the civilian population. Military operations in Nagaland, too, resulted in civilian fatalities and large-scale displacement. In Assam, in the beginning of the 1990s, two military operations, Operation Rhino and Operation Bajrang, were launched against U.L.F.A. militants. These forced U.L.F.A. to move out of the state and locate itself in areas outside the country. However, such operations have not been able to post conclusive gains against militancy in any of the states. In states like Manipur, militants have been able to carve out vast stretches of "liberated zones" where only their laws and dictates hold sway.

Acts, Rules & Regulations

Assam Rifles Act (Act V of 1941) (March 17th 1941): An act to provide for the regulation of and the maintenance of discipline in the Assam Rifles.Where as it is expedient to provide for the regulations of and the maintenance of discipline in the Assam Rifles.

- Section 1: Short title, extent and application.
- Section 2: Definitions.
- Section 3: General Superintendence and Control of the Force.
- Section 4: Appointment and Discharge.
- Section 5: Class and Rank.
- Section 6: Heinous offences.
- Section 7: Other offences including acts prejudicial to good order and discipline.
- Section 8: Minor Offences and Punishment.
- Section 9: Manner of imprisonment.
- Section 10: Privileges of, and protection for acts done by, Commandant, Assistant Commandant etc.
- Section 11: Members of the Assam Rifles to be deemed part of the Indian Army for certain purposes.

- Section 12: Power of Central Covernment to make rules.
- Section 13: Cesser of Assam Rifles Act 1 of 1920 and of appointment of rifleman as Police Officers.

The Assam Rifles Rules, 1985: In the exercise of the powers conferred by Section 3 and 12 of the Assam Rifles Act, 1941 (5 of 1941), the Central government made The Assam Rifles Rules, 1985.

- Section 1: Short title and commencement.
- Section 2: Definitions
- Section 3: General Superintendent and Control
- Section 4: Powers of the Central Government and Certain Officers of the Force.
- Section 5: Organization
- Section 6: Classification.
- Section 7: Particulars of services etc to be performed
- Section 8: Command
- Section 9: Disqualification
- Section 10: Ineligibility of Aliens
- Section 11: Attestation on Oath or affirmation
- Section 12: Enrolling Officer
- Section 13: Procedure for enrolment as a rifleman
- Section 14: Signing of statement in the Schedule to the Act
- Section 15: Discharge
- Section 16: Discharge Certificate
- Section 17: Other conditions of Service
- Section 18: Transitory Provisions
- Section 19: Repeal and Saving

Weapons and Equipments

Light weaponry includes FN 35 and Glock 17.9 mm pistols, Heckler & Koch MP5 sub-machine guns, INSAS 5.56 mm assault rifles. INSAS 5.56 mm light machine guns, AGS-17 Plamya 30 mm automatic grenade launcher and AK 47, AK 74 sub machine guns. Type 81 Assault rifles, AKM rifles, INSAS 5. 56 MM Assault rifle, G3A3 Battle rifle, MP5 Submachine-gun ; Uzi submachinegun, M9 pistol ; RPG `7 Rocket-propelled grenade launchers ; and M67 hand-grenades. CRPF also uses landmine detectors ; Light Machine-Guns and Heavy-Machine-Guns.

Vehicles used by Assam rifles are; BMP-2 Armoured Amphibious Dozer and Engineer Reconnaissance Vehicle (ERV), Casspir - mine protected vehicles (165), Tata LPTA 1621 TC - 6x6 truck, Mahindra - light multi-role 4x4, Rampar - amphibious 4x4.

Recruitment

Officers: Assam Rifles take its officers from Indian Army on deputation.

Other Ranks: recruitment is held every year in all states. Male candidates and ex-servicemen can apply. Recruitment is held for enrolment to 45 posts in the categories of rifleman (general duty)/ driver, PA/steno (personal assistant), clerk, Operation Room Assistant (ORA), plumber, pharmacist, electrician, B&R JCO (Bridge and Road), radio mechanic, electrical fitter signal (EFS), safai, carpenter and washerman. Candidates have to undergo the physical/medical/written test and interview. The duration of test will be a minimum of six days. There are vacancies for the same state Ex-Servicemen in the categories of rifleman (general duty)/ driver, electrician, electrical fitter signal (EFS) and carpenter.

Training: Selected and medically fit candidates are required to undergo basic training at Assam Rifles Training Centre & Schools

Famous Operations

World War-I: During the World War I, Assam Military Police troopers were part of the Indian forces that fought for Britain in Europe and Middle East. They fought valiantly, earning many honours and awards. The name Assam Rifles was assigned in 1917 as recognition of their part in the war.

Battle of Kohima: Kohima was a tiny hill station, dominating the lone road which led from the supply base at Dimapur, down onto the Imphal plain, where the main part of 14th Army was awaiting the Japanese invasion of India from Burma, which was composed of British, Commonwealth and Indian troops.

14th Army was led by General William Slim, who is probably the best British commander of WWII, and could easily be counted as one of the best commanders of WWII on any side. Fighting in a neglected theatre that was almost always last on the list for any resources, 14th Army bitterly adopted the nickname 'Forgotten Army'. Later this became a badge of pride.

The Japanese did invade, and so began the long battle on the Imphal plain, in which Slim's surrounded 14th Army was supplied by air. It was such a complex battle that Slim's superior said afterwards he had difficulty understanding the report of it, and Slim had to resort to the idea of imagining the battle as a clockface, taking each of the actions in turn around it, although they were all simultaneous and had effects on each other.

However, at Kohima Slim had made one of his few mistakes, which he freely admitted afterwards. He and his staff had believed that the Japanese would only be able to send a single regiment through the terrible terrain northeast of Imphal, where they would cut the supply road from Dimapur that ran around the hill-station and village of Kohima.

This is an area of mountainous jungle, with some of the highest rainfall in the world. But as it happened, the Japanese commanders sent an entire *division* up to this area, and their objective was to capture Kohima, with a view to advancing further into India, depending on how the main action at Imphal went.

Kohima was defended by the 1st Assam Regiment, an Indian regiment, and also had a few hundred convalescents and administrative staff. Realising the size of the force advancing towards them, the 1st Assam Regiment fought several valiant delaying actions and the 50th Indian Parachute Regiment (mostly Gurkhas) which was posted northeast of Kohima sacrificed itself at Sangshak to delay the Japanese advance for a week. These actions at Sangshak, Jessami, Kharasom and Phek deserve their own place in the litany of last stands, but I'm trying not to stray too far from the main topic here.

Slim realised the danger, and did something practically unprecedented: he managed to scrape together enough planes to airlift the entire veteran British 2nd Division to Dimapur, straight from its successful offensive in the Arakan, and sending it down the road towards Kohima.

The desperate delaying actions by the 1st Assam and the sacrifice of the 50th Indian Parachute Regiment only half-worked. The remnants of the 1st Assam trickled bit by bit back to Kohima, where they began to organize for defence. They consisted of 266 men. With them were those couple of hundred convalescent and administrative staff. Towards them and around both sides of Kohima came about 13, 000 Japanese soldiers.

And then 440 men of the 4th Royal West Kents raced ahead of the advancing 2nd British Division and on 5th April managed to enter the perimeter just as the jaws closed around Kohima. They were surrounded, and the Japanese set up roadblock after roadblock to stop the rest of 2nd British Division from reaching them. The tiny garrison now had to survive until relief came.

Even being generous with the unknown number of administrative staff, the garrison itself consisted of about a thousand men. This placed the odds at about 13-1. This may not be entirely fair, as of course the Japanese also had the advancing 2nd British Division to contend with, but for the most part they simply set up roadblocks and detached forces to delay the advancing British. Their objective was the capture of the commanding position of Kohima, and that was the main focus of their efforts.

For two weeks, in pouring rain and under continual bombardment, the British and Indian garrison held on. They were slowly driven back, from one position after another, to the hill itself, which consisted of a series of flat 'steps' leading up to its summit. Here, in the District Commissioner's Bungalow the defenders had their Headquarters. A few 'steps' further down from here was the attached tennis court. This became the infamous scene of the 'battle within a battle', the Battle of the Tennis Court. The British and Indians were literally dug in on one side of the tennis court, the Japanese on the other, exchanging grenades, rifle fire and machine-gun fire, interspersed with desperate hand to hand fighting with bayonets when the Japanese made wild assaults of almost suicidal bravery. The defenders built barricades from the piled bodies of the attackers, the entire area eventually becoming a thick carpet of blackened and rotting corpses. When digging in, they found often themselves digging through the dead before hitting earth. One British officer digging in through the corpses on ground that had see-sawed back and forth in possession with the enemy found his friend's body this way. He had disappeared after leading a desparate counterattack three days before. The officer only recognized him from his watch and identity discs.

The perimeter had shrunk to 600 yards and was under constant bombardment by artillery. There were so many wounded that the dressing stations didn't have enough space, and dozens of the wounded had to be left lying outside in scraped out trenches to await their turn for treatment, where the bombardment wounded many a second and third time, killing others.

On 14th April, Lt-Col John Laverty, commanding the 4th Royal West Kents, reported to the garrison commander, Colonel Hugh Richards, that 'The men's spirits are all right, but there aren't many of us left, ' and that if help was not received within forty-eight hours, Kohima would fall.

5 days later, on the 19th April, the perimeter had shrunk to 350 yards square, but still included the shattered corpse-covered tennis court. The terrain had been blasted to mud by the constant shellfire, shattered trees hung with the ghostly remnants of parachutes: the garrison had been supplied by air. On this day, the 2nd British Division finally managed to batter their way through to their trapped brothers in Kohima. They were confronted by the exhausted remains of the garrison who were described as 'filthy, bearded, bedraggled scarecrows'. They were also horrified by the desolation of Kohima Ridge. 'The stench of festering corpses... the earth ploughed by shell-fire... human remains lay rotting as the battle raged over them... flies swarmed everywhere and multiplied with incredible speed... Men retched as they dug in... the stink hung in the air and permeated clothes and hair... We were profoundly shocked by the conditions on Garrison Hill.'

One of the generals of 2nd British Division had served in the First World War as a junior officer on the Western Front, being wounded three times and winning the Military Cross. When he saw the battlefield at Kohima, he whispered that it was worse than anything he had ever seen.

As it turned out, the tennis court was the high-tide mark of the Japanese attacks on Kohima. That was as far as they could get. They showed incredible bravery in their attacks that astonished the defenders time and time again. And now the Battle of Kohima continued as the Japanese went on the defensive, and held on for weeks with as much tenacious courage in that awful terrain as the defenders of Kohima had, while the 2nd British Division relieved the garrison and continued battering their way south to reach the rest of the embattled 14th Army at Imphal.

How such a tiny garrison held on for so long against the numbers and assaults that were thrown at it can only really be explained by the fact that this was probably some of the most perfect defensive terrain in the world. Pouring rain, slicked mud, steep stepped hillsides all contributed to the defenders' victory, but this is in no way a disparagement of their achievement. But at the same time, the sheer ferocious tenacity and incredible courage of the Japanese soldiers in pressing home their attacks despite sometimes staggering casualties should be recognized.

Role in 1950 Earthquake in Assam: In the disastrous 1950 earthquake in Upper Assam, 2 AR jawans rendered immediate and invaluable help in the reconstruction, resettlement and rehabilitation of the victims.

Safe Conduct of Dalai Lama: In 1959, it was the forward elements of this Force that received His Holiness The Dalai Lama and his entourage fleeing into India, and ensured their safe passage up to Misamari.

Indo-China War: The initial onslaught of the Chinese in 1962 was borne by delaying elements of the AR. They gave a good account of themselves in this delaying role to enable the army to take up whatever defences that it was able to manage in the event.

Operation Pawan: The 22nd, 23rd and 26th AR Battalions were committed for Operation Pawan in Sri Lanka from December 1988 to February 1990. They were under the direct operational control of the army. Adept in the counter insurgency type operations undertaken there, they were on home ground and as such came out with colours flying very high.

Operations in Kashmir Valley: Two battalions of AR, the 7th and the 26th, have operated in the Srinagar Valley with great success. Their catches were more than those of the adjoining army units and formation commanders rated their performance very high.

Awards

Gallantry Awards

Award Name	*No. of Awards Received*
Ashok Chakra (AC)	3
Vir Chakra (Vrc)	5
Kirti Chakra (KC)	29
Shaurya Chakra (SC)	118
Param Vishisht Seva Medal(PVSM)	5
Ati Vishisht Seva Medal (AVSM)	11
Sena Medal	178
Vishisht Seva Medal (VSM)	73
Others	2869

Civil Awards

Award Name	*No. of Awards Received*
Presidents Police Medal for Gallantry	3
Presidents Police Medal for Distinguish Service	5
Prime Minister Police Medal for Life Saving	6
Police Medal for Gallantry	20
Governor's Gold Medal	386
Police Medal for Meritorious Service	226

Modernization

Modern training is given for adapting to style of command, in view of the changing aspirations of the soldiers in present socio-economic milieu. There are issues pertaining to operational preparedness, administrative efficiency and modernization plan of the oldest Paramilitary Force in the country.

Workshops are organized for rationalisation of manpower, man management issues, civic action programmes, improvement in communication and transit facilities, prompt disposal of disciplinary cases, appropriate action to dilute anomalies in pay and allowances, improved state of accommodation and medical care, greater educational opportunities and enhanced financial benefits for the serving and retired personnel of the Force.

The Assam Rifles, hailed as the Sentinels of the North-East, has embarked on a vigorous modernization drive to give it more fire power. The modernization plans of the senior-most Paramilitary Force of the nation include procuring state-of-the-art weapons and latest gadgets to boost operational efficiency of the troops. Assam Rifles has 65, 000 troops at present, having grown in strength of just 750 combatants at the time of its inception.

Miscellaneous

Assam rifles is involved with various welfare activities like IGNOU Assam Rifles Educational Project, Prime Minister's Scholarship Scheme, Assam Rifles Group Insurance Scheme and many more. It is also involved with various cultural activities and sports activities. It conduct various sports events at state level and its players also take part in various Armed Forces sports contests.

REFERENCES

Bamzai, Prithvi Nath Kaul: Kashmir and Power Politics: From Lake Success to Tashkent, Metropolitan Book Co., Delhi, 1966.

Bose, Sumantra: The Kashmir Challenge, Sage, New Delhi, 1997.

Coffee Land News, Jan. 2000.

Deccan Herald, July 10, 1987.

Dte General, Assam Rifles, Shillong.

Employment News.

Frontier India Defence & Strategic News Service, 16 May, 2008.

Frontline, Aug. 28 - Sep. 10, 1999.

India Today, Oct. 11, 1999.

Indian Express, Aug. 12, 1997.

Indian Express, Dec. 16, 1997.

Indian Express, Dec. 6, 1999.

Indian Express, July 6, 1999.

Indian Express, July 24, 1999.

Indian Express, May 1, 2000.

Indian Express, May 8, 1999.

Indian Express, May. 18, 1999.

Nayar K. K. and Amar Jawan - A Book of Remembrance, India Book House.

Singh, Harjeet (Col.), Doda: An insurgency in the Wilderness.

The Assam Tribune July 14, 2001.

The Daily Excelsior, July 30, 1999.

The Daily Excelsior, Oct. 15, 1999.

The Doon City Cronicle, June 1999.

The Hindu, Jan. 27, 1997.

The Hindu, Mar. 21, 2008.

The Tribune, Aug. 20, 1998.

The Tribune, July 16, 1999.

5

Border Security Force

"Duty unto Death"

Introduction

Border Security Force (BSF) raised in 1965, is entrusted with the task of maintaining permanent vigilance on India's international borders. The present strength of BSF is 157 battalions and guards a total of 6, 385.36 km of international borders, spread over mountains, inhospitable deserts, riverine, and snow bound and marshy areas. BSF has been assigned the role of promoting a sense of security amongst the people living in the border areas and preventing trans-border crimes, such as smuggling, infiltration/exfiltration and other illegal activities.

India shares 14, 000 kilometres of land frontier with six nations: Pakistan, China, Nepal, Bhutan, Bangladesh, and Burma. India claims an exclusive economic zone of 200 nautical miles.

In the mid-1990s, India had boundary disagreements with Pakistan, China, and Bangladesh; border distances are therefore approximations. The partition of India in 1947 established two India-Pakistan frontiers:

one on the west and one on the east (East Pakistan became Bangladesh in 1971) Disputes over the state of Jammu and Kashmir led to hostilities between India and Pakistan in 1947. On 01 January 1949 a cease-fire arranged by the United Nations (UN) divided control of Kashmir.

India controls Jammu, the Valley of Kashmir, and the capital, Srinagar, while Pakistan controls the mountainous area to the northwest. Neither side accepts a divided Kashmir as a permanent solution. India regards as illegal the 1963 China-Pakistan border agreement, which ceded to China a portion of Pakistani-controlled Kashmir. The two sides also dispute the Siachen Glacier near the Karakoram Pass. Further India-Pakistan hostilities in the 1965 war were settled through the Soviet-brokered Tashkent Declaration.

In 1968 an international tribunal settled the dispute over the Rann of Kutch, a region of salt flats that is submerged for six months of the year in the state of Gujarat. The following year, a new border was demarcated that recognized Pakistan's claim to about 10 percent of the area. In 1992 India completed fencing most of the 547-kilometre-long section of the boundary between the Indian state of Punjab and the Pakistani province of Punjab.

This measure was undertaken because of the continuing unrest in the region caused by both ethnic and religious disputes among the local Indian population and infiltrators from both sides of the frontier. The more rugged terrain north of Punjab along the entire cease-fire line between India and Pakistan in Jammu and Kashmir continues to be subject to infiltration and local strife.

The 2, 000-kilometre-long border with China has eastern, central, and western sections. In the western section, the border regions of Jammu and Kashmir have been the scene of conflicting claims since the nineteenth century. China has not accepted India's definitions of the boundary and has carried out defense and economic activities in parts of eastern Kashmir since the 1950s. In the 1960s, China finished construction of a motor road across Aksai Chin (a region under dispute between India and China), the main transportation route linking China's Xinjiang-Uygur Autonomous Region and Tibet. In the eastern section, the China-India boundary follows the McMahon Line laid down in 1914 by Sir Arthur Henry McMahon, the British plenipotentiary to a conference of Indian, British, and Chinese representatives at Simla (now known as Shimla, Himachal Pradesh).

The Simla Convention, as the agreement is known, set the boundary between India and Tibet. Although the British and Tibetan representatives signed the agreement on July 3, 1914, the Chinese delegate declined to sign. The line agreed to by Britain and Tibet generally follows the crest of the eastern Himalayas from Bhutan to Burma. It serves as a legal boundary, although the Chinese have never formally accepted it. China continued to claim roughly the entire area of Arunachal Pradesh south of the McMahon Line in the early 1990s. In 1962 China and India fought a brief border war in this region, and China occupied certain areas south of the line for several months.

India and China took a major step toward resolving their border disputes in 1981 by opening negotiations on the issue. Agreements and talks held in 1993 and 1995 eased tensions along the India-China border. Sikkim, which became an Indian state in 1975, forms the small central section of India's northern border and lies between Nepal and Bhutan. India's border with Bangladesh is essentially the same as it was before East Pakistan became Bangladesh in 1971.

Some minor disputes continued to occur over the size and number of the numerous enclaves each country had on either side of the border. These enclaves were established during the period from 1661 to 1712 during fighting between the Mughal Empire and the principality of Cooch Behar. This complex pattern of enclaves was preserved by the British administration and passed on intact to India and Pakistan.

The 2001 Indian-Bangladeshi border conflict was a short conflict between border guards of India and Bangladesh over the poorly marked border during 2001. Though there had been previous incidents of border violations, this one was significantly greater in scale.

Sovereignty over two separated pieces of territory was contested during the Sino-Indian War. One is Aksai Chin is located either in the Indian province of Kashmir or the Chinese province of Xinjiang in the west. It is a virtually uninhabited high-altitude wasteland crossed by the Xinjiang-Tibet Highway. The other disputed area lies to the east is referred to as Arunachal Pradesh by India and South Tibet by China. It is a sparsely inhabited area with numerous local tribes.

History

Need: Till mid sixties India-Pakistan borders were patrolled by the State Armed Police Battalions of the respective states. On 9 April, 1965 Pakistan attacked Sardar Post, Chhar Bet and Beria Bet in Kutch. These

Police Battalions proved ineffeicient and this exposed the inadequacy of the State Armed Police to handle this kind of situation. That is when Government of India felt the requirement for a dedicated centrally controlled Force, which would be well equipped and well skilled to man the International Border with Pakistan. As a result of the recommendations of the Committee of Secretaries, the Border Security Force came into existence on 01 Dec 1965 with K. F. Rustamji as its first chief and founding father.

Origin: Uptil the year 1965, India-Pakistan borders were manned by the State Armed Police Battalion. Pakistan attacked Sardar Post, Chhar Bet and Beria Bet on 9 April 1965 in Kutch. State Armed Police were unable to cope with armed aggression, so Indian Government felt the need for a specialized centrally controlled Border Security Force, which would be armed and trained to man the International Border with Pakistan. As a result of the recommendations of the Committee of Secretaries, the Border Security Force came into existence on 01 December 1965 with Shri K. F. Rustamji as the first commanding officer.

The Border Security Force (BSF) is responsible for guarding India's land borders during peacetime and prevent trans-border crimes. BSF has an extensive intelligence network to support these missions. Total strength of the BSF is approsimately 180, 000. Nearly, one third of the BSF is deployed in Jammu & Kashmir.

As part of its occupation of Kashmir, the Indian Government has deployed more than half a million soldiers and a quarter of a million Paramilitary Forces. Beginning in 1990 the Indian central government deployed the full range of Paramilitary Forces to Kashmir, as the Army was unwilling to commit its forces to the counter-insurgency operation. The BSF had never been committed for this type of operation.

The BSF has transformed itself from a border force to a counter-insurgency formation, and established an intelligence network in the area. However, more units of the force were deployed without the required specialised equipment and training. The first three years of BSF search, cordon, detention and killings produced an increase in the incidence violence in the Valley.

At least fifty-six of 148 battalions of Border Security Forces - each including one thousand men - are engaged in Kashmir. Thirty-nine in the valley and seven in Doda District are involved in counter-insurgency operations, and ten along the line of control are involved in border security operations. Security forces committed an estimated 100-200 killings of suspected militants in Jammu and Kashmir during 1997.

Countermilitants are former separatist militants who have surrendered to government forces but have retained their arms and paramilitary organization. Although precise numbers are unavailable, progovernment countermilitants may have committed 100 to 200 killings in Jammu and Kashmir during 1997.

Under the auspices of the UN and with USG encouragement, counter narcotic officials of India and Pakistan have continued the cooperation begun in 1994. Indian and Pakistani officials met three times in 1995 and agreed to speedy exchange of information and contacts. Narcotics representatives also participate in the quarterly meetings between the Indian Border Security Force and the Pakistani Rangers.

Few tangible results have yet come out of these meetings at times of general elections to Lok Sabha and to the Legislative Assemblies, the State Governments generally seek assistance of the Central Government Offices and Departments located in the States for deployment of their employees in connection with the conduct of elections. The civil employees of Border Security Force also participate in such election duty.

Key Dates in History

01 Dec 1965	Force came into existence
5-6 Dec. 1971	BSF Exemplary Courage in Battle of Longewala
25 May 1971	BSF sacrificed many soldiers during Pakistan attack on Dhallu Post
24 Sep. 1984	BSF sacrificed many soldiers during Terrorist attack on their Post in Punjab
May-July 1999	Kargil conflict
26 Jan. 2001	During the earthquake Gujarat, the BSF was the first to reach out to help the distressed people.
August 2003	Elimination of Terrorist Ghazi Baba
Nov. 2007	UN peacekeeping Mission in Sudan

Present Scenario

Personnel Strength: The BSF has strength of approximately 200, 000 troops and 165 battalions. The force is led by a Director General aided by an Additional Director General. A. K. Mitra is the present Director General of BSF.

Bases: The Force is commanded by an officer of the rank of Director General. The highest Headquarter of the force is located at New Delhi.

Two sector Headquarters are located in Kolkotta, Bengal and Nagpur, Maharashtra. Each is headed by an officer of rank of Add. Director General.

There are 165 Battalions of BSF.

Organizational Structure

Organizational setup of BSF from top to bottom is:

- Director General
- Additional Director General
- Inspector General
- Deputy Inspector General
- Additional Deputy Inspector General
- Commandant
- Second-in-Command
- Deputy Commandant
- Assistant Commandant
- Subedar Major
- Inspector
- Sub-Inspector
- Asstt Sub Inspector
- Head Constable
- Constable
- Enrolled Follower

Notable Chiefs of BSF

- Shri R. S. Mooshahary
- A. K. Mitra
- G. S. Gill

Duties and Functions

Motto: BSF motto is ***"Duty unto Death"*** showing their courage and determination. Its ethos is **"Any task, any time, any where"**

Maxim: BSF maxim in peace time and war time is:

- Promote a sense of security among the people living in the border areas.
- Prevent trans border crimes, unauthorized entry into or exit from the territory of India.
- Prevent smuggling and any other illegal activity.
- deployment for counter insurgency and internal security duties
- Holding ground in less threatened sectors.
- Protection of vital installations.
- Assistance in control of refugees.
- Anti-infiltration duties in specified areas.

Border Vigilance: Presently BSF guards a total of 6, 385.36 km of international borders, spread over mountains, inhospitable deserts, riverine, and snow bound and marshy areas. BSF has been assigned the role of promoting a sense of security amongst the people living in the border areas and preventing trans-border crimes, such as smuggling, infiltration/exfiltration and other illegal activities.

Counterinsurgency Operations: The BSF has transformed itself from a border force to a counter-insurgency formation, and established an intelligence network in the disturbed areas. The troops are very courageous and know how to perform the job. Their battle hardiness is as good as that of the regular Infantry battalions. Its battalions are adept in counter insurgency operations, where their performance has been better than before.

They are especially proficient in the un-orthodox type of small-scale missions to seek and destroy/apprehend hostiles. At present the Force is deployed all over India. It is helping out the civil administration in the maintenance of law and order, assisting the army in counter insurgency duties, and the general welfare of the locals and development of the inaccessible areas. It has proved itself more than a match for army units engaged in counterinsurgency and border surveillance roles.

Amarnath Yatra: Amarnath Yatra is a challenge which BSF takes seriously. BSF by virtue of its assimilation with border population do not face any problem in carrying out the security duty in Shri Amarnath Ji Yatra since 1994 by providing route security, medical assistance and other social services. Approximately five battalions were deployed on both axis i.e. Chandanwari to Holy cave and Baltal to Holy Cave by pressing into services of the Dog Squads, QRT's, electronic gadgets and more than that an effective surveillance system.

In Amarnath Yatra, BSF has focused its role towards medical aid which is as essential as security. BSF deployes Medical Officers assisted Para Medical staff, mobile teams with medicines and at critical points. The role of BSF medical staff is highly appreciated by the pilgrims.

Elections Duties: The election duties are another challenge given to BSF. BSF provided security during Assembly elections in the Kashmir state. In the 2002, Assembly elections, BSF was made a nodal agency in entire valley. True to its traditions, it played a crucial role alongwith JKP and other SFs in the conduct of a free and fair election despite the threats. BSF has sacrificed many lives of Jawans for carrying out this onerous task. This tradition and professional spirit was repeated during Parliamentary and Municipal elections.

VIP Duties: It is to the credit of the BSF that flag hoisting was done amidst challenge by militants at Lal Chowk in Srinagar on 26 January in year 1992. This tradition was continued by BSF on every Independence Day and Republic Day despite serious threats, BSF played key role in ensuring incident free Independence Day. BSF made extra efforts in facilitating security cover alongwith JKP and other SFs during many VVIP visits like –President, Prime Minister, Home Minister and other VVIPs visits Srinagar and other place in the valley.

Aid During Avalanches: During heavy snowfall during in winters, the BSF men extend a helping hand to the local civilians by deploying medical teams, manning medical aid posts and organizing mobile medical groups. Besides clearing several road stretches in remote areas, BSF supplies ration, Kerosene Oil, medicines etc to the remote villages, thus saving many lives.

Civic Programs: While fighting militancy with an iron hand, BSF has also adopted a compassionate touch in the strategy by carrying out civic action programmes. On the civic action front BSF adopted 10 schools providing them furniture items, stationery items, uniforms besides medical assistance.

Bharat Darshan Tour: Realising the need of winning the hearts and minds of the people, BSF conducted Bharat Darshan Tour, covering up to Kanyakumari for the youth in the age group of 10-15 giving a wide exposure about the nation. So far 330 children from various parts of Kashmir including children of victims of militancy, children from remote area and from poor families have availed this opportunity.

Srinagar-Muzaffrabad Bus Service: BSF played vital role in ensuring incident free bus service from Srinagar to Muzaffrabad by deploying ROPs and corridor security covering a stretch of 94 Kms out of 148 Kms stretch.

Welfare Activities: BSF since its induction in valley had recognized the aspect of human approach as since qua non in its anti-militancy strategy. It has to change it strategy in tune with the social behaviours and social structure. Thus, importance for human rights became a part of the curriculum. While BSF was ruthless against the militants, its attitude towards public, innocent, children, women and elders and quite sympathetic, accommodative and co-operative.

The training programme of all Jawans and officers included topics relating to human rights by eminent personalities and agencies. There is no gain saying that the Human Right Violation cases against BSF has been lowest among on the SFs and BSF did have no compunction in punishing the guilty. One of the principles followed by BSF in its operations is avoidance of collateral damage and if compelled to do so, to be minimal. This is one of the strong points which helped the BSF troops in carrying out their operations in a most surgical manner.

Training Overseas: BSF has the unique distinction of training large number of trainees from foreign Countries like Bhutan, Nepal, Mauritius, Kenya, Malaysia, Palestine etc. Till 1999, BSF has trained 298 personnel of various categories from foreign Countries in addition to training approximately 9000 to 10000 (400 to 500) recruits and 4000 to 5000 service personnel from their own organization in our training institutions.

Acts, Rules & Regulations

Border Security Force Act 1968: It is an Act to provide for the constitution and regulation of an Armed Force of the Union for ensuring the security of the borders of India and for matters connected therewith.

- Section 1: Short title and commencement.
- Section 2: Definitions.
- Section 3: Persons subject to this Act.
- Section 4: Constitution of the Force.
- Section 5: Control direction, etc.
- Section 6: Enrolment.
- Section 7: Liability for service outside India.

- Section 8: Resignation and withdrawal from the post.
- Section 9: Tenure of service under the Act.
- Section 10: Termination of service by Central Government.
- Section 11: Dismissal removal of reduction by the Director General and by other officers.
- Section 12: Certificate of termination of service.
- Section 12: Certificate of termination of service.
- Section 13: Restrictions respecting right to form association, freedom of speech, etc.
- Section 14: Offences in relation to the enemy and punishable with death.
- Section 15: Offences in relation to the enemy and not punishable with death.
- Section 16: Offences punishable more severely on active duty than at other times.
- Section 17: Mutiny.
- Section 18: Desertion and aiding desertion.
- Section 19: Absence without leave
- Section 20: Striking or threatening superior officers.
- Section 21: Disobedience to superior officer.
- Section 22: Insubordination and obstruction.
- Section 23: False answers on enrolment.
- Section 24: Certain forms of disgraceful conduct.
- Section 25: Ill-treating a subordinate.
- Section 26: Intoxication.
- Section 27: Permitting escape of person in custody.
- Section 28: Irregularity in connection with arrest or confinement.
- Section 29: Escape from custody.
- Section 30: Offences in respect of property.
- Section 31: Extortion and corruption
- Section 32: Making away with equipment.
- Section 33: Injury to property.

- Section 34: False accusations.
- Section 35: Falsifying official documents and false declarations.
- Section 36: Signing in blank and failure to report.
- Section 37: Offences relating to Security Force Court.
- Section 38: False evidence.
- Section 39: Unlawful detention of pay.
- Section 40: Violation of good order and discipline.
- Section 41: Miscellaneous offences.
- Section 42: Attempt.
- Section 43: Abetment of offences that have been committed.
- Section 44: Abetment of offences punishable with death and not committed.
- Section 45: Abetment of offences punishable with imprisonment and not committed.
- Section 46: Civil offences.
- Section 47: Civil offences not triable by a Security Force Court.
- Section 48: Punishments awardable by Security Force Courts.
- Section 49: Alternative punishments awardable by Security Force Courts.
- Section 50: Combination of punishments.
- Section 51: Retention in the Force of a person convicted on active duty.
- Section 52: Punishments otherwise than by Security Force Courts.
- Section 53: Minor punishments.
- Section 54: Limit of punishments under section 53:
- Section 55: Punishment of persons of and below the rank of subordinate officers by Deputy Inspectors-General and others
- Section 56: Collective fines.
- Section 57: Custody of offenders.
- Section 58: Duty of Commandant in regard to detention.
- Section 59: Interval between committal and trial
- Section 60: Arrest by civil authorities.

- Section 61: Capture of deserters.
- Section 62: Inquiry into absence without leave.
- Section 63: Force police officers.
- Section 64: Kinds of Security Force Courts.
- Section 65: Power to convence a General Security Force Court.
- Section 66: Power to convence a Petty Security Force Court.
- Section 67: Contents of warrants issued under sections 65 and 66:
- Section 68: Composition of General Security Force Court.
- Section 69: Composition of a Petty Security Force Court.
- Section 70: Summary Security Force Court.
- Section 71: Dissolution of a Security Force Court.
- Section 72: Power of a General Security Force Court.
- 73: Powers of a Petty Security Force Court.
- 74: Power of a Summary Security Force Court.
- Section 75: Prohibition of second trial.
- Section 76: Period of limitation for trial for an offence of desertion in certain cases.
- Section 77: Trial, etc., of offender who ceases to be subject to this Act.
- Section 78: Application of Act during term of sentence
- Section 79: Place of trial.
- Section 80: Choice between criminal court and Security Force Court.
- Section 81: Power of criminal court to require delivery of offender.
- Section 82: Presiding officer.
- Section 83: Law officers.
- Section 84: Challenges
- Section 85: Oaths of member, Law Officer and witness.
- Section 86: Voting by members.
- Section 87: General rule as to evidence.
- Section 88: Judicial notice.

- Section 89: Summoning witnesses.
- Section 90: Documents exempted from production.
- Section 91: Commissions for examination of witnesses.
- Section 92: Examination of a witness on commission.
- Section 93: Conviction of offence not charged.
- Section 94: Presumption as to signatures.
- Section 95: Enrolment paper.
- Section 96: Presumption as to certain documents.
- Section 97: Reference by accused to Government Officer.
- Section 98: Evidence of previous convictions and general character.
- Section 99: Lunacy of accused.
- Section 100: Subsequent fitness of lunatic accused for trial.
- Section 101: Transmission to Central Government of orders under section 100:
- Section 102: Release of lunatic accused.
- Section 103: Delivery of lunatic accused to relatives.
- Section 104: Order for custody and disposal of property pending trial.
- Section 105: Order for disposal of property regarding which offence is committed.
- Section 106: Powers of Security Force Court in relation to proceedings under this Act.
- Section 107: Finding and sentence not valid, unless confirmed.
- Section 108: Power to confirm finding and sentence of General Security Force Court.
- Section 109: Power to confirm finding and sentence of Petty Security Force Court.
- Section 110: Limitation of powers of confirming authority.
- Section 111: Power of confirming authority to mitigate, remit or commute sentences.
- Section 112: Confirming of findings and sentences on board a ship.
- Section 113: Revision of finding of sentence.

- Section 114: Finding and sentence of a Summary Security Force Court.
- Section 115: Transmission of proceedings of Summary Security Force Courts.
- Section 116: Alteration of finding or sentence in certain cases
- Section 117: Remedy against order, finding or sentence of Security force Court.
- Section 118: Annulment of proceedings.
- Section 119: Form of sentence of death.
- Section 120: Commencement of sentence of imprisonment.
- Section 121: Execution of sentence of imprisonment.
- Section 122: Temporary custody of offender.
- Section 123: Execution of sentence of imprisonment in special cases.
- Section 124: Conveyance of prisoner from place to place.
- Section 125: Communication of certain orders to prison officers.
- Section 126: Execution of sentence of fine.
- Section 127: Informality or error in the order or warrant.
- Section 128: Pardon and remission.
- Section 129: Cancellation of conditional pardon, release on parole or remission.
- Section 130: Suspension of sentence of imprisonment.
- Section 131: Orders pending suspension.
- Section 132: Release on suspension.
- Section 133: Computation of period of suspension.
- Section 134: Order after suspension.
- Section 135: Reconsideration of case after suspension.
- Section 136: Fresh sentence after suspension.
- Section 137: Scope of power of suspension.
- Section.138: Effect of suspension and remission on dismissal.
- Section 139: Powers and duties conferrable and imposable on members of the Force.

- Section 140: Protection for acts of members of the Force.
- Section 141: Power to make rules.
- Section 142: Provisions as to existing Border Security Force.

Weapons and Equipments

Light weaponry includes FN 35 and Glock 17.9 mm pistols, Heckler & Koch MP5 sub-machine guns, INSAS 5.56 mm assault rifles. INSAS 5.56 mm light machine guns, AGS-17 Plamya 30 mm automatic grenade launcher and AK 47, AK 74 sub machine guns. Type 81 Assault rifles, AKM rifles, INSAS 5. 56 MM Assault rifle, G3A3 Battle rifle, MP5 Submachine-gun ; Uzi submachinegun, M9 pistol ; RPG 7 Rocket-propelled grenade launchers ; and M67 hand-grenades. CRPF also uses landmine detectors ; Light Machine-Guns and Heavy-Machine-Guns.

Recruitment

Officers: The recruitment of officers into the BSF is carried out twice in a year to match with the dates of commencement of basic training at their Academy. The applications for the post of Assistant Commandant is advertised through National Dailies, Employment Exchange and Website. The preliminary selections of the candidates is conducted at Delhi, Mumbai, Chennai and Kolkatta by conduct of Mental Ability Test and an Interview.

These shortlisted candidates are invited to face Selection Board. The selection procedure followed is a three pronged system, where in candidates are assessed for officer like qualities by three different techniques. The system is similar to the one followed by Army. Those who are recommended by the Board and found medically fit are offered the appointment as per merit viz-a-viz number of vacancies.

These officers are also given a short course on personality development prior sending them for basic training.

The qualifications required to become an officer in the BSF are: 10+2+degree with BSc degree with Physics and Maths to join Mechanical/ Electrical/ Electronics Engineering for the Technical branches.

Other Ranks: Recruitment to the OR is done bi-annually. Candidates can join one of many branches. Entry to the done through a Mental Ability Test, entrance test and an interview. Qualified candidates undergo a medical examination and those who pass are selected on the basis of merit. Candidates undergo a written test, followed by an interview, followed by a medical examination.

Training: Border Security Force, one of the largest Paramilitary Forces in the World, is a versatile force, which is responsible for guarding round the clock vast and volatile borders not only against trans-border criminals but also against heavily armed trans-border terrorism as well.

Though guarding the borders is the prime commitment, security forces remain heavily and decisively involved in the interior as well in combating insurgency and militancy in various parts of the country. Because of its friendly and human face, BSF remains the much sough after Force for combating and containing serious law and order situations in the trouble prone States. And in case of hot War, BSF works as a force multiplier and contributes substantially towards over all War efforts of the nation as a credible front line Force.

By virtue of this unique dual role, the Border-men more commonly known as "Prahari" is required to be a perfect Policeman during peace and a professional soldier during War. Management of borders (International Border), restoration of law and order situation in the interior and fighting a Conventional/unconventional War are the three challenging assignments which a border-man is required to carryout.

In short, these fundamental essentials make the "Training Trilogy" of BSF. Professional proficiency of any Force is directly related to the standard of Training of that Force and it is Primarily due to this commitment that BSF refuses to compromise on its training assignments irrespective of handicaps and heavy orders. BSF believes in sweating during peace to ensure that it does not bleed during War or War like situation.

For organising and carrying out normal training and professional training, BSF have three main training Institutions, five Special Training Schools and eleven STCs/BTCs spread across the Country. Three main training Institutions are:

- BSF academy, Tekanpur
- Training centre and school, Meru.
- Central school of weapons and tactic, Indore.
- National training centre for dogs, Gwalior
- Signal training school, New Delhi
- Signal training school, Bangalore

In addition to main Training Institutions, BSF has eleven Subsidiary Training Centres/Basic Training Centres. Basically these are the breeding and training centres for various field formations. These are the nodal training Centres where 400-500 recruits always remain under training, thus training approximately 5000 recruits every year.

Famous Operations

Anti Smuggling Activities on Indo-Pak Border: On 11/12 December 2006 BSF naka deployed on border under Faridkot sensed some movement and also heard sound of movement. Sentry on duty alerted the naka and reached the spot and on searching, naka party discovered one packet lying about 15 meters from the fence on home side. The naka party informed the Post Commander and Company commander about the same who organized further search of the area and recovered 2 more packets of heroin and a Chinese Pistol loaded with 4 rounds on other side of fence. The smugglers however succeeded in escaping taking advantage of thick fog. Besides narcotics, BSF has seized fake Indian currency and weapons. Many intruders have been killed and Pakistan nationals apprehended while they were trying to infiltrate in India side.

In Congo: BSF conducted a special mission for maintenance of law and order and conduct of elections in Congo. Known for playing crucial role in containing insurgency in Jammu& Kashmir and North -East, BSF was stationed in Democratic Republic of Congo, Africa. The challenging task in this mission was for restoration of law and order and to create a conducive atmosphere for holding elections in a land riddled with multi faceted internal contradictions and conflicts.

True to the ethos of BSF in accepting challenges with proven experience in Jammu Kashmir and other parts of the country, this mission was another step for BSF, the largest border guarding force in the world in contributing to security management on foreign soil.

A unit of 125 personnel from BSF is deployed in Kinshasa. The officers of the India Formed Police Units extracted from life threatening situations over 100 individuals, including UN Staff, members of the diplomatic community as well as other civilians. Their professional competence has been recognized among the representatives of the international community in Kinshasa, as well as at all levels within the United Nations. The secretariat has commended the personnel of BSF unit for their dedication. BSF has taken part in several Peacekeeping Missions in Namibia, Cambodia, Bosnia, Sudan, Kosovo etc.

Anti-terrorist Operations in Kashmir: BSF in the recent past include neutralizing militant leaders of top hierarchical level, notable being Gazi Baba, the Jaish Chief, Rashid Bhai code Suhail Bhai, Janbaz, Dy Ops Chief of Jaish, Manzoor Zahid Choudhary (mastermind of Akshardham attack), Ghulam Hassan Khan at Saiful Islam, Dy Supreme Chief and Ops Comdr of HM, Mohd Yousuf Hazam, Comn Chief HM, Shaukat Ahmed Ganai at Crush India, HM, Ghulam Mustafa Jatta, JKFF and Abu Umair of LET, involved in Nadimarg Attack.

BSF had been instrumental in neutralizing the top hierarchy of HM, LET and JEM etc. The elimination of Gazi Baba, the terrorist of the decade, was a turning point in the canvas of anti-terrorist ops. With these calibrated and surgical operations, BSF has proved to be a force excelled by few and equalled by none. To its credit in Kashmir Valley, BSF accounted for neutralization of 2749 militants including 1096 foreigners (mostly Pakistanis), apprehended 9798 which includes senior militant leaders like Ghulam Rasool Shah code General Abdullah present chief of JUM, Maulana Masood Azhar, chief of JEM and Mustaq Latram Zargar, Al-Umar. 929 militants surrendered before BSF till October 2007

Awards

Gallantry Awards

Mahavir Chakra	01
Param Vishisht Seva Medal	01
Kirti Chakra	04
Vir Chakra	11
Ati Vishisht Seva Medal	01
Shaurya Chakra	10
Others	1240

Other Awards

Padma Bhushan	02
Padamshri	05
Arjuna Awards	12

Modernization

The future model of force would have numerous dimensions – environment would be Information Warfare oriented, operational and tactical situations would call for speedy decision making and integration with other services would be vital. Enhanced intelligence, training skills, flexibility and adaptability have become increasingly important as the army equipment and weapon systems have become sophisticated and complex.

It would harness advanced technologies to enable forces to read the environment instantly and respond either individually or as a tactical team with speed, precision, lethality and agility exploiting all the supporting combat components. The force should have multi terrain, multi environment capability to fight as an autonomous combat platform networked into the overall war fighting system architecture.

India's Border Security Force (BSF) would soon be making use of remote sensing and digital technologies to improve intelligence, curb infiltration and protect sensitive installations. Remote sensing and satellite technologies have become an essential part of security world wide, particularly in the field of defence. Most of the border areas are inhospitable terrain like ice-capped mountains of Himalayas or swift rivulets. Infiltration become easy in these areas if inadequately attended.

Objective of the training on use of satellite imaging and digital data is to put forward a suggestion on border management that can be improved and automated to the maximum possible extent. Developments in remote sensing, GIS, GPS and others can thus be fully exploited to safeguard our borders obtaining high resolution multi-sensor imagery and integrating at near real time with geographic information system to give that critical edge to security personnel.

The Border Security Force have been allocated Rs 435 crore for modernization of its communication network, Stressing the need for upgradation of communication techniques to gain an upper hand over militants. The technological advancement and deceiving methods adopted by the BSF will we be able to succeed.

Miscellaneous

BSF is involved in various welfare activities for its personnel and their families. Some of these are:

- Financial benefits to families of BSF personnel.
- Six Senior Secondary Schools, 61 Primary Schools and 3 Polytechnics are being run by the BSF out of Central Education Fund.
- An Institute of Rehabilitation and Re-settlement has been established at BSF Academy Tekanpur to impart vocational training to BSF widows on the following for re-settlement:

- Garment making course.
- Home products making course
- Multi-purpose Ayas/Nursing Staff Nurse
- Computer application/office Management Course.
- Rehabilitation training for disabled BSF Jawans. BSF had approached Queen Mary's Technical Institute (QMTI), Pune to organize rehabilitation training for disabled BSF Jawans. This institute which is a Private trust imparts vocational training to disabled personnel with a view to rehabilitate them.
- The facility being offered by QMTI cater to post medical rehabilitation vocational training i.e. after the disabled are adequately medically treated (acquired prosthesis were necessary) and are capable of undergoing one to two years of training in various skills. Hostel facilities are also offered. Personnel with more than 40% disability are only accepted by QMTI. At present 20 disabled personnel have completed their training and 4 candidates are undergoing training at QMTI, Pune.
- Remarriages of 38 widows of deceased BSF personnel have been arranged till date.
- 50 Plots have allotted to widows/disabled personnel at BSF Academy Tekanpur.
- 547 widows/dependents of deceased personnel have been given Govt. employment in BSF as Peons, follower, Clerk, Daftry, etc and 284 widows have been given employment in the various projects run out of BSF Welfare Fund.
- BSF has constructed 111 quarters at different location for allotment to the widows.
- Rustamji Institute of Technology (RJIT) is the first Engineering College in India established by Paramilitary Force. Due to deployment of the bulk of the Border Security Force (BSF) personnel in militancy-affected areas, the majorities of the force personnel stay separated from their families and are unable to look after the education of their children. A number of personnel are laying down their lives in the fight against anti national elements every day.

The Rustamji Institute of Technology (RJIT) has been set up with the objective of giving an opportunity to the children of serving BSF personnel as well as for those who have laid down their lives in service to the nation, for acquiring higher technical qualification. The Border Security Force education fund sponsored the development of the institute.

REFERENCES

Annual Report 2002-2003, Ministry of Home Affairs, Government of India.

Ashok Krishna: Examples of Learning in Counter-Insurgency, IDSA 2000.

Bose, Sumantra: The Kashmir Challenge, Sage, New Delhi, 1997.

Bruce Elleman: Sino-Soviet Relations and the Feb 1979 Sino-Vietnamese Conflict. (20 Apr 96).

Christian. F. Ostermann: New Evidence on the Sino-Soviet Border Dispute, Cold War International History Project Bulletin Issue 5 (Spring 1995).

Col. Ahrnam Singh. Doda: Insurgency in the Wilderness. Lancer, New Delhi 1999.

Dte General, BSF, New Delhi.

Employment News.

Free Press Journal, March 13, 2000.

Gupta, Sisir: Kashmir, Asia Publishing House, Bombay, 1966.

Indian Express. March 27, 2000.

Kumar, Raj: Encyclopaedia of Military Systems in India, Commonwealth Publishers, New Delhi, 2004.

Major General Arjun Ray: Kashmir Diary, Manas, New Delhi 1996.

Manoj Joshi: The Lost Rebellion. Penguin India, New Delhi 1997.

Ministry of Home Affairs.

Ramesh Thakur and Carlyyle Thayer: Soviet Relations with India and Vietnam. New York. St Martin Press, 1992.

Robert A. Scalapino: The Political Influence of the USSR in Asia in Donald. S. Zagoria ed. Soviet Policy in East Asia. New Haven, Yale University Press 1982.

The Hindu, Aug. 10, 1999.

The Hindu, Feb. 15, 2000.

Tribune, Dec. 07, 1999.

Tribune, Nov. 25, 1998.

6

Central Industrial Security Force

"Protection and Security"

Introduction

The Central Industrial Security Force (CISF)was established in its current shape on June 15, 1983 is a paramilitary security force in India. It was set up under an act of Parliament on 10 March 1969 with a strength of 2, 800 personnel. CISF was subsequently made an armed force of the Union of India by another act of Parliament passed on 15 June 1983. Its current strength is 105, 000. It is directly under the Ministry of Home Affairs and its headquarters are at New Delhi.

The CISF provides security cover to over two hundred industrial units located all over India. Industrial sectors like atomic power plants, space installations, defence production units, mints, oil fields and refineries, major ports, heavy engineering, steel plants, barrages, fertilizer units, airports and hydro electric/thermal power plants are protected by

CISF. Most of these installations are located in difficult terrains of the country with harsh climatic conditions. CISF also provides consultancy services to private industries as well as other organizations within the Indian government for security purposes.

The consulting wing has amongst its clients some of the renowned business houses and organizations of India including TISCO Jamshedpur; SEBI Hqrs. Mumbai; Vidhana Soudha, Bangalore; Orissa Mining Co., Bhubaneswar; AP Assembly, Hyderabad; Bangalore Metropolitan Transport Corp., HIL Kerala, IARI, Delhi; NBRI, Lucknow and Infosys, Bangalore. The scope of CISF's consulting practice includes security consulting and fire protection consulting.

History

Need: In sixties, with the industrial development of India going on a very fast pace, it was felt that big industries needed separate security. With emerging scenario of insurgency in country, a need for dedicated security force for protection of vital industrial complexes was felt. Other forces could not be burdened with this task. So a force was set up by act of parliament in 1969.

Origin: In the beginning this force was made of only 2800 personnel, but today it consists of more than 100, 000 personnel. As the name suggests, it was created for the better protection and security of Industrial Undertakings. There was a limitation though, that industries to be provided protection should be wholly owned by the Central Government, which has since been modified so that the industries can now be a joint venture with the Central Government.

However the role of CISF has undergone a diversification and it now also protects airports, seaports, metro rail networks, government buildings, heritage monuments, nuclear power plants, and space installations apart from industries. The Taj Mahal is also protected by the CISF. It has also moved into the fields of VIP security as well as Disaster Management.

The Force was constituted in such manner, that it consists of such number of Supervisory Officers, Subordinate Officers, under Officers and other enrolled Members of the Force.

The various duties of member of the Force is to Promptly obey and execute all orders lawfully issued to him by his superior authority, to protect and safeguard the Industrial Undertaking owned by the Central Government together with such other installations as are specified by that Government to be vital for the carrying on of work in those Undertakings, situate within the local limits of his jurisdiction: Provided that before any installation not owned or controlled by the Central Government is so specified, the Central Government shall obtain the consent of the Government of the State in which such installation is situate, to protect and safeguard such other Industrial Undertakings and installation for the protection and security of which he is deputed, to protect and safeguard the employees of the Industrial Undertakings and installations, to do any other act conducive to the better protection and security of the industrial undertakings and installations, to provide technical consultancy services relating to security of any private sector industrial establishment, to protect and safeguard the organizations owned or funded by the Govt and the employees of such organizations as may be entrusted to him by the Central Govt. and any other duty which may be entrusted to him by the Central Govt. from time to time.

Key Dates in History

10 March 1969	Conception of CISF
1969	Induction of Fire Wing
16 April 1970	First Fire Induction
15 June 1983	CISF in its present form
07 Dec. 2001	Consultancy services launched

Present Scenario

Personnel Strength: The CISF has strength of approximately 105, 000 troops. The force is headed by a Director General. He is helped by an Addl. Director General and one Insp. General. Ranjit Kumar Das is the present Director General of CISF.

Force Headquarters has six Deputy Inspectors General, one each for Intelligence and Operations Wing, Personnel Wing, Administration Wing, Fire Wing, Training, Wing and Induction and Planning Wing. Directorate General is located in New Delhi.

Bases: The country is divided into four sectors; North, South-West, East and North-East. An IG heads each sector.

There are many zones in each sector headed by DIGs.

There are eight reserve Battalions of CISF

Organizational Structure

Organizational setup of CISF from top to bottom is:

- Director General
- Additional Director General
- Inspector General
- Deputy Inspector General
- Additional Deputy Inspector General
- Commandant
- Deputy Commandant
- Assistant Commandant
- Subedar Major
- Inspector
- Sub-Inspector
- Asstt Sub Inspector
- Head Constable
- Constable
- Follower

Notable Chiefs of CISF

- Ravi Kant Sharma
- K. M. Singh
- Digvijay Kumar Singh
- H. J. Dora
- S. I. S. Ahmed
- Ranjit Kumar Das

Duties and Functions

Motto: ***"Protection and Security"*** is CISF motto.

Maxim: To Promptly obey and execute all orders lawfully issued to him by his superior authority.

- To protect and safeguard the Industrial Undertaking owned by the Central Government together with such other installations as are specified by that Government.

- To protect and safeguard such other Industrial Undertakings and installation for the protection and security of which he is deputed.
- To protect and safeguard the employees of the Industrial Undertakings and installations.
- To do any other act conducive to the better protection and security of the industrial undertakings and installations, to provide technical consultancy services relating to security of any private sector industrial establishment.
- To protect and safeguard the organizations owned or funded by the Govt and the employees of such organizations as may be entrusted to him by the Central Govt. and any other duty which may be entrusted to him by the Central Govt. from time to time.

Description of Duties: CISF is responsible for conducting instruction, presentations and exercises in accordance with the guidelines and directives set forth by the Department of State Diplomatic Security Antiterrorism Assistance Program (ATA). Responsible for ensuring only current ATA approved training materials (lesson plans, participant handouts, videos, case studies, etc.) are used in the delivery of ATA courses.

Airport Security: Airport security refers to the techniques and methods used in protecting airports and by extension aircraft from crime and terrorism. Large numbers of people pass through airports every day. Such a large gathering of people presents a natural target for terrorism and other forms of crime due to the number of people located in a small area. Similarly, the high concentration of people on large airliners, the potential high lethality rate of attacks on aircraft, and the ability to use a hijacked airplane as a lethal weapon provide an alluring target for terrorism.

Airport security provides a first line of defence by attempting to stop would-be attackers from bringing weapons or bombs into the airport. If they can succeed in this, then the chances of these devices getting on to aircraft are greatly reduced. As such, airport security serves two purposes: To protect the airport from attacks and crime and to protect the aircraft from attack.

India stepped up its airport security after the 1999 Kandahar hijacking. The Central Industrial Security Force is in charge of airport security. CISF formed an Airport Security Group this security force is dedicated to protect Indian airports. Each and every airport has now been given an APSU (Airport Security Unit), a highly trained unit to counter unlawful interference with civil aviation, apart from the CISF every airline has a highly trained aviation security force which is a separate department.

Terrorist threats and narcotics are the main threats in Indian airports. Another problem that some airports face is the proliferation of slums around the airport boundaries in places like Mumbai. Before boarding an aeroplane, searching of hand luggage is compulsory.

The CISF controls airport security at all commercial airports in India. Airport security, in the past, was under the control of the Airport Police (under the State Government). However, following the hijacking of Indian Airlines Flight 814 in 1999, the topic of handing over security of the airports to the CISF was first proposed.

While this proposal lay low for the next two years, the Central Government woke up to the security threat after the September 11, 2001 attacks in the United States of America and decided to implement the suggestion. The Netaji Subhash Chandra Bose International Airport in Kolkata was the first airport that came under the CISF's control. Following this majority of the commercial airports in India were brought under its purview. As of now CISF is protecting a total of 54 international and domestic airports in the country.

Many past tragedies were the result of travellers being permitted to carry either weapons or items that could be used as weapons on board aircraft so that they can hijack the plane. Travellers are quickly screened by a *metal detector*. More advanced explosive detection machines are being used in screening. Passengers must be screened to discourage the carrying of bombs aboard an aircraft. X-ray machines are often used to speed up this process. Explosive detection machines can also used for both carry on and checked baggage. These detect volatile compounds given off from explosives using a kind of gas chromatography. A recent development is the use of backscatter X-ray scanners to detect hidden weapons and explosives on passengers. These devices, which use Compton scattering, require that the passenger stand close to a flat panel and produce a high resolution image.

Generally people are screened through airport security into the concourses, where the gates are all located. This area is often called a secure or sterile area, and is referred to as airside. Passengers are discharged from airliners into the sterile area so that they usually will not have to be re screened if disembarking from a domestic flight; however they are still subject to search at any time. Eating establishments have started using plastic glasses and utensils as opposed to glasses made out of glass and utensils made out of metal to reduce the usefulness of such items as weapons. Traditionally, non-passengers were allowed on the concourses to meet arriving friends or relatives at their gates, but this is greatly restricted now in the interest of security in India. Non-passengers must obtain a gate pass to enter the secure area of the airport. The most common reasons that a non-passenger may obtain a gate pass is to assist children and the elderly as well as for attending business meetings that take place in the secure area of the airport. In India, at least 24 hours notice is generally required for those planning to attend a business meeting inside the secure area of the airport.

CISF sometimes use trained individuals who engage passengers in a conversation to detect threats rather than solely relying on equipment to find threats. CISF has run several dummy tests in several major airports to measure the success of catching people with bombs. The tests are done by using undercover agents to carry fake bombs/parts in their carry on luggage and counting how many are successful with getting through security checkpoints. CISF runs covert tests everyday and when a screener misses an undercover agent carrying dangerous items, they are immediately sent to remedial training.

CISF primary personnel in airport security include:

- Airport Security Unit
- A branch of the local police department stationed at the airport
- Members of the local police department assigned to the airport as their normal patrol area
- Members of a country's airport protection service
- Police dog services for explosive detection, drug detection and other purposes

Industry Security: The CISF is providing security cover to 267 PSUs located all over the country. This list comprises vital industrial sectors like atomic power plants, space installations, defence production units, mints, oil fields and refineries, major ports, heavy engineering, steel plants, barrages, fertilizer units, airports and hydro electric/thermal power plants.

Consultancy Services: In the year 1999, the Indian Parliament, further widened the charter of duties of CISF by allowing its deployment even in Joint Ventures as also permitting it to provide consultancy services in fields of Security & Fire Protection to even private sector, among others. The then Deputy Prime Minister of India, Mr. L K Advani, formally launched the Consultancy Services of CISF at a glittering function in New Delhi on 7th December 2001. The CISF Consultancy Wing has since provided consultancy to over 50 clients which include big names in private and public sectors.

Fire Wing: Fire fighting is the act of extinguishing destructive fires. A firefighter fights these fires to prevent destruction of life, property and the environment. Fire fighting is a highly technical profession which requires years of training and education in order to become proficient. Besides providing protection, safety, and security to Industrial undertaking/installations, CISF also offers protection against Fire hazards. CISF has a highly specialised, trained and fully equipped fire wing. The first fire wing unit with a strength of 53 personnel was Inducted in Cochin. As on date, the fire wing has been inducted in 81 units. The present strength of the Fire Wing is 5028 personnel. The Fire wing which is an integral part of Central Industrial Security Force is the largest, well trained and equipped, fire fighting force in the Government Sector.

It is known as an outstanding fire fighting force having an enviable record. It is providing fire coverage to establishments varying from power plants, refineries, petro-chemicals, fertilizers, steel plants surface transport, heavy industries, space application centre etc. Fire wing Induction in the Undertaking is not limited to providing manpower to fight fire alone. It also ensures availability of proper and adequate devices for fire prevention and fire fighting along with the fire fighting staff.

CISF Fire-fighters work by

- Eliminating exposure of fuel that may be ignited by nearby flames or radiant heat
- Cooling the fuel below flashpoint (The temperature when a fuel is combustible)
- Containing and extinguishing the fire
- Removing debris and extinguishing all hidden fires to prevent rekindling

Their goal is to save life, property and the environment. A fire can rapidly spread and endanger many lives; however, with modern fire fighting techniques, catastrophe is usually, but not always, avoided. To prevent fires from starting a fire-fighter's duties include public education and conducting fire inspections. Because fire-fighters are often the first responders to people in critical conditions, fire-fighters provide basic life support as emergency medical technicians or advanced life support as licensed paramedics.

CISF Fire Wing has the distinction of training large number of trainees from foreign Countries like Mauritius, Kenya, Palestine etc. Till 2007, it has trained 540 personnel from foreign Countries.

Acts, Rules & Regulations

The CISF is governed by The Central Industrial Security Force Act, 1968, The Act consists of 22 sections in all.

- Section 1: Short title, extent and commencement
- Section 2: Definitions
- Section 3: Constitution of the Force
- Section 4: Appointment and powers of supervisory officers
- Section 5: Appointment of enrolled members of the Force
- Section 6: Certificates of Members of the Force
- Section 7: Superintendence and administration of the Force
- Section 8: Dismissal, removal etc
- Section 9: Appeal and revision
- Section 10: Duties of member of the Force
- Section 11: Power to arrest without warrant
- Section 12: Power to search without warrant
- Section 13: Procedure to be followed after arrest
- Section 14: Deputation of the Force to Industrial undertaking in public
- Section 15: Officers and Members of the Force to be considered always on duty and liable to be employed anywhere in India
- Section 16: Responsibilities of member of the Force during suspension
- Section 17: Surrender of certificate arms etc. by persons ceasing to be members of the Force
- Section 18: Penalties for neglect of duty etc
- Section 19: Application of Act 22 of 1922 to member of the Force

- Section 20: Certain Acts not to apply to Members of the Force
- Section 21: Protection of acts of members of the Force
- Section 22: Power to make rules

CISF Rules: These rules are called The Central Industrial Security Force Rules, 2001. There are 92 Sections in all.

- Section 1: Short title and commencement
- Section 2: Definitions
- Section 3: Constitution of the Force
- Section 4: Composition of the Force
- Section 5: Conferment of local rank
- Section 6: Duties of Director General
- Section 7: Duties of Sector Inspectors General in Central Industrial Security Force
- Section 8: Duties of Deputy Inspector General
- Section 9: Duties of Managing Director and General Manager
- Section 10: Duties of Commandant
- Section 11: Duties of Deputy Commandant
- Section 12: Duties of Assistant Commandant
- Section 13: Arrest
- Section 14: Search
- Section 15: Prescribed rank
- Section 16: Powers of appointment
- Section 17: Conditions of eligibility for appointment to the Force
- Section 18: Disqualification
- Section 19: Name of the posts, their classification and scales of pay
- Section 20: Method of recruitment, age limits and other qualifications
- Section 21: Agreement
- Section 22: Cadre
- Section 23: During the period of deputation, the officer on deputation shall be governed by the provisions of the Act and the rules and regulations made thereunder

- Section 24: Promotion
- Section 25: Probation
- Section 26: Termination
- Section 27: Special provision for certain categories of persons
- Section 28: Power to relax
- Section 29: Manuals
- Section 30: Solemn affirmation of allegiance
- Section 31: Rules governing discipline
- Section 32: Disciplinary Authority
- Section 33: Suspension
- Section 34: Nature of Penalties
- Section 35: Petty punishments
- Section 36: Procedure for imposing major penalties
- Section 37: Procedure for imposing minor
- Section 38: Procedure for imposing petty
- Section 39: Special procedure in certain cases
- Section 40: Provisions regarding enrolled members of the Force borrowed from State Governments etc
- Section 41: Provisions regarding enrolled member of the Force lent to state Government etc
- Section 42: Reduction in rank etc.
- Section 43: Withholding of increment
- Section 44: Appeal against order of suspension
- Section 45: Orders against which no appeal lies
- Section 46: Appeal against order imposing penalties
- Section 47: Period of limitation for appeals
- Section 48: Form and contents of appeal
- Section 49: Submission of Appeals authority which made the order appealed against.
- Section 50: Withholding of appeals
- Section 51: Transmission of appeals
- Section 52: Consideration of appeals

- Section 53: Implementation of orders in appeal
- Section 54: Revision
- Section 55: Dies-non
- Section 56: Petitions
- Section 57: Other methods forbidden
- Section 58: Resignation
- Section 59: Discharge Certificate
- Section 60: Surrender of certificate of appointment
- Section 61: Free Accommodation
- Section 62: Medical facilities
- Section 63: Leave
- Section 64: Recall from Leave
- Section 65: Free Leave Pass and Leave Travel Concession
- Section 66: Power to grant monetary
- Section 67: Eligibility for monetary rewards
- Section 68: Authorities competent to grant monetary rewards
- Section 69: Monetary rewards offered by the Managing Director of the Industrial undertakings
- Section 70: Benefits on account of risk of "office"/special Risk of "office
- Section 71: Superannuation etc
- Section 72: Transfer
- Section 73: Payment of charges
- Section 74: Non-applicability of rules in certain cases
- Section 75: Award of Director General's Commendation Disc
- Section 76: Ministerial staff
- Section 77: Other conditions of service
- Section 78: Magisterial Powers
- Section 79: Judicial trials
- Section 80: Magistrate
- Section 81: Language to be used in the proceedings before Commandant

- Section 82: Magistrate not to try enrolled members of the Force
- Section 83: Magistrate to give notice
- Section 84: Magistrate to be informed of the trial of the accused
- Section 85: Unit Commander to deliver the accused to the Magistrate
- Section 86: Manner of imprisonment
- Section 87: Force Custody
- Section 88: Promulgation of sentence
- Section 89: Transmission of proceedings
- Section 90: Appeals
- Section 91: Technical consultancy services to the industrial establishments in the private sector
- Section 92: Repeal and Saving

Weapons and Equipments

Weapons: Light weaponry includes FN 35 and Glock 17.9 mm pistols, Heckler & Koch MP5 sub-machine guns, INSAS 5.56 mm assault rifles. INSAS 5.56 mm light machine guns, AGS-17 Plamya 30 mm automatic grenade launcher and AK 47, AK 74 sub machine guns. Type 81 Assault rifles, AKM rifles, INSAS 5. 56 MM Assault rifle, G3A3 Battle rifle, MP5 Submachine-gun ; Uzi submachinegun, M9 pistol ; RPG 7 Rocket-propelled grenade launchers ; and M67 hand-grenades. CRPF also uses landmine detectors ; Light Machine-Guns and Heavy-Machine-Guns.

Equipments: Nomex and Kevlar protective pants, jump suits, Crew Boss brush coats, safety vests and chain saw chaps, Hot Shield face protector, fire helmets,

Recruitment

Officers: The recruitment of officers into the CISF is carried out every year. The applications for the post of Assistant Commandant and Sub Inspector is advertised through National Dailies, Employment Exchange and Website. Selection is through Limited Departmental Competitive Examination. These officers are also given a short prior sending them for basic training. The qualifications required to become an officer in the CISF is graduation.

Other Ranks: Recruitment for followers and constables is done annually. Entry is through a Mental Ability Test, entrance test and an interview. Qualified candidates undergo a medical examination and those who pass are selected on the basis of merit. Candidates undergo a written test, followed by an interview, followed by a medical examination.

Training: The CISF training college, initially established at Partapur (Meerut) in 1969 was shifted to Shivrampally, Hyderabad in 1971, In 1987, the college moved into the present premises at Hakimpet, Secundrabad (A.P) and was upgraded into an academy on 8 Dec. 1990 with Dy Inspector General as its head. This academy now has the capacity to train 848 trainees at a given point of time. NISA was declared "Centre of Excellence" by the Ministry of Home Affairs (GOI) in the field of Industrial Security on 30.09.1999. Keeping in view of the increasing role of NISA in conducting not only the basic as well as in–service courses for CISF officers, but various courses and seminars for the officers of others organization also, the pose of Director NISA has been upgraded and the Academy is now being headed by an officer of the rank of Inspector General.

The National Industrial Security Academy (NISA) was established primarily to conduct the basic induction training of directly recruited Assistant Commandants and to function as an organ of the CISF to cultivate professionalism and expertise in Industrial Security Management. The academy has been imparting professional and specialised training to officers and men of CISF and other Police organizations and public sector undertakings in addition to the primary task of grooming the Assistant Commandant (Probationers) and other direct recruits of the Force.

The academy is also organizing prestigious In-Service Course like Vertical Interaction Courses for IPS Officers, Disaster Management Course for District Level Officers and Integrated Industrial Security Management Course for Commandants and Deputy Commandants and equivalent ranks of Police and Paramilitary Forces and PSUS. The Academy provides following training to Personnel:

- Disaster Management Course for District Level officers
- Vertical Interaction Course for IPS officers of state and CPOS
- Duties of quarter master/provisioning and procurement action for DC/ACs
- Safety awareness course for DC/ACs/ Inspectors.

- Legal and Establishment course for DC/ACs
- Course on computer and MIS for DC/ACs/ Inspectors
- Staff officer course for DCs
- DDO Course for DC/ACs
- Yoga and Meditation course for DC/ACs
- Intelligence course for ACs/ Inspectors
- Integrated Industrial Security Management course CO/DC of CPOs.
- TTC on aviation security for GOs and SOs.
- Senior level industrial Security course for Comdt./Dy.Comdt./ ACs of States/Uts/CPOs.
- Refresher course for AC
- Departmental Inquiry course for SOs
- JLIS course for SOs /ASOs of States/CPOs
- Aviation Security Course for SO's
- Pre-Promotion course for GOs upto the rank of IG
- Promotion cadre course for SI/EXE, SI/MIN
- Promotion cadre course for ASI/CLK
- Yoga and Medication Course for SOs nand ORs
- QM course for SOs
- Legal and Establishment course for DC/AC/Inspr.
- Indoor Instructor course
- Tactical and WT course for GOs and SOs
- Training of trainer course for SOs
- Computer Course for Sos
- Human Right Course for Gos
- Assistant Commandant (DA) Basic Course
- SI/Exe Basic Course
- HC/CLK and SI/Steno Basic Course
- Disaster Management Course for District Level Officers
- Vertical Interaction Course for IPS Officer
- Integrated Industrial Security Management course for DC/AC, CPOS and State Police

- Senior level Industrial Security Management course for DC/ ACS for CPOS
- Junior level Industrial Security course for Inspectors/SI of state and CPOS
- Junior level Industrial Security Course for Parliament security officers
- Junior Level Industrial Security course for DAE Security officers

CISF Recruit Training Centre Bhilai was established at sector-3 of Bhilai Steel Plant on 15-2-1975 on bifurcation from CISF training College Shivram Palli (NPA) at Hyderabad.

Initially, the training centre was headed by an Assistant Commandant as Principal and was under the command, control and supervision of DIG BSP Bhilai. The training capacity was to train only 270 personnel at a given time.

The RTC Bhilai was upgraded in Feb.1988 along with other training centres and its training capacity was enhanced to 500 trainees. The existing infrastructure facilities and the total land area available at sector-3, Bhilai were inadequate for the training centre to impart training for 500 personnel.

The Recruit Training Centre, Arakkonam has been established near the village called Nagarikuppam by in the year 1988. The Campus is called "Suraksha Campus". CISF 6th Reserve Battalions Hqrs is also located in the same campus.

This RTC is one of the best among other training centers of CISF. This RTC is headed by an officer of the rank of Additional Dy. Inspector General This RTC is having a training capacity of 1008 trainees at any given time.

RTC Barwaha is located near to Badali river from which the name of the place Barwaha was derived. During the reign of Mughal emperor Shahjahan, Rana Durjansal of Tomar Dynasty received the Zamindari of Jaitpuri (Barwaha) in the year 1646. In the year 1758 Shivaji Rao Holkar of Holkar Dynasty built the longest palace of Asia the "Dariya Mahal" at Barwaha which is having 198 rooms and five palaces these are being used for residential and official purpose. In August 1968 CRPF established their RTC in Dariya Mahal and the surrounding areas. In 1984, the 1st Res. Batallion of CISF was shifted from Deoli and took charge of the area from CRPF. On 1st April 1985, CISF established its Recruit Training Centre here. Following courses are conducted here:

- Basic Course of Constable (Male.)recruits
- Basic Course of Constable(Female) recruits
- HC/GD to ASI/Exe
- Constable to HC/GD
- STF Commando Course
- Short Commando course for direct SI/Exe
- WT & Tactics course
- QRT course
- UAC Course
- Drill and WT Instructors courses

Recruit Training Centre–I Deoli, is located in one of the oldest cantonment having great history. Since its birth as a cantonment of British Army, existing campus of this training centre has gone through different phases. First of all, a part of Kotah contingent an Auxiliary Force raised by the Darbar Kotah Maharaja Ram Singh Ji, was established here in 1855. When this contingent joined the mutiny in 1857, a new Mina Battalion was raised. Later on, when agency was established in Deoli in 1859, this battalion become the Infantry of the Deoli Irregular Force. In 1903, it became the 42nd Deoli Regiment, which was disbanded at the end of the Great war 1921 and in 1922 a new Mina corps was raised.

In its Second Phase during 1931 this campus was used to detain about 500 Bengali leaders arrested from Bengal and was guarded by Royal Garhwal Rifles.

In 1940, when freedom movement got its momentum, this campus was again opened to detain the well known freedom fighters, under the protection of special armed force of U.P. and later on in 1942, security of this detention camp was handed over to CRP(Crown Representative Police). At that time, well known freedom fighters such as S/Shri Jai Prakash Naryan, S.S.Batliwala, Rahul Sanskrutyan, S.K.Dange, Sudhir Ghosh, Keshav Dutt Malviya, Harish Dutt Malviya, Sardar Mota Singh and Dr.Fakharudin were detained here. During Second World War, Japaneese, Italians and Germans were kept here who were released after the World War and the camp was closed on 28.02.1947. In its third phase it was reopened on 1.1.1948 and was used to accommodate about 10, 000 Sindhi Refugees who had migrated from Pakistan.

In 1957, CRP (Central Reserve Police) took over this camp and its 4th and 9th battalion were stationed here but again this camp was converted into a detention camp to accommodate about 3000 prisoners and was known as Chinese camp. From 1967 onward it was used as rehabilitation camp. Again in 1979, 79 Batallion of CRP took over the camp.

On 10.3.1980, Ist Reserve Battalion of CISF took over the charge of this historical complex and finally, CISF RTC was established here on 01.08.1984.Subsequently, Ist Reserve Battalion of CISF was shifted to Barwaha, Madhya Pradesh. This RTC is headed by an officer of the rank of Additional Dy. Inspector General. This RTC is having a training capacity of 500 trainees at any given time.

Famous Operations

Fighting fire in Travancore: A blazing fire was subdued at Fertilizers and Chemicals factory in Travancore, Cochin on 16 April, 1970 with 53 personnel.

Fighting fire at MGCC Nagothane: In a fire incident at MGCC Nagothane in 1990, the CISF lost 9 personnel but saved property worth Rs.1000 crores

Naxalite Encounter: On 9th February 2006, at a unit of National Mineral Development Cooperation Ltd. in iron ore field of Baladila, Dantewada, Chhatisgarh, Shri DNP Singh, S.I., CISF was on duty with 8 personnel guarding the area including an Explosive store when a group of 500 Naxlites attacked the barrack shouting slogans and demanding fire arms. Shri Singh took stock of the situation and started firing at them. The Naxlites fired heavily with grenades and petrol bombs causing grievous injuries to many personnel. Shri Singh didn't lose courage and continued to return fire.

Meanwhile, the Naxlites managed to blast off the asbestos roof of barrack using landmines. Undeterred by the barrage of fire, the CISF personnel under the leadership of Shri Singh did not lose courage and prevented the Naxlites to enter the barracks. Despite collapse of the roof of the barrack and serious injuries on his body, Shri Singh continued to confront the Naxlites and resisted their advances to capture the building. The Naxlites blasted the barrack and captured the buildings. They asked Shri Singh to surrender, who however refused to lay down arms and continued the fight. He was then shot dead by the Naxlites.

UN Peacekeeping Missions: CISF has been a part of the Indian contingents to UN peacekeeping missions and was deployed in these missions to Cambodia, Mozambique, Angola and Bosnia.

In the year 2006-2007, the CISF detected 7646 cases of theft from PSUs involving property worth Rs 3.30 crores, apprehended 918 persons, and recovered stolen goods (including unclaimed property) worth Rs. 7.48 crores. Of the 257 PSUs under them, the CISF has made 173 crime free. In a fire incident at MGCC Nagothane in 1990, the CISF lost 9 personnel but saved property worth Rs.1000 crores. At a fire incident at Hindustan Petro-Chemicals Limited (HPCL), Visakhapatnam, 9 personnel died but saved property worth Rs.75 crores. In the last five years, the CISF has attended to 12, 496 fire alarms.

Awards

Gallantry Awards

President's Police Medals for Gallantry	4
President's Police Medals for Distinguished Service	39
Others	432

Other Awards

Arjun Award	8

Modernization

CISF is providing modern training to its personnels, in view of the changing scenario of todays security situations. There are issues pertaining to operational preparedness, administrative efficiency and modernization plan. Workshops are organized for rationalisation of manpower, man management issues, improvement in communication and transit facilities, improved equipments and training, greater educational opportunities for personnel of the Force.

Objective of the training on use of modern equipments on fire management that can be improved and automated to the maximum possible extent. Developments in techniques and others can thus be fully exploited to safeguard our PSUs. CISF have been allocated Rs 200 crore for modernization of its Fire Wing, communication network, Stressing the need for upgradation of communication techniques to gain an upper hand over security at Airports.. The technological advancement adopted by the CISF will we be able to succeed.

Miscellaneous

CISF players had bagged over 200 medals over the years in various sports events. CISF had won the National Taekwondo Championships. Its weightlifting, boxing, judo, gymnastics and wrestling teams have done proud to organization while shooting team has lifted the trophy many times.

REFERENCES

A Reference Annual, New Delhi: Ministry of Information & Broadcasting 1996.

Annual Report 2002-2003, Ministry of Home Affairs, Government of India. Border Security Force.

B.Prasad ed.: Official History of the Indian Armed Forces in the Second World War-Expansion of Armed Forces and Defence Organization.

Datta, Civil Defence - Problems & Prospects.

Dte General, CISF, New Delhi.

Employment News.

Government of India: Civil Defence Handbook No. 1,New Delhi.

Government of India: India 1995 - A Reference Annual.

Government of India: Ministry of Defence Annual Report 1995-1996.

Baranwal J.: The Military Yearbook 1992-1993, New Delhi: Guide Publications.

Baranwal J.: The Military Yearbook 1993-1994, New Delhi: Guide Publications.

Malhotra V. P.: Encyclopaedia of Indian Army, Anmol, New Delhi 2006.

P. Singh, Civil Defence in the Nuclear Age.

Prasad, Expansion of Armed Forces and Defence Organization.

Datta R.: Civil Defence - Problems & Prospects, New Delhi: Sehgal Publishers 1991.

Prasad R.: India's Civil Defence in the Nuclear Age.

Baranwal S. P.: Military Yearbook 1974, New Delhi: Guide Publications 1974.

The Hindu, Nov. 11, 2004.

The Tribune, Jan. 28, 2001.

Xinhua News Agency, Oct. 02, 2006.

7

Central Reserve Police Force

"CRPF Sada Ajay, Bhrat Mata Ki Jai"

Introduction

The Central Reserve Police Force (CRPF) is a paramilitary security Force functioning under the Ministry of Home Affairs, Government of India. The CRPF's primary role lies in assisting the State/Union Territories in police operations to maintain law and order and contain insurgency. It came into existence as the Crown Representative's Police on July 27, 1939. After Indian Independence, it became the Central Reserve Police Force on enactment of the CRPF Act on December 28, 1949.

The Force from the point of view of its functions and activities has not only remained a Police Force for the mere purpose of helping the states in their anti dacoity operations and in maintaining internal law and order, but today its duties extend, much beyond its original scope, to fight terrorism and insurgency. CRPF was originally created as CRP(Crown Representative Police) on 27 July, 1939, with two Battalions. Its primary duty at that time was to protect the British residents in sensitive states. In 1949, Sardar Patel had it renamed as CRPF under the CRPF Act.

It has completed 67 years of glorious history. The Force has grown into a big organization with 191 Battalions (173 executive Battalions including two Mahila Battalions, ten RAF Battalions, five Signal Battalions and one Special Duty Group) 35 Group Centres including a Signal GC, ten training Institutions, three Base Hospitals and one 100 bed composite Hospital with a backup of well knit administrative set up covering the entire geography of the country.

Besides Law and Order and counter insurgency duties, the role of CRPF in the General Elections, held repeatedly during the past few years, has been very significant and vital. This is especially true for the trouble torn states of J&K, Bihar and in the North-East. During the Parliamentary elections of September 1999, the CRPF played a major role in the security arrangements. This is the largest Paramilitary Force in the world with 200 battalions besides various establishments.Of late, CRPF contingents are also being deployed in UN missions.

Central Reserve Police Force is a versatile Force of all India character. The Force is primarily used to aid and assist the States and thus contemporary internal security scenario of the country has a direct bearing on its operational commitments and responsibilities.

Depending upon the internal security situations cropping up in different parts of the country, the Force is rushed at short notice by quickest available means to tackle the situation. The Force has the distinction of undertaking such frequent and cross country operational moves at short notice and thus plays a vital role towards maintenance of security and integrity of the country.

History

Need: Its primary duty at the time of its conception was to protect the British residents in sensitive states. In 1949, Sardar Patel had it renamed as CRPF under the CRPF Act. After independence, to control law situations in civil areas, need for such a force was felt and CRPF accomplished this act very well.

Origin: CRPF was originally created as CRP(Crown Representative Police) on 27th July, 1939, with 2 Battalions. Its primary duty at that time was to protect the British residents in sensitive states. In 1949, Sardar Patel had it renamed as CRPF under the CRPF Act. The Sixties saw major expansion of CRPF in which many State Reserve Police Battalions were merged with CRPF. Today, the force has 200 Battalions. CRPF has been active against foreign invasion and domestic insurgency. On 21 October 1959, Dy.S.P. Karam Singh and his 20 soldiers were attacked by the Chinese Army, at Hot Springs in Ladakh. 10 were killed and the rest were taken prisoners. 21st October is now remembered across the country as Police Commemoration Day. In the 1965 India-Pakistan war, two companies (approx. 150 men) of the 2nd Battalion of CRPF defeated an Infantry brigade (approx. 1600 men) of Pakistan Army at Kanjar Kot in Gujarat.

The CRPF guarded the India-Pakistan border until 1965, at which point the Border Security Force was created for that purpose. On 13th December, 2001, the CRPF troopers killed all five terrorists who had entered the premises of the Indian Parliament at New Delhi. In 2005, the CRPF troops killed all terrorists who had stormed the Ram Temple at Ayodhya.

In recent years, the Central Government has decided to follow up on recommendations of the Cabinet to use each security agency for its mandated purpose. Therefore, the counterinsurgency operations in India has been entrusted to the CRPF. The CRPF is currently charged with securing the Kashmir valley. Recently CRPF have completely relieved the Border Security Force in the Kashmir Valley of its Internal Security duties.

Key Dates in History

27 July 1939	Created as Crown Representative Police
28 Dec. 1949	Renamed as Central Reserve Police Force
21 Oct. 1959	Hot Springs incident, now celebrated as Police Commemoration Day
8-9 Apr. 1961	The Battle of Sardar Post
13 Dec. 2001	CRPF Personnel killed terrorists who had entered the premises of the Indian Parliament
5 July 2005	CRPF Personnel killed terrorists who had entered the premises of Ram Temple, Ayodhya

Present Scenario

Personnel Strength: At present there are around 300, 000 CRPF personnel and 200 CRPF battalions commanded by an officer designated as Commandant and consists of seven CRPF companies. The Companies are in charge of Assistant Commandants. S. I. S. Ahmed is the present Director General of CRPF.

The headquarters of Central Reserve Police Force is located in New Delhi. It is headed by Director General, who is assisted by Addl. Director General (Hqr), Three Inspectors General of Police, a Financial Adviser and Director (Medical).

Various branches in the force are as under:

- Personnel and Administration: The personnel and Administration branches are functioning under officers of the rank of DIG known as DIG (Pers) and DIG (Adm) respectively, under the overall supervision of IG (Pers & Hqr). The DIG(Pers) has one Addl. DIG (Pers) and two Commandants to assist him. Similarly the DIG (Adm) has one Addl. DIG (Adm) and two civilian officers known as Asstt. Director (Adm/Accts) and Asstt. Director (Legal) to assist him in his day to day functioning.
- Operations and Training: The operations and Training Branches are functioning under officers of the rank of DI known as DIG (Ops) and DIG (Trg) respectively, under the overall supervision of IG(Ops & Trg). The DIG (Ops) has one Addl. DIG (Ops) to assist him. Similarly, DIG (Trg) has one Addl. DIG (Trg) and one Comdt (Sports) to assist him in his day to day functioning.
- Provisioning and Works: The Provisioning and Works Branches are functioning under the overall supervision of IG (Prov & Works). He is assisted by one Addl. DIG (Prov), Commandant (MT), Commandant (Works) and one Assistant Director (Prov/Accts).
- Communication: The Communication Branch is functioning under a DIG known as DIG (Comn). The DIG (Comn) is assisted by two officers viz. Addl. DIGP (Comn) and Commandant (EDP).
- Medical: The Medical Branch is functioning under overall charge of an officer equivalent to the rank of IG known as Director (Medical)
- PAO and Finance: The Pay & Accounts and Finance Branch are functioning under civilian officers known as Dy. Director (Accts) and Dy. Financial Adviser. The Dy. Director (Accts) is assisted by two officers viz. Asstt. Director (Accts) and Asstt. Director (Accts/Pension). Similarly, the Dy. Financial Adviser

has one Jt. Asstt. Director(Audit/Budget) and six Jt. Asstt. Director (Audit) to assist him in his day to day functioning.

- Field Formation: CRPF have ten Administration and four Operations sectors. Each Administration sector is headed by an officer of the rank of IGP. Each Adm Sector has two to three ranges, each range headed by a DIGP. Each range has one Group Centre headed by an Addl. DIGP and 4 battalions, each headed by an officer of the rank of Commandant.

Bases: There are ten sectors namely; North-West, Central, East, North, West, North-East, South, Bihar sector, RAF sector and one Special sector.

Group Centres of Central Reserve Police Force which are located in different parts of the Country are responsible to maintain service records of the personnel of Units those are attached to them. Group Centres are also responsible for payment of all type of dues to the personnel of Units attached with it. Regular monthly pay bills are centrally prepared by EDP Cell at Force Hqrs New Delhi and are sent to all field units along with drafts/cheques so that the payment of monthly pay and allowances to the men /women is made by the last working day of the same month. For payment of bills a centralised Pay and Accounts office is functioning at Force Hqrs. at New Delhi which is responsible for clearing payment of all types of claim of the personnel.

Organizational Structure

Organizational setup of CRPF from top to bottom is:

- Director General
- Additional Director General
- Inspector General
- Deputy Inspector General
- Additional Deputy Inspector General
- Commandant
- Deputy Commandant
- Assistant Commandant
- Subedar Major
- Inspector
- Sub-Inspector
- Asstt Sub Inspector

- Head Constable
- Constable
- Naik
- Lance Naik
- Buglars
- Follower

Notable Chiefs of CRPF

- J. K. Dutt
- V. K. Joshi
- S. C. Chaube
- Dr. Trinath Mishra
- J. K. Sinha
- S. I. S. Ahmed

Rapid Action Force

The increasing communal tensions and riots during the early nineties had been putting a serious strain on the secular structure of Indian Society. Consequently the Government took a well considered decision to set up a special anti-riot force which could reach the place of occurrence with the quickest possible speed and deal with communal riot or riot-like situation in an absolutely objective and non-partisan manner. The RAF was raised by converting ten existing CRPF battalions. Young CRPF personnel with quick reflexes, maturity and un-biased views were selected and posted to these battalions. Five battalions became functional during October 1992 while the remaining five became operational in April 1994. The area of responsibility of each RAF battalion is approximately 400 Kms. The special features of the RAF are that each team is independently operational and mobile.

They have a distinctive uniform and have to act in zero response time. Each Company has a Mahila component and additional Para-medical staff for first aid, rescue and relief. In between spells of duty, RAF undertake intensive familiarization exercises in communally sensitive areas to familiarise themselves with the area. To make bridges with the public, RAF also undertakes socially useful work such as children education, adult literacy, tree plantation, medical camps, hygiene education etc. and also adoption of villages for all round focused development. RAF was recently deployed in highly sensitive situations in Mumbai during Ganesh Utsava, in Karnataka after kidnapping of Kannada film star Raj Kumar and in Malpura (Rajasthan) during communal riot to maintain law and order.

Role of Rapid Action Force: To rush to a place of communal incidents with 'Zero response time' and deal with such situations with the dexterity and expertise, to be especially acquired by the Force. To render succour to the innocent persons ravaged by riots. To be deployed for short spells. Prolonged deployment at any particular place to be avoided under all circumstances. To be deployed to deal with other internal security duties only during certain emergent needs for short durations- and thereafter return to their base Hqrs.

Composition of RAF: The following points were kept in view in composition of RAF:

- Age group of constabulary to be between 20-27 years and junior leaders to be between 30-35 years to keep the perpetually young.
- Inclusion of personnel already having a few years of service with qualities of direction and drive to ensure that the personnel have the required maturity for the delicate duties required to be performed.
- A composite character with fair representation of minorities and weaker sections to be maintained by re-grouping and re-shuffling the personnel from other battalions of the CRPF.

RAF Activities: 100 Battalion RAF went through its first test in 1994 when it assisted the Civil Administration in Surat (Gujrat) during the out break of Plague which had assumed gignatic proportions. RAF proved its worth in dealing with such type of natural calamity by evacuating a large number of plague victims to hospitals and assisted civil and para medical staff in tackling the gruesome situation.

RAF Units have been in the forefront in organising Medical Relief Camps. The following relief camps were organized:

Organized medical relief camp in Allahabad during Kumbh Mela in 1995 and provided medical aid to a large number of pilgrims.

Organized medical camps at Natthupura, Karwalnagar, and Sabhapur and provided medicines to sick and needy people in 1995.

Organized medical relief and public awareness camp at Ghaziabad. which was attended by more than 400 villagers who were provided with free medicines in 1995.

When Dengue fever epidemic spread all over the capital, 3 medical camps were established by RAF Batallion at Mehrauli, Gokulpuri and Sultanpuri where more than 5, 000 patients were educated and provided with preventive medicines.

All RAF Units are organising routine Medical camps in their respective location on the occasions of Pulse Polio Eradication Programme.

Three Days Medical camps were organized at Nand Nagari (East Delhi) and at Rajiv Gandhi Smrithi Van (Sarai Kale Khan) South Delhi in November 1999 under the arrangements of RAF Sector to provide medical aid to poor people living in slum areas of the city. As many as 8, 577 patients were provided medical treatment free of cost.

On 11.6.95, a tourist party consisting of two men and woman were washed away in heavy currents of Narmada river at Neelkantheshwar Mahedev Mandir in Bharuch (Guj). Personnel of B/107 RAF, deployed in that area, jumped immediately into the river without caring for their own lives, and rescued all of them.

On 13.7.95, a powerful bomb exploded in a private bus in Saharanpur (UP). A contingent of D/108 RAF conducting familiarisation exercise close by, immediately rushed to the site and rescued the injured passengers from the burning bus and evacuated them to hospital, thus saving many precious lives.

On 20.8.95, a major train accident took place between the Purshottam and Kalindi Express near Firozabad railway station. Two Companys of 101 Batallion RAF which were deployed in Faizabad, immediately rushed to the accident site to extricate the casualties and evacuated the injured passengers to hospital.

On 3.9.95, a three storied Hotel collapsed in heavy rain in Meerut. Personnel of D/108 RAF rushed to the site and assisted local authorities in extricating three severely wounded persons. Five dead bodies were also traced and pulled out from the debris.

Personnel of 101 Batallion RAF rescued victims trapped in a wall collapse in Ayodhya (U. P) on 26 March 1996, and evacuated them to hospital.

On 11 June 1998, the RAF contingent gave valuable assistance to the people and Government of Gujrat, in relief and rescue work around Kandla Port in West Gujrat which was struck by a devastating cyclone. One Company of 100 Batallion RAF was rushed to the area, carried out rescue and relief work up to 20th June 1998, earning a good name for the Force.

A Company of 106 Batallion RAF carried out rescue and relief operations for 45 days in Gangtok (Sikkim) which had been severely hit by devastating land slides. The Company rescued a number of people and salvaged large amounts of cash, valuables etc.

In 1998 the RAF organized two Medical Camps in Sultanpuri and Gokulpuri areas of Delhi in its effort to assist Civil Administration to contain the spread of Dropsy, Dengue and other contagious diseases. More than 5, 000 patients turned up for medical check up and blood testing. They were also provided with preventive medicines and educated on the awareness of various diseases.

On 1/4/99, a sudden fire broke out in Sanjay Market, Jamshedpur. Personnel of D/Company 106 Batallion RAF rushed to the spot and despite injuries, gave valuable assistance in relief and rescue work.

Four Companys of 99 Batallion and 2 Companys of 106 Batallion RAF actively assisted the Civil Administration in Orissa in the relief and rescue operation after the devastating cyclone hit the State in October 1999. The personnel worked tirelessly to rescue marooned and affected personnel and provided them succour. The relief provided included: Distributed 104 truck loads of rescue and relief materials in 105 Gram Panchayats feeding approximately 1, 25, 000 families. Organized medical camps in different areas providing medical aid to about 9, 031 patients.

Besides the above, CRPF units deployed in J&K and NES have carried out Civic Action Programmes in far-flung and interiors of such areas. Free medicines, books, study materials, sports items were distributed, apart from construction of temporary/semi permanent buildings for schools, bathrooms/toilets etc. by CRPF Units, which has been much appreciated by the local administration and local people. By conducting Civic Action Programmes, CRPF have taken a step forward for consolidation of peace gained the confidence of the local populace.

Mahila Battalion

With increasing participation of women in politics, agitation and crime, policemen have been feeling handicapped in handling women agitations especially because even a small, real or alleged misdemeanour on their part in dealing with any matter related to women has the potential of turning into a serious law & order problem. To cope with such eventualities the first Mahila battalion in CRPF, the 88(M) battalion was created in 1986 with Headquarters in Delhi. The successful experiment of the 88 (Mahila) battalion and the ever increasing requirement of a Mahila component in dealing with emerging law and order situation necessitated the raising of the second Mahila battalion the 135(M) battalion with Headquarters at Gandhinagar (Gujrat) in 1995.

Green Force: Another specialised outfit of the CRPF is the Green Force. The force has been able to effectively check environmental degradation and sustain the regeneration of local flora and fauna. Every year Green Force personnel plant lakhs (hundreds of thousands) of trees in various parts of the country.

Duties and Functions

Motto: CRPF motto is ***"CRPF Sada Ajay, Bhrat Mata Ki Jai"*** meaning **"CRPF is always victorious, long live Mother India"**.

Maxim: Place country above self.

Uphold constitution and rule of Law.

Obey all lawful commands.

Be disciplined, courageous and alert.

Be mutually supportive, compassionate and considerate

Respect Human Rights

Perform duties promptly, impartially and courageously.

Acquire and upgrade professional skills for your tasks.

Rise above caste, creed and religion.

Have pride in the force and respect the motto "Service and Loyalty"

Description of Duties: The Central Reserve Police Force is an armed Force of the Union of India, with the basic role of striking reserve to assist the State/Union Territories in Police operations to maintain law and order and contain insurgency. Its role is that of a catalyst in maintaining law & order, and returns to barracks once this objective is achieved.

The force is also being used for various police duties in various States. It is All India in character, both in deployment and in its composition. Due to its unique capability to quickly adapt to various situational requirements, and also, to work in perfect harmony with the State Police, CRPF has, over the years, acquired the distinction of being perhaps the most acceptable Force, by the people and the State administrations.

Besides Law and Order and counter insurgency duties, the role of CRPF in the General Elections, held repeatedly during the past few years, has been very significant and vital. This is especially true for the trouble torn States of J&K, Bihar and States of North-East.

During the Parliamentary elections of Septtember 1999, the CRPF played a major role in the security arrangements. One of the vital roles of the CRPF, which is not very evident, is guarding vital Central Govt. installations such as airport, power houses, bridges, doordarshan kendras, all India radio stations, residence of governors and chief ministers, nationalized banks and other government establishments in insurgency affected states. The CRPF is ensuring the safety of the democratic institutions, and preventing the take over of civil society by the militants, in these highly disturbed areas.

This contribution of the CRPF, though not very visible, is nonetheless very vital. 7.5% of the Force is deployed for the security of VIPs mostly in North-Eastern States, J&K, Bihar and Andhra Pradesh which include Governors, Chief Ministers, Ministers, MPs and MLAs of J&K, Assam, Arunachal Pradesh, Manipur and Nagaland, Tripura and Mizoram. CRPF is also providing security at the residence/office of Prime Minister of India, various Union Ministers and MPs and other dignitaries. 17.5% of the Force is deputed for guarding the important installations of Central and State Govts mostly in insurgency affected areas which includes Secretariats, Doordarshan Kendras, Telephone exchanges, Banks, Hydroelectric projects, Jails etc.

CRPF is also deployed for the security of Parliament House. Ten Companies of CRPF are deployed for the security of three sensitive shrines i.e. Krishna Janma Bhoomi, Shahi Idgah Masjid complex (Mathura), Ram Janma Bhoomi- Barbi Masjid complex (Ayodhya) and Kashi Vishwanath Temple- Gyanvapi Mosque (Varanasi). Four Companies of the Force are deputed for the security of Mata Vaishno Devi Shrine, Katra, Jammu (J&K). CRPF is the only Paramilitary Force in the Country which has two Ladies (Mahila) Battalions. After its training in March 1987, 88(M) Battalion won laurels for its work assisting the Meerut riots and later with the IPKF in Srilanka.

Personnel of second Mahila battalion (135 Batallion) performed creditably during the Lok Sabha elections 1996 in many states. At present mahila personnel are deployed in active duty in Jammu & Kashmir, Ayodhya, Manipur, Assam and other parts of the country where they are doing commendable job. In addition each RAF battalion has a Mahila (Ladies) component consisting of 96 personnel.

UN Peace Keeping Missions: The role of the CRPF and its services rendered have extended beyond the nation's borders as well. The services rendered by the CRPF in Sri Lanka as part of IPKF, as part of the UN Peace Keeping Force in Namibia, Somalia, Haiti, Maldives and also in Bosnia speaks volumes about the ability, agility, versatility and dependability of the Force to adapt to any conflict-situation round the globe. Presently a contingent of 240 personnel of RAF are deployed in KOSOVO as UN Mission in Kosovo is to provide protection and security to the UN officials/UN civil police/ Crowd control etc. RAF Companys will also assist local Police to control /mob during violent demonstration, humanitarian and to assist the activities of the ICTY.

Acts, Rules & Regulations

The CRPF is governed by the CRPF Act 1949. The Act consists 19 sections in all.

- Section 1: Title
- Section 2: Definitions
- Section 3: Constitution of the Force
- Section 4: Appointment and Powers of Superior Officers
- Section 5: Enrolment
- Section 6: Resignation and withdrawal from the Force
- Section 7: General Duties of member of the force.
- Section 8: Superintendence, Control and Administration of the Force
- Section 9: More heinous offences.
- Section 10: Less heinous offences
- Section 11: Minor punishments.
- Section 12: Place of imprisonment and liability to dismissal on imprisonment
- Section 13: Deduction from pay and allowance
- Section 14: Collective fine

- Section 15: Arrest
- Section 16: Powers and duties conferrable and imposable on member of the force.
- Section 17: Protection for acts of members of the Force
- Section 18: Power to make rules.
- Section 19: Validation of Acts done before commencement Act.

The Central Reserve Police Force Rules/Regulations/Scheme, 1955: The CRPF follows The Central Reserve Police Force Rules/ Regulations/Scheme, 1955. It has 111 Sections in all.

- Section 1: Title
- Section 2: Definitions
- Section 3: Interpretation
- Section 4: Powers of the Central Government and Certain Officers of the Force
- Section 5: Battalion other than Signal Battalion
- Section 6: Members of the Force
- Section 7: Appointments other than that of Superior Officers
- Section 8: Seniority
- Section 9: Attestation of oath or affirmation
- Section 10: Recruitment
- Section 11: Enlistment Standards
- Section 12: Health Certificate
- Section 13: Recruiting Roll
- Section 14: Verification
- Section 15: Plural Marriages
- Section 16: Period of Service
- Section 17: Discharge
- Section 18: Discharge Certificate
- Section 19: Travelling allowance to men discharged at their own request
- Section 20: Travelling Allowance admissible to men discharged otherwise than at their own request

- Section 21: Travelling allowance admissible to members of his family in the event of member of the Force being declared medically unfit
- Section 22: Legal Privileges and Powers of member of the Force
- Section 23: Organization
- Section 24: Service Companies
- Section 25: Primary Duties of the Force
- Section 26: Standard of Training
- Section 27: Procedure for the Award of Punishments
- Section 28: Appeal
- Section 29: Revision
- Section 30: Petitions
- Section 31: Desertion and Absence without leave
- Section 32: Orderly Room
- Section 33: Entry of Punishment in Service Roll
- Section 34: Report on Judicial Proceedings
- Section 35: Loss or Damage to Arms, Ammunition and Property
- Section 36: Judicial Trials
- Section 37: Character and Service Roll
- Section 38: Clerical Staff
- Section 39: System of Accounts
- Section 40: Scale of pay and Allowances
- Section 41: Free Accommodation
- Section 42: Pension
- Section 43: Superannuation
- Section 44: Special Pay
- Section 45: Officiating Pay
- Section 46: Pay and allowances on Detachments and under Training
- Section 47: Free transport on enlistment
- Section 48: Recruit's Subsistence Allowance

- Section 49: Discharge of Head Constable, Naiks and Constables on pension or superannuation
- Section 50: Death of Member of Force
- Section 51: Former military service and military pensions
- Section 52: Wound, injury or family pension or gratuities
- Section 53: Financial powers
- Section 53: Rewards
- Section 54: Force deductions
- Section 55: Merit
- Section 56: Seniority
- Section 57: Determination of Seniority of Members of the Force other than the Gazetted Officers
- Section 58: Probationary Period
- Section 59: Officiating Promotions
- Section 60: The following examinations and courses shall be held to enable Under Officers and Constables to qualify for promotion
- Section 61: Maintenance of Lists of Approved Candidates
- Section 62: Preparation of Lists of Approved Candidates
- Section 63: Selection Board
- Section 64: Educational Qualification for Promotion to the Rank of Sub-Inspector
- Section 65: Confidential Reports
- Section 66: Additions to and Removals from Approved Lists
- Section 67: Head Constables
- Section 68: Naiks
- Section 69: Lance Naiks
- Section 70: Special Promotion to Naik and Head Constable
- Section 71: Special Qualification for Promotion
- Section 72: Withholding of Increment
- Section 73: Subedars (Inspectors) and Sub Inspectors
- Section 74: Head Constables, Naiks and Head Constables
- Section 75: How to be made

- Section 76: Supersession
- Section 77: Subedar (Inspector) Major
- Section 78: Sub-Inspector Adjutant
- Section 79: Quarter Master Sub-Inspector
- Section 80: Head Constables
- Section 81: Nominal Roll of the Central Reserve Police Force-Particulars
- Section 82: Order of Seniority
- Section 83: Maintenance of Promotion and Reversion Roll
- Section 84: Incorporation of Entries in the Promotion and Reversion Rolls
- Section 85: Army Officers
- Section 86: Other Superior Officers
- Section 87: Other Police Officers on Deputation from other Services
- Section 88: Other Superior Officers and Members of the Force
- Section 89: Leave Sanctioning Authorities
- Section 90: Recall from leave
- Section 91: Free Passage to Families
- Section 92: Free Leave Pass Concessions
- Section 93: Dress Regulations
- Section 94: Superior Officers
- Section 95: Scale of Uniform
- Section 96: Initial issue and replacement of Uniform
- Section 97: Periodical Inspections
- Section 98: Uniform Stock Registers
- Section 99: Authorised Scales
- Section 100: Accoutrements
- Section 101: Accoutrements of Subordinate Officers
- Section 102: Other conditions of Service
- Section 103: Cadre Regulations
- Section 104: Classification

- Section 105: Appointment and Promotion of Superior Officers
- Section 106: Training
- Section 107: Tenure
- Section 108: Probation and Confirmation
- Section 109: Transfers
- Section 110: Discipline and Appeal
- Section 111: Pensions and Pensionary Benefits

Weapons and Equipments

CRPF uses basic Infantry weapons such as Type 56 Assault rifles, Type 81 Assault rifles, AKM rifles, INSAS 5. 56 MM Assault rifle, G3A3 Battle rifle, MP5 Submachine-gun ; Uzi submachinegun, M9 pistol ; RPG 7 Rocket-propelled grenade launchers ; and M67 hand-grenades. CRPF also uses landmine detectors ; Light Machine-Guns and Heavy-Machine-Guns.

Recruitment

Officers: The recruitment of officers into the CRPF is carried out whenever needed. The applications for the post are advertised through National Dailies, Employment Exchange and Website. Selection is through written examination, interview and physical test. These officers are also given a short prior sending them for basic training. Graduates from any stream can apply if they fall in the 19 to 25 years age group. They begin their careers, on selection, as Assistant Commandants/ Company Commanders, Quartermasters and Deputy Superintendents. The prescribed qualification is a 1st Class/2nd Class Bachelor's degree with 50% marks. Special relaxation in marks is made for graduates who have the 'B' or 'C' certificates of N.C.C, outstanding sports or atheletics certificates is an added qualification. For officer cadres preference is given to 'C' certificate holders. Selection is made through a written examination, physical efficiency test (PET) and an Interview.

Other Ranks: Recruitment for OR is done annually. Entry is through a Mental Ability Test, entrance test and an interview. Qualified candidates undergo a medical examination and those who pass are selected on the basis of merit.

Training: CRPF has its training academies for officers and men where post selection training as well as inservice training is imparted Officers are trained at Neemuch in Madhya Pradesh while the constabulary is trained at Srinagar in the north, Thiruvananthapuram and

Avadi in the South, Neemuch in Central India. Avadi is also a training centre for sub-inspectors.

Training Institutes: The Internal Security Academy was established under the aegis of Ministry of Home Affairs, Government of India at Mount Abu (a hill station at an altitude of approximately 1200 mtrs in the Aravali ranges in Rajasthan).

The Academy has been identified as Centre of Excellence in the matters of Internal Security & related issues. It also offers facilities for research studies on Internal Security and related subjects and will expand its source base through tie-ups with similar institutions in and outside the country. The Academy conducts the following Internal Security Courses:

1. Junior Level Internal Security Course for Dy.S.P/ SDMs of States / CPOs.)
2. Senior Level Internal Security Course for S.P. / D.M. / Commandants of States / CPOs.
3. Internal Security Strategy Management Course for Deputy Inspectors General of Police of States / CPOs.
4. Vertical Interaction Course on Internal Security for IPS officers.

The Central Training College-I, CRPF Neemuch, a premier Police training Institution in the country, was established on the 1st December'1960. It is oldest training Institution of Central Reserve Police Force. The Institution has been conducting regular courses for CRPF personnel as also for other State and Central Police Organizations and departments like Narcotics, Parliament Security, I.B and Indian Air Lines.

The Central Training College-II has finally shifted to Coimbatore (Tamilnadu) from Avadi (Chennai) on 1st May'1 2000 due to increased training responsibilities and lack of adequate training area and other administrative constrains.

The Central Training College-III was established in May'1994 with the specific requirement of the Force in training Directly Appointed Subordinate Officers of Ministerial Cadre, Group 'C' & 'D' Hospital staff and organising promotional cadres for personnel at the level of Under Officers and Subordinate Officers besides some inservice and specialist courses of training. Its sprawling campus of 400 acres has completed 1st phase of construction.

The Central Training College-III is located at Mudkhed at a distance of 40 Kms from Nanded in Maharastra. It is linked by rail and road. The distance is about 850 Kms from Delhi.

Recruits Training Centre-I

Neemuch (M.P.), established during Sept 1968

Recruits Training Centre-II

Avadi, Chennai (Tamilnadu). Established during Feb 1969.

Recruit Training Centre-III

Pallipuram, Trivandrum (Kerala). Established during October 1986.

Recruit Training Centre-IV

Humhuma, Srinagar, J&K. Established during March 1990.

Famous Operations

Operation at Hot Spring: In the early days one of the most hazardous of the tasks entrusted to CRPF were on the Indo-Tibetan border, abreast of Aksaichin. From 1953 onwards, Leh (Ladakh) and its frontier check posts had been the sacred trust of one company of CRPF.

The wilderness of Aksai area, the inhospitable terrain, the loneliness of the barren mountains, the icy cold winds did not deter the CRPF men from policing the border day and night in defence of their motherland. It was on one such day, conscious of the heightened Chinese movement, and the danger that lurked around, a small patrol party of CRPF moved out along the border with Tibet, unmindful of the fact that they were scripting history for themselves.

It was on 21 October 1959, when a small but dedicated group of soldiers came under heavy fire from automatic weapons of Chinese troops at a place called "Hot Springs". Each one of them fought bravely with only one thought in their minds that they must at all costs hold back the aggressor in defence of their motherland.

The CRPF patrol gave a very bold account of itself even though vastly outnumbered by a trained army having much superior weaponry. Ten jawans laid down their lives for a cause dearest to their hearts. The incident made "Hot Springs" a holy place to CRPF and the day a martyrs day for entire Police Force of the Country.

The Battle of Sardar Post: During early 1965, four companies of 2 Battalion CRPF were ordered to set up border posts. In the darkness of intervening night of 8 & 9 April, 3500 men of 51st Infantry Brigade of Pakistan, comprising of 18 Punjab Battalion, 8 Frontier Rifles and 6 Baluch Battalion stealthily launched operation "Desert Hawk" against border posts.

While the planners of operation "Desert Hawk" had taken great care to plan and left nothing to chance, they failed to calculate the grit and determination of a small group of CRPF. CRPF men guarding the Sardar Post were not asleep despite the Pakistani strategy to lull them by proposal of peace talks.

Head Constable Ranjit Singh was on duty manning a machine gun at that time at Sardar post. He sensed some movement about 50 to 100 yards to his North, perceiving it to be enemy movement, he challenged the intruders and the response was a hail of bullets, which was a signal for Pakistani forces to open up with mortars and shells of 25 pounders. A simultaneous attack of a brigade strength began on Sardar arid TAK post manned by 4 Companys of 2 Batallion, CRPF.

The personnel in the posts took up positions and to conserve the available supply of ammunition till the last moment, they held their fire with baited breath and allowed the enemy to close in. The death like silence made the Pakistanis to think that all the personnel manning the post have been killed or wounded in the shelltng. It was to the credit of Shiv Ram of Sardar Post to detect the enemy observation post 600 yards away directing the deadly artillery and mortar fire. Once detected, Subedar Balbir Singh was quick enough to direct own mortar fire to destroy this enemy.

The attacking columns by now fanned out and the post was surrounded, from close quarters. There was no sign of life in the post. At this stage twenty of the attacking column stepped closer when all the three machine guns of the post came to life and with a sharp hail of murderous fire flattened the enemy, all of them lay dead in an instant. Another wave of the enemy attack from the rear met the fate of their predecessors who fell in the front. In this wave 14 lay dead and 4 were captured alive.

The enemy, however, achieved a fleeting success when the machine gun at the North-East corner of the post jammed, but the CRPF men rallied swiftly and mounted a counter attack and threw back the enemy. Although the enemy retreated, they were successful in taking 19 CRPF men captive including the post commander Maj.

Sardar Karnail Singh. The exchange of fire lasted one hour during which the enemy made three attempts to over run the post but was repulsed with heavy casualties. It was to the valour of Head Constable Bhawana Ram deployed on the eastern parameter of Sardar Post who even when the MMG in his locality was silenced, collected all the grenades in his post and kept throwing one after the other at the enemy attempting to close in.

His gallant act was to a great extent instrumental in demoralising the intruders and forcing them to retreat from the post. The retaliation by the CRPF men was such a profound shock to the enemy that despite their numerical and armament superiority, they dared not venture another attack.

Attack on Indian Parliament: The Jawans of the CRPF tested their mettle when a suicidal attack was done on Parliament House by militants on December 13, 2001. In exchange of fire between the CRPF and militants that continued for about 30 minutes, all the five militants were eliminated.

In the skirmish one Mahila Constable, while showing exemplary courage and presence of mind sacrificed her life at the call of duty. The both houses of Parliament including the Prime Minister and Home Minister have applauded the role of CRPF Jawans in the operation. In recognition of the valour displayed in this encounter, Late Mahila Constable has been awarded "Ashoka Chakra" and 4 Jawans have been awarded "Shaurya Chakra" on 26 January. 2002.

UN Peacekeeping Missions: The role of the CRPF and its services rendered have extended beyond the nation's borders as well. The services rendered by the CRPF in Sri Lanka as part of IPKF, as part of the UN Peace Keeping Force in Namibia, Somalia, Haiti, Maldives and also in Bosnia speaks volumes about the ability, agility, versatility and dependability of the Force to adapt to any conflict-situation round the globe.

Presently a contingent of 240 personnel of RAF are deployed in KOSOVO as UN Mission in Kosovo is to provide protection and security to the UN officials/UN civil police/ Crowd control etc. RAF Companys will also assist local Police to control /mob during violent demonstration, humanitarian and to assist the activities of the ICTY.

Awards

Gallantry Awards

George Cross	01
Kings Police Medal for Gallantry	03
Ashok Chakra	01
Veer Chakr	01
Shurya Chakra	04
Vishit Seva Medal	04
Sena Medal	05

Other Awards

Yudh Seva Medal	01
Jeevan Raksha Padak	01
Padam Shree	01
PPFSMG	49
President Police Medal for Gallantry	103
Police Medal for Gallantry	542
IPMG	05
PM's Life Saving Medal	80
Jeevan Raksha Padak	01
Bar to PPFSMG	01
Bar to PMG	14
Meritorious Service Medal	1186
Distinguished Service Medal	119

Modernization

CISF has started a vigorous modernization drive to give it more fire power. The modernization plans of this Paramilitary Force of the nation include procuring state-of-the-art weapons and latest gadgets to boost operational efficiency of the troops.

Miscellaneous

Mountaineering Expeditions: After successfully conducting a chain of adventure. sports including an expedition to Mount Jogin - I (6456 Mtrs.) and Jogin-3 (6116 Mtrs.), CRPF launched an expedition to Mount. Sri Kailas (6932 Mtrs) in Garhwal Himalayas to mark the culmination of Diamond Jubilee celebrations of the Force.

The expedition which comprised of sixteen members included five Gazetted Officers and eleven other ranks. In this expedition for the first time four women including two Gazetted Officers participated. They were ably supported by one Medical Officer, one Nursing Assistant, two Radio Operators and one Cook. Mount Sri Kailash (22737 ft) situated in Himalayan range of Garhwal region is the second highest Peak which offers tremendous excitement to any Mountaineer.

Though second highest in the region, it offers tremendous challenge to the Mountaineers due to its conical shape, long and difficult approach march. Large glacier track with wide crevices and generally prevailing bad weather conditions over the Peak. The CRPF Mountaineers having been flagged off on 24 April 2000 commenced their approach march from Gangotri. The road head, and having established 7 camps enroute finally reached the Summit Camp at an altitude of 21200 feet on 18 May 2000.

The first attempt to scale the peak was made under the leadership of Sunand Kumar with seven other members including two Mahilas namely Sima Tolia and Sukhla Das. Their first attempt had to be called off mid way due to extremely bad weather conditions and wide crevices enroute which could not be bridged Undeterred, the team made second attempt on next day and at 0945 hours on 20 May 2000 they successfully planted the National tricolour and the CRPF Flag on top of Mount Sri Kailash. Motivated by the success of first group, the second party under Shri B. C. Sharma with Indrani Yadav and five other Mountaineers moved from camp-3 to Summit Camp on the same day and successfully summated Mount Sri Kailas on 21 May 2000 at 1250 hrs. Thus CRPF was able to put fifteen Mountaineers on top of Mount Shri Kailas.

Sports: Over the years CRPF has produced many outstanding sportsmen and athletes, who have brought great honour and appreciation both within the country and abroad. There have been outstanding sportsmen like S/Shirr G S Randhawa, R.S.Bal and Hari Chand, in athletics, Khazan Singh, Raja Ram Tokas and Radhakrishanan in swimming and lately Ms. Kunjarani Devi, Jeevan Jyoti Manitombi Devi and Neelam Laxmi in weight lifting Insp. Ragzen Angmo in Marathons.

REFERENCES

Annual Report 2003-2004, Ministry of Home Affairs, Government of India.

Ashok Krishna: Examples of Learning in Counter-Insurgency. IDSA 2000.

Central Reserve Police Force: Backgrounder, July 27, 2004.

Col. Ahrnam Singh. Doda: Insurgency in the Wilderness. Lancer, New Delhi 1999.

Counter-Insurgency Operations Forces Breathe Life Into Valley, Free Press Journal, 13 March, 2000.

CRPF Samachar, Vol. 16, No. 8, 31 Dec., 2003.

D.G. Mohapatra,"CRPF in its New Avatar: A Protector of Environment.

D.G. Mohapatra: CRPF: The Peacekeepers of Nation.

Detailed Demands for Grants (Vol.I) of Ministry of Home Affairs for 2004-2005.

Dte General, CRPF, New Delhi.

Employment News.

Hindustan Times, Dec. 27, 2003.

Indian Express. 27 March, 2000.

Major General Arjun Ray: Kashmir Diary, Manas, New Delhi 1996.

Manoj Joshi: The Lost Rebellion, Penguin India, New Delhi 1997.

The Hindu, Aug. 10, 1999.

The Hindu, Feb. 15, 2000.

The Hindu, Oct. 16, 2004.

The Tribune, Jan. 26, 2004.

Tribune, Dec. 07, 1999.

Tribune, Nov. 25, 1998.

8

Indo-Tibetan Border Police

"Shaurya-Dridhata-Karm Nishtha"

Introduction

The ITBP was founded on Oct. 21, 1962, after the Sino-Indian War as an integrated intelligence/signal/pioneer/engineering/medical and guerrilla unit and was initially placed under the Intelligence Bureau for operational control. In 1975 the force's primary task was to check illegal immigration and trans-border crimes. It has the responsibility of providing security, communication and medical assistance to the pilgrims visiting the Hindu holy sites Mount Kailash and Lake Mansarovar located in Tibet, besides being the Nodal Agency for Disaster Management in the Central and Western Himalayan region.

The ITBP was initially raised under the CRPF Act, however in 1992, the parliament enacted the ITBPF Act, and rules thereunder were framed in 1994. ITBP is a multi-dimensional force and is main functions are to keep vigil on northern borders, to detect and prevent border violation, promcte sense of security among the local populace. To check illegal immigration, trans-border smuggling and crimes. To provide security to sensitive installations, banks and protected persons. To restore and preserve order in any area in the event of disturbance. In border patrolling, the ITBP mans forward border posts at altitudes ranging from 9000 to 18000 feet. Most of the forward posts remain cut off by the surface route during winter months. The border posts are exposed to the fury and violence of nature like snow blizzards, avalanches, landslides, besides the hazards of high altitude and extreme cold where temperature normally remains below minus 40 degrees Celsius.

The force, besides guarding the border, is heavily engaged in fighting Pakistan-sponsored terrorism in the State of Jammu & Kashmir. The "Himveers", as the personnel are nicknamed, also provide security cover to installations and to VIPs in Delhi. Each year ITBP personnel are deployed to UN Peace Keeping Missions in Bosnia, Kosovo, Herzegovina, Angola & Western Sahara.

History

Need: After the Sino-Indian War of 1962 India found a hole in the security of its northern border. The situation at the border was so bad that all the tribal population living along the border remained cut off from the rest of the country for years. In this aftermath a force was required to keep special vigil on Indo-China border. Indian Government raised this force keeping this requirement in mind.

Origin: Indo-Tibetan Border Police was conceived on October 24, 1962. ITBP was initially raised under the CRPF Act, however in 1992, the parliament enacted the ITBP Act and rules there under were framed in 1994. The Indo Tibetan Border Police Force was conceived on October 24, 1962 for the security of the frontiers along the Indo-Tibetan Border covering 2115 kilometres from Karakoram Pass to Lipulekh Pass and Tri junction of India, Nepal and China. Initially, only four battalions were assigned with filling up the security vacuum that was prevalent at that time along the Indo-Tibet border.

Later in view of additional responsibilities and a task redefined in 1976, the Force was restructured in 1978. In its border vigil task, the ITBP keep vigilance on forward border posts at altitudes ranging from 9000 to 18000 feet. Most of the forward posts remain cut off by the surface route during winter months.

The border posts are exposed to the fury and violence of nature like snow blizzards, avalanches, landslides, besides the hazards of high altitude and extreme cold where temperature normally remains below minus 40 degrees Celsius. The force, besides guarding the border, is heavily engaged in fighting Pakistan-sponsored terrorism in the State of Jammu & Kashmir. The Himveers, as the personnel are nicknamed, also provide security cover to installations and to VIPs in Delhi.each year ITBP personnel are deployed to UN Peace Keeping Missions in Bosnia, Kosovo, Herzegovina, Angola & Western Sahara. From the ranks of ITBP come world class mountaineers who have scaled more than a hundred Himalayan peaks, including the Mount Everest, four times.

Its skiers have been national champions and have taken part in the Winter Olympics. Its river rafters have rafted through the turbulent white waters of the Brahmaputra, the Indus and the Ganga.

The Force became the first Central Paramilitary Force to grab up the Best Marching Contingent Trophy in the Republic Day parades in 1998, 1999 and 2000. In 1998, it sent the first ever police tableau of the country to participate in the Republic Day Parade. The ITBP is at the forefront of the movement for the preservation of Himalayan environment & ecology. ITBP has taken up the task of greening the Himalayan regions especially in Inner Himalayas. Being the only human presence in these forward areas, it has taken on itself the task of maintaining the delicate balance of flora and fauna. ITBP being deployed in mountains has developed expertise in mountain rescue & relief operations, which entail different specialized skills of very high standard. ITBP extends rescue & relief in case of natural calamity.

ITBP conducts a large number of medical civic action programmes in remote border and terrorist affected areas to provide free and expert medical, health and hygiene care to the civilian population in remote villages. The ITBP is the only police force in the country that possesses expertise in policing the mountains of the Himalayas. The annual pilgrimage to Mount Kailash and Holy Mansarovar Lake in Tibet (China) is conducted under the wings of ITBP

Key Dates in History

24 Oct. 1962	Force came into existence
May 1981	Start of Security of Kailash Mansarovar Yatra
1 Sep. 1992	The Indo-Tibetan Border Police Force Act, 1992 came into force
10 May 1996	ITBP team conquered Mt. Everest
2 Nov. !998	Encounter with Terrorists
Nov. 2005	United Nation Mission in Congo

Present Scenario

Personnel Strength: At present there are around 57, 715 ITBP personnel and 29 ITBP battalions. Vikram Srivastava is the present Director-General of Indo-Tibetan Border Police.

Bases: There are four zones; UA & HP Zone under which comes Ladakh Sector, Himachal Pradesh Sector and Kumaon Sector. NE Zone under which comes NE-I Sector and NE-II Sector. L&C Zone having L&C Sector and lastly Training Zone Each zone is headed by one Inspector General and each sector is headed by Deputy Inspector General. Besides these there are four special battalions namely; Telecom Battalion, Transport Battalion, Service and Supply Battalion and Spt Battalion. Each battalion is headed by an officer of the rank of Commandant.

Organizational Structure

- Director General
- Additional Director General
- Inspector General
- Deputy Inspector General
- Additional Deputy Inspector General
- Commandant Second in Command
- Deputy Commandant
- Assistant Commandant
- Subedar Major
- Inspector
- Sub-Inspector
- Asstt Sub Inspector
- Head Constable
- Constable
- Naik
- Lance Naik
- Enrolled Person

Chiefs of ITBP

- Sh. Balbir Singh, IG, (02-02-1963 to 02-06-1964)
- Sh. B. Chatterjee, IG, (02-06-1964 to 31-08-1974)

- Sh. R. N. Sheopory, IG, (03-09-1974 to 22-12-1980)
- Sh. K. Ramamurthy, IG, (22-12-1980 to 31-01-1981)
- Sh. Shivraj Bahadur, DG, (04-06-1981 to 31-12-1983)
- Sh. Shivraj Swarup, DG, (01-01-1984 to 19-03-1984)
- Sh. M. C. Misra, DG, (19-03-1984 to 28-03-1985)
- Sh. O. P. Bhutani, DG, (28-03-1985 to 28-02-1987)
- Sh. J. M. Qureshi, DG, (28-02-1987 to 02-03-1988)
- Sh. G. S. Mander, DG, (02-03-1988 to 08-07-1988)
- Sh. D. V. L. N. Ramakrishna Rao, DG, (28-07-1988 to 31-01-1992)
- Sh. R. K. Wadehra, DG, (31-01-1992 to 31-01-1993)
- Sh. D. K. Arya, DG, (03-02-1993 to 31-01-1994)
- Sh. S. C. Mehta, DG, (03-01-1994 to 16-04-1994)
- Dr. R. C. Jha, DG, (16-04-1994 to 31-01-1995)
- Sh. Joginder Singh, DG, (31-01-1995 to 10-04-1996)
- Sh. R. K. Sharma, DG, (10-04-1996 to 10-01-1997)
- Sh. B. B. Nandy, DG, (10-01-1997 to 03-04-1997)
- Sh. Nikhil Kumar, DG, (03-04-1997 to 03-12-1997)
- Pt. Gautam Kaul, DG, (01-06-1998 to 31-03-2001)
- Sh. S. C. Chaube, DG, (03-04-2001 to 31-12-2002)
- Sh. R. C. Agarwal, DG, (01-01-2003 to 30-06-2004)
- Sh. K. J. Singh, DG, (01-07-2004 to 30-04-2005)
- Sh. S. K. Kain, DG, (05-05-2005 to 31-10-2005)
- Sh. V. K. Joshi, DG, (20-01-2006 to 07-05-2008)
- Sh. Vikram Srivastava, DG, (07-05-2008 onwards)

Duties and Functions

Motto: ITBP motto is ***"Shaurya-Dridhata-Karm Nishtha"*** meaning **"Valour-Determination-Devotion to Duty"**.

Maxim: To keep vigil on northern borders, detection and prevention of border violation, and promotion of sense of security among the local populace.

To check illegal immigration, trans-border smuggling and crimes.

To give security to sensitive installations, banks and protected persons.

To restore and preserve order in any area in the event of disturbance.

Description of Duties: ITBP is a multi-facetedl force. Presently Battalions of ITBP posted on borders from Karakoram Pass in Ladakh to Diphu La in Arunachal Pradesh covering 3488 km of India China Border are manning border out posts at an altitude ranging from 9000' to 18500' in the Western, Middle & Eastern Sector of India China Border. ITBP is basically a mountain trained Force and most of the officers & men are professionally trained Mountaineers and Skiers. The force is under an expansion plan at the moment in order to provide relief to its troops from constant deployment in high altitude areas. The border posts manned by ITBP are exposed to high velocity storms, snow blizzards, avalanches, and landslides, besides the hazards of high altitude and extreme cold, where temperature dips up to minus 40 degree Celsius.

ITBP conducts Long Range and Short Range patrols to keep an effective vigil on inaccessible and unmanned areas on the border. To maintain optimum operational efficiency of troops, periodical tactical exercises are conducted independently as well as jointly with Army. The ITBP has recently taken on a disaster management role. Being the first responder for natural Disaster in Himalayas, ITBP was the first to establish 06 (Now 08) Regional Response Centres in HP, Uttaranchal and North-East and carried out numerous rescue and relief operations in various disaster situations, which took place in ITBP areas of responsibility as well as other parts of the country.

ITBP has already trained 1032 personnel in Disaster Management including 98 personnel in Radiological and Chemical/biological emergencies. ITBP has established a National Centre for Training in Search, Rescue & Disaster response at Bhanu, Haryana which is imparting training to personnel of ITBP and other paramilitary / State Police Forces. There is also a training centre for the Dogs at Basic Training centre situated at Bhanu. The centre is known as NICD. ITBP Commando units provide security to the Embassy and consulates of India in Afghanistan. Besides this two Companies of the ITBP are providing security in Afghanistan.

ITBP has also excelled in UN peace keeping operation. The Force personnel have been deployed for peacekeeping operations in Angola, Namibia, Cambodia, Bosnia & Herzegovina, Mozambique and Kosovo. Presently 01 Company of ITBP is deployed in United Nation Mission in Congo since November, 2005. A National Centre for UNCIVPOL training has been setup at ITBP Camp, Tigri, New Delhi for providing systematic training to Indian Police Officers for deployment in UN Mission. Sh S R Roy, Comdt, served in Western Sahara as police commissioner and remained instrumental in imparting pre induction training to Indian Police Officers. Sh Sanjeev Raina, ADIG has been one of the pioneer officer of ITBP, who remained with UN Missions both in Europe as well as in Africa and imparted training and helped the local police in achieving self relinace for maintaining law and order.

A number of other officers such as Sh M K Singh, Comdt, Sh R S Pathania, DIG, Sh Jaspal Singh, Comdt, Sh A J Rasool, Comdt etc has served various UN Missions with distinction. Indeed ITBP has achieved glorious standards in international policing also. ITBP is also providing security to the pilgrims during Annual Kailash Mansarovar Yatra from 1981. ITBP provides communication, security and medical cover to the yatries from Gunji to Lipulekh Pass and back to Gunji in co-ordination with MEA and Kumaon Mandal vikas Nigam. Indo Tibetan Border Police Force was conceived on 24th October, 1962 for the security of our frontiers along the Indo - Tibetan Border covering 2115 km from Karakoram Pass to Lipulekh Pass and Tri junction of India, Nepal and China.

Incredible though it may sound, only four battalions were sanctioned to begin with to fill up the security vacuum that was prevalent at that time on the Indo - Tibet border. Later in view of the additional responsibilities and the task redefined in 1976, the Force was restructured in 1978. Each year ITBP personnel are deployed to UN Peace Keeping Missions in Bosnia, Kosovo, Herzegovina, Angola & Western Sahara. Adventure and dare-devilry are the required professional skill for ITBP and therefore from its ranks come world class mountaineers who have scaled more than a hundred Himalayan peaks, including the Mount Everest, four times. Its skiers have been national champions, who have done India proud in the winter Olympics. Its river rafters have created international history in rafting through the turbulent white waters of the mighty Brahmaputra, the Indus and the Ganga. The Force has created a milestone by becoming the first Central Paramilitary Force to grab up the Best Marching Contingent Trophy in the Republic Day parades in 1998, 1999 and 2000.

Keeping Vigilance on Northern Borders: It restore and preserve order in any area in the event of disturbance. In border vigil task ITBP mans forward border posts at altitudes ranging from 9000 feet to 18000 feet. Most of the forward posts remain cut off by the surface route during winter months. The border posts are exposed to the fury and violence of nature like snow blizzards, avalanches, landslides, besides the hazards of high altitude and extreme cold where temperature normally remains below minus 40 degrees Celsius. The force besides guarding the border, is heavily engaged in fighting Pakistan sponsored terrorism in the State of Jammu & Kashmir, where it has displayed exemplary nerve and gallantry. The Himveers also provide security cover to installations and to VIPs in Delhi.

Prevention of Border Violation: The main theme in performance of the multifarious duties assigned to ITBP have always been to maintain strict vigilance by taking timely security and preventive measures so that the possibilities of trans-border crime, incident of smuggling and other law and order problems are not allowed to take place and flourish. It is because of this philosophy of ITBP that wherever this Force is deployed, minimum such incidents have taken place and the officers and men of ITBP are ever willing to serve the nation and in doing so much supreme sacrifices. The ITBP has also made pioneering efforts in introducing the use of Solar Energy and Wind Mill in the border area for the purpose of electrification, battery charging and telecommunication.

Security of Sensitive Installations and Protected Persons: Because of combat capability, high standard of discipline and fortitude, the ITBP has been regarded as an elite force in the country even by the foreign observers. The commandos of the ITBP are also providing special security cover to the Indian High Commission in Srilanka since 1988. As many as 174 major branches of the nationalised banks having currency chests or repositories all over the State of Punjab are being guarded by ITBP including the movement of cash remittance since April 1988. The ITBP is also guarding banks and many vital installations in the State of Jammu and Kashmir, Union Territory of Chandigarh and Leh-Ladakh.

Election Duties: The ITBP has been also helping Central as well as various State Governments by carrying out internal security duties, election duties during Lok Sabha and Assembly Elections. During the Lok Sabha and Assembly Elections of 1989, as many as 40 Companies of ITBP were deployed for election duties in various States. During 1991 & 1996 elections, they were again called for duty of various places. Currently 4 companies are also doing antinaxalite duties in Andhra Pradesh

UN Peace Keeping Missions: The role of the ITBP and its services rendered have extended beyond the nation's borders as well.. ITBP also takes part in UN peace keeping operation. The Force personnel have been deployed for peacekeeping operations in Angola, Namibia, Cambodia, Bosnia & Herzegovina, Mozambique and Kosovo. Presently 01 Company of ITBP is deployed in United Nation Mission in Congo since November, 2005.

Duties during Kailash Mansarovar Yatra: Mt. Kailash, 6, 740 m. is situated to the north of the Himalayan barrier, wholly within Tibet. It is the spiritual centre for four great religions: Tibetan Buddhism, Hinduism, the Jain religion and the pre-Buddhist animistic religion-Bonpo.

It is said that a stream from the mountain pours into a nearby lake and from here rivers flow in the four cardinal directions. The River of the Lion Mouth to the North, the River of the Horse Mouth to the east, the River of the Peacock Mouth to the south and the River of the Elephant Mouth to the West. Strangely enough, four major rivers do indeed originate near Kailash, the Indus, the Yarlung Tsangpo (Brahmaputra), the Karnali and the Sutlej. Tibetans believe that it is the residence of Demchog, a fierce looking tantric deity who lives there with his consort, Dorje Phagmo.

For the Tibetans also, it is a particularly special place in that their poet saint Milarepa, spent several years here meditating in a cave. For the Hindus Mount Kailash is the earthly manifestation of Mt. Meru, their spritual centre of the universe, described as a fantastic world pillar 84, 000 miles high, around which all else revolves, its roots in the lowest hell and its summit kissing the heavens.

On the top lives their most revered God, Shiva, and his consort Parvati. For the Jains, an Indian religious group, Kailash is the site where their first prophet achieved enlightenment. For the older, more ancient religion of Bon, it is the site where its founder Shanrab is said to have descended from heaven.

It was formerly the spiritual centre of Zhang Zung, the ancient Bon Empire that once included all of western Tibet. Bon people walk around the mountain in a counter clockwise manner, unlike the other religions. Over the centuries pilgrims have constantly journeyed immense distances to achieve enlightenment or cleanse themselves of sin, braving enormous distances, particularly harsh weather and bandit attacks.

ITBP discharges pious responsibility and provides comforts and succour to old and young pilgrims during their tire some trek to their holy destination. ITBP performs following duties during Mansarovar Kailash Yatra:

- To provide detailed Medical check up of pilgrims before commencement of pilgrimage at ITBP Base Hospital Delhi.
- At Gunji the escort duties are taken over by Indo-Tibetan Border Police.
- High altitude Medical check up of pilgrims by ITBP panel of Doctors at Gunji.
- Escort and security of pilgrims from Gunji to Lipulekh Pass on way to China and return from Lipulekh Pass to Gunji.
- Communication facilities between Gunji to Lipulekh Pass while on way to China and on return from Lipulekh pass to Gunji.
- Provide Medical care between Gunji to Lipulekh pass.
- Communication and co-ordination with the agencies connected with this pilgrimage.
- To attend to any emergency or evacuation due to natural hazards.

Acts, Rules & Regulations

The ITBP is governed by the ITBP Act 1992. The Act consists 157 sections in all.

- Section 1: Short title and commencement
- Section 2: Definitions
- Section 3: Persons subject to this Act
- Section 4: Constitution of the Force
- Section 5: Control, direction, etc
- Section 6: Enrolment
- Section 7: Liability for service outside India
- Section 8: Resignation and withdrawal from the post
- Section 9: Tenure of service under the Act
- Section 10: Termination of service by Central Government
- Section 11: Dismissal, removal or reduction by the Director-General and by other officers

- Section 12: Certificate of termination of service
- Section 13: Restrictions respecting right to form association, freedom of speech, etc
- Section 14: Remedy of aggrieved persons other than officers
- Section 15: Remedy of aggrieved officers
- Section 16: Offences in relation to the enemy or terrorist and punishable with death
- Section 17: Offences in relation to the enemy and not punishable with death
- Section 18: Offences punishable more severely on active duty than at other times
- Section 19: Mutiny
- Section 20: Desertion and aiding desertion
- Section 21: Absence without leave
- Section 22: Striking or threatening superior officer
- Section 23: Disobedience to superior officer
- Section 24: Insubordination and obstruction
- Section 25: False answers-on enrolment
- Section 26: Unbecoming conduct
- Section 27: Certain forms of disgraceful conduct
- Section 28: Ill-treating a subordinate
- Section 29: Intoxication
- Section 30: Permitting escape of person in custody
- Section 31: Irregularity in connection with arrest or confinement
- Section 32: Escape from custody
- Section 33: Offences in respect of property
- Section 34: Extortion and exaction
- Section 35: Making away with equipment
- Section 36: Injury to property
- Section 37: False accusations
- Section 38: Falsifying official documents and false declarations
- Section 39: Signing in blank and failure to report

- Section 40: Offences relating to Force Court
- Section 41: False evidence
- Section 42: Unlawful detention of pay
- Section 43: Violation of good order and discipline
- Section 44: Miscellaneous offences
- Section 45: Attempt
- Section 46: Abetment of offences that have been committed
- Section 47: Abetment of offences punishable with death and not committed
- Section 48: Abetment of offences punishable with imprisonment and not committed
- Section 49: Civil offences
- Section 50: Civil offences not triable by a Force Court
- Section 51: Punishment awardable by Force Courts
- Section 52: Alternative punishments awardable by Force Courts
- Section 53: Combination of punishments
- Section 54: Retention in the Force of a person convicted on active duty
- Section 55: Punishments otherwise than by Force Courts
- Section 56: Minor punishments
- Section 57: Limit of punishments under Section 56
- Section 58: Punishment of persons of or below the rank of Commandant by Inspectors-General and others
- Section 59: Review of proceedings
- Section 60: Collective fines
- Section 61: Deductions from pay and allowances of persons subject to this Act
- Section 62: Pay and allowances during trial
- Section 63: Limit of certain deductions
- Section 64: Deduction from public money due to a person
- Section 65: Pay and allowances of prisoner of war during inquiry into his conduct
- Section 66: Remission of deductions

- Section 67: Provision for dependants of prisoner of war from his remitted deductions and pay and allowances
- Section 68: Period during which a person is deemed to be a prisoner of war
- Section 69: Custody of offenders
- Section 70: Duty of commanding officer in regard to detention
- Section 71: Interval between committal and trial
- Section 72: Arrest by civil authorities
- Section 73: Capture of deserters
- Section 74: Inquiry into absence without leave
- Section 75: Force Police Officers
- Section 76: Kinds of Force Courts
- Section 77: Power to convene a General Force Court
- Section 78: Power to convene a Petty Force Court
- Section 79: Contents of warrants issue under Sections 77 and 78
- Section 80: Composition of a General Force Court
- Section 81: Composition of a Petty Force Court
- Section 82: Summary Force Court
- Section 83: Dissolution of a Force Court
- Section 84: Power of It General Force Court
- Section 85: Power of a Petty Force Court
- Section 86: Power of a Summary Force Court
- Section 87: Prohibition of second trial
- Section 88: Period of limitation for trial
- Section 89: Trial, etc:, of offender who ceases to be subject to this Act
- Section 90: Application of Act during term of sentence
- Section 91: Place of trial
- Section 92: Choice between criminal court and Force Court
- Section 93: Power of criminal court to require delivery of offender
- Section 94: Presiding officer

- Section 95: Judge Attorneys
- Section 96: Challenges
- Section 97: Oaths of member, Judge Attorney and witness
- Section 98: Voting by members
- Section 99: General rule as to evidence
- Section 100: Judicial notice
- Section 101: Summoning Witnesses
- Section 102: Documents exempted from production
- Section 103: Commissions for examination of witnesses
- Section 104: Examination of a witness on Commission
- Section 105: Conviction for offences not charged
- Section 106: Presumption as to signatures
- Section 107: Enrolment paper
- Section 108: Presumption as to certain documents
- Section 109: Reference by accused to Government officer
- Section 110: Evidence of previous convictions and general character
- Section 111: Lunacy of accused
- Section 112: Subsequent fitness of lunatic accused for trial
- Section 113: Transmission to Central Government of orders under Section 112
- Section 114: Release of lunatic accused
- Section 115: Delivery of lunatic accused to relatives
- Section 116: Order for custody and disposal of property pending trial
- Section 117: Order for disposal of property regarding which offence is committed
- Section 118: Powers of Force Court in relation to proceedings under this Act
- Section 119: Tender of pardon to accomplice
- Section 120: Trial of person not complying with conditions of pardon
- Section 121: Finding and sentence not valid unless confirmed

- Section 122: Power to confirm finding and sentence of General Force Court
- Section 123: Power to confirm finding and sentence of Petty Force Court
- Section 124: Limitation of powers of confirming authority
- Section 125: Power of confirming authority to mitigate, remit or commute sentences
- Section 126 Confirming of findings and sentences on board a ship
- Section 127: Revision of finding or sentence
- Section 128: Finding and sentence of a Summary Force Court
- Section 129: Transmission of proceedings of Summary Force Court
- Section 130: Alteration of finding or sentence in certain cases
- Section 131: Remedy against order, finding or sentence of Force Court
- Section 132: Annulment of proceedings
- Section 133: Form of sentence of death
- Section 134: Commencement of sentence of imprisonment
- Section 135: Execution of sentence of imprisonment
- Section 136: Temporary custody of offender
- Section 137: Execution of sentence of imprisonment in special cases
- Section 138: Conveyance of prisoner from place to place
- Section 139: Communication of certain orders to prison officers
- Section 140: Execution of sentence of fine
- Section 141: Informality or error in the order or warrant
- Section 142: Pardon and remission
- Section 143: Cancellation of conditional pardons, release on parole or remission
- Section 144: Suspension of sentence of imprisonment
- Section 145: Orders pending suspension
- Section 146: Release on suspension
- Section 147: Computation of period of suspension

- Section 148: Order after suspension
- Section 149: Reconsideration of case after suspension
- Section 150: Fresh sentence after suspension
- Section 151: Scope of power of suspension
- Section 152: Effect of suspension and remission on dismissal
- Section 153: Rank structure
- Section 154: Powers and duties conferrable and imposable on members of the Force
- Section 155: Protection for acts of members of the Force
- Section 156: Power to make rules
- Section 157: Provisions as to existing Indo-Tibetan Border Police Force

The Indo-Tibet Border Police Rules 1994: The ITBP follows The Indo-Tibet Border Police Rules 1994. It has 187 sections in all.

- Section 1: Short title, commencement and application
- Section 2: Definitions
- Section 3: Reports and applications
- Section 4: Forms in appendices
- Section 5: Exercise of power vested in holder of an office in the Force
- Section 6: Case un-provided for
- Section 7: Constitution of the Force
- Section 8: The task of the Force and Command and Control thereto
- Section 9: Command
- Section 10: Ineligibility
- Section 11: Ineligibility of aliens
- Section 12: Appointment of officers
- Section 13: Appointment of Subordinate Officers and Enrolled Persons
- Section 14: Probation
- Section 15: Procedure for enrolment, mode of enrolment and other matters connected therewith

- Section 16: Liability of Service
- Section 17: Termination of service
- Section 18: Termination of service of officers by the Central Government on account of misconduct
- Section 19: Termination of service of Officers by the Central Government on grounds of un-suitability
- Section 20: Termination of service of persons, other than officers on account of misconduct
- Section 21: Discharge from service on grounds of unsatisfactory progress in training
- Section 22: Termination of service on grounds of furnishing false / incorrect information at the time of appointment
- Section 23: Retirement/discharge/release of officers on grounds of physical unfitness
- Section 24: Termination of service of subordinate officers by the authorities as specified in rule 17 on the grounds of unsuitability
- Section 25: Termination of service of enrolled persons on the grounds of unsuitability
- Section 26: Retirement: discharge of subordinate officers and enrolled persons on grounds of physical unfitness
- Section 27: Resignation
- Section 28: Appeal against orders of dismissal, removal or retirement
- Section 29: Date of dismissal, removal, discharge or retirement
- Section 30: Forms of arrest
- Section 31: Authority to order arrest
- Section 32: Arrest, how imposed-(A) Close arrest (B) Open arrest
- Section 33: Release from arrest during investigation
- Section 34: Release without prejudice to re-arrest
- Section 35: Arrest, when to be imposed
- Section 36: Special provision in case of arrest of a drunken person

- Section 37: Arrest in case of persons whose trial has been ordered
- Section 38: Delay Report
- Section 39: Rights of a person under arrest
- Section 40: Suspension
- Section 41: Trial of cases either by Force Court or Criminal Court
- Section 42: Cases which may' not be tried by Force Court
- Section 43: Statement of allegations
- Section 44: Hearing by an officer not below the rank of Assistant Commandant
- Section 45: Hearing by the Commanding Officer
- Section 46: Procedure for summary disposal of charge against officers
- Section 47: Summary disposal of charges against subordinate officer
- Section 48: Attachment to another unit
- Section 49: Charges not to be dealt with summarily
- Section 50: Record of evidence
- Section 51: Abstract of evidence
- Section 52: Investigation of cases by Police
- Section 53: Disposal of case by Commanding Officer After record or abstract of evidence
- Section 54: Application for a Court
- Section 55: Charge-sheet
- Section 56: Charges
- Section 57: Joint Charges
- Section 58: Validity of charge-sheet
- Section 59: Amendment of the charge by the Force Court
- Section 60: Amendment of Charge by Convening Officer
- Section 61: Action by a Superior Authority on receiving an application for convening a Court
- Section 62: Disqualification of officers for serving on General and Petty Force Courts

- Section 63: Composition of General and Petty Force Courts
- Section 64: Duties of convening officer when convening courts
- Section 65: Preparation of defence by the accused
- Section 66: Summoning of Defence Witnesses
- Section 67: Assembly and swearing of Court
- Section 68: Commencement of Trial
- Section 69: Swearing or affirming of members
- Section 70: Swearing or affirmation of Judge Attorney and other officers
- Section 71: Objection to Interpreter or Shorthand Writer
- Section 72: Objection to Judge Attorney and Prosecutor
- Section 73: Arraignment
- Section 74: Plea to Jurisdiction
- Section 75: Objection to the charge
- Section 76: Plea in bar of trial
- Section 77: Application for separate trial
- Section 78: Application for trial an separate charge-sheet
- Section 79: Pleading to the charge
- Section 80: Acceptance of plea of guilty
- Section 81: Plea en alternative charge
- Section 82: Order of trial where plea of guilty and not guilty
- Section 83: Change of plea
- Section 84: Procedure on plea (s) of not guilty
- Section 85: Opening address
- Section 86: Additional witness
- Section 87: Dropping witnesses
- Section 88: Withdrawal of witnesses
- Section 89: Examination of witness
- Section 90: Questioning by the Court
- Section 91: Reading over of evidence
- Section 92: Calling or recalling witnesses by the Court
- Section 93: Submission of no case to answer and stopping of cases

- Section 94: Case for the defence
- Section 95: Witnesses for defence
- Section 96: Witness in reply
- Section 97: Closing address
- Section 98: Summing up by Judge Attorney
- Section 99: Deliberation on finding
- Section 100: Record and announcement of finding
- Section 101: Procedure on acquittal
- Section 102: Procedure on conviction
- Section 103: Sentence
- Section 104: Recommendation far mercy
- Section 105: Announcement of sentence and signing and transmission of proceedings
- Section 106: Revision
- Section 107: Confirmation and Promulgation
- Section 108: Seating of members
- Section 109: Responsibility of Presiding Officer
- Section 110: Power of Court over address of prosecutor and accused
- Section 111: Sitting in closed Court
- Section 112: Continuity of trial and adjournment of Court
- Section 113: Suspension of trial
- Section 114: Proceedings on death or illness of accused
- Section 115: Death, retirement or absence of presiding officer
- Section 116: Presence of all members of Court
- Section 117: Taking of opinions of members of Court
- Section 118: Procedure on incidental questions
- Section 119: Evidence: when to be translated
- Section 120: Record in Proceedings of transactions of a Force Court
- Section 121: Custody and inspection of proceedings
- Section 122: Review of General /Petty Force Court proceedings

- Section 123: Defending Officer, friend of accused and counsel
- Section 124: Requirement for appearance of counsel
- Section 125: Disqualification of Judge Attorney
- Section 126: Substitution on death, illness or absence of Judge Attorney
- Section 127: Power and duties of Judge Attorney
- Section 128: Finding of insanity
- Section 129: Preservation of proceedings
- Section 130: Right of person tried to copies of proceedings
- Section 131: Copy of proceedings not to be given in certain cases
- Section 132: Loss of proceedings
- Section 133: Offences by witnesses and others
- Section 134: Proceedings
- Section 135: Evidence when to be translated
- Section 136: Assembly
- Section 137: Swearing or affirming of court and interpreter
- Section 138: Swearing of Court to try several accused persons
- Section 139: Arraignment of accused
- Section 140: Objection by accused to charge
- Section 141: Amendment of charge
- Section 142: Special pleas
- Section 143: General plea of "Guilty" or "Not Guilty"
- Section 144: Procedure after plea of "Guilty"
- Section 145: Withdrawal of plea of "Not Guilty"
- Section 146: Procedure after plea of "Not Guilty"
- Section 147: Witnesses in reply to defence
- Section 148: Evidence of witnesses
- Section 149: Record and announcement of finding
- Section 150: Procedure on acquittal
- Section 151: Procedure on finding of "Guilty"
- Section 152: Sentence

- Section 153: Signing of proceedings
- Section 154: Charges in different charge sheets
- Section 155: Clearing the Court
- Section 156: Adjournment
- Section 157: Friend cf the accused
- Section 158: Memorandum to be attached to proceedings
- Section 159: Promulgation
- Section 160: Review of proceedings
- Section 161: Action by the Deputy Inspector General or the Additional Deputy Inspector General
- Section 162: Rules which shall not apply to trial by Summary Force Court
- Section 163: Direction about Sentence of imprisonment
- Section 164: Warrants
- Section 165: Warrant in case of sentence of death
- Section 166: Changes in sentence
- Section 167: Sentence of dismissal
- Section 168: Petitions against finding and sentence of Court
- Section 169: Period of Limitation
- Section 170: Mode of submitting petitions
- Section 171: Composition
- Section 172: Assembly order
- Section 173: Members of Court not to be sworn or affirmed
- Section 174: Procedure of Courts of Inquiry
- Section 175: Courts of Inquiry, when to be held
- Section 176: Action on the proceedings of a Court of Inquiry
- Section 177: Copies of Court of Inquiry Proceedings
- Section 178: Prescribed Officer under Section 11
- Section 179: Authority prescribed for the purpose of Section 13
- Section 180: Prescribed Officer under sections 61 and 62
- Section 181: Prescribed authorities under section 66

- Section 182: Prescribed Officer under section 75
- Section 183: Prescribed manner of custody and prescribed officer under sections 111 and 112
- Section 184: Prescribed Officer under section 132
- Section 185: Authorised deductions
- Section 186: Repeal and Savings
- Section 187: Transitory provision

Weapons and Equipments

ITBP uses basic Infantry weapons such as Type 56 Assault rifles, Type 81 Assault rifles, AKM rifles, INSAS 5. 56 MM Assault rifle, G3A3 Battle rifle, MP5 Submachine-gun ; Uzi submachinegun, M9 pistol ; RPG 7 Rocket-propelled grenade launchers ; and M67 hand-grenades. CRPF also uses landmine detectors ; Light Machine-Guns and Heavy-Machine-Guns.

Besides, personnel also use special equipment for high altitudes such as; Rope, cord and webbing, Carabiners, Quickdraws, Harnesses, Belay devices, Rappel, devices, Ascenders, Slings, Protection devices, Specialist clothing, Climbing shoes, Belay gloves, Helmet and Webbing.

Recruitment

Officers: The Central Government may appoint suitable persons as officers in the Force in the following manner:

- By direct recruitment
- By transfer on deputation from the All India Services. Defence Forces; any other armed forces of the Union, State Police, any other department of the Central Government or of the State Government or autonomous bodies
- By promotion as may be prescribed from time to time
- By transfer
- By re-employment

Other Ranks: Appointment to the posts of Subedar-Majors or Subedars may be made by the Inspector-General of Sub-Inspectors by the Deputy Inspector-General or Additional Deputy Inspector General, and of enrolled persons by the Commandant or any other officer of the

Force who may be appointed as enrolling officer by the Director General, respectively in the following manner:

- By direct recruitment
- By transfer on deputation from the Defence Forces, any other armed forces of the Union, State Police, any other department of the Central Government or of the State Government or autonomous bodies
- By promotion as may be prescribed from time to time
- By transfer
- By re-employment

Training: ITBP give training to trainees to develop professional skills, esprit de corps, and leadership, Values of integrity, impartiality and respect for all castes, creed and religion Highest tradition of supreme sacrifice in the service of motherland Respect for human rights so as to make us a formidable force in maintaining the security & territorial integrity of India The Basic Training Centre at Bhanu, ITBP Academy at Mussourie, and the Mountaineering & Skiing Institute at Auli run the training programmes and conduct indoor and outdoor training activities, in pursuance of this mission.

The ITBP Academy consists of two wings viz. Adm Wing and Combat Wing. The Adm Wing of ITBP Academy is the erstwhile 'Specialist Training Centre of ITBP, which was situated in Nowgaon (M. P) prior to the year-1976. Similarly, the 'Advanced Training Centre', which was earlier located in Shivpuri (MP) is now forms Combat Wing. Both these establishments had separate strength and command structure. However, after the reorganization of the Force in 1978 these were amalgamated and restructured on functional basis as Adm Wing and Combat Wing, These wings under their respective commandants work within the over all control and supervision of Director.

For the day-to-day administration, he is assisted by one Addl Dy. Inspector General. The two wings of ITBP Academy are spread over an area of 243 acres of land where training infra-structure like firing ranges, obstacle course, area for field craft, tactics etc have been established. Adm Wing is responsible to provide administrative cover to Academy and Combat Wing for conducting the training in Academy. Besides conducting the basic training of directly recruited Asstt Commandants and Sub-Inspectors, the ITBP Academy organizes in-service Courses on conventional warfare, intelligence, field engineering, VIP security and commando operations, counter-insurgency operations, administration, computers, karate, map reading, rock climbing and staff duties etc for all ranks of the Force and of CPOs/ State Police Forces. ITBP Academy has been given the status of 'Centre of Excellence' by the Government of India and now is on the path of modernization of its training infra-structure.

Famous Operations

Operation Against Hizbul-Mujahideen: ITBP team in an encounter with Hizbul-Mujahideen terrorists, in District Anantnag in the state of Jammu & Kashmir, killed all terrorists. Constable Suresh Kumar was killed in action. He was posthumously decorated with Presidents Police Medal for Gallantry.

Scaling Mt. Everest from North Side: Sonam Palzore was the first ITBP person who reached the summit in 1984 as one of the members of 4th Indian Expedition. Hukam Singh led first all ITBP expedition on Everest in 1992 Thereafter, the highest peak was scaled by ITBP mountaineers in 1993, 1996 and 1999. Ms Santosh Yadav made three successful attempts on Mt. Everest. Sh Mohinder Singh made a history by leading successful expedition on Everest from North Cole- from China side in 1996.

Operation against Lashkar-e-Toiba: On 02-11-1998 at Chirwar, District Anantnag, J & K, Ashok Kumar Rana, Assistant Commandant was leading a troop of ITBP when he encountered Lashkar-e-Toiba terrorists. There was a bloody battle in which all terrorists were killed. He sacrificed his life in this encounter. In the encounter he killed 3 terrorists. He was Posthumously decorated with the Shaurya Chakra.

Awards

Shaurya chakra	1
Sena medal	1
Presidents police medal for gallantry	11
Police medal for gallantry	61

Modernization

The ITBP has embarked on a major modernization campaign to bring itself up to the expected level of a modern military force. The latest weapons and equipments required on the modern battlefield are under development or are coming into service. In the near future, the ITBP will be able to conduct sustained independent operations at high altitudes.

Miscellaneous

Adventure and dare-devilry are the trademark of ITBP and therefore from its ranks come the world class mountaineers who have scaled more than a hundred Himalayan peaks, including the Mount Everest, four times. Its skiers have been national champions, who have done India proud in the winter Olympics. Its river rafters have created international history in rafting through the turbulent white waters of the mighty Brahmaputra, the Indus and the Ganga.

ITBP has taken up the task of greening the Himalayan regions. It has taken on itself the task of maintaining the delicate balance of flora and fauna. ITBP being deployed in mountains has developed the expertise in rescue & relief operations in mountains, which entail different specialized skills of very high standard. It is always first in extending rescue & relief in case of natural calamity.

ITBP conducts a large number of medical civic action programmes in remote border and terrorist affected areas to provide free and expert medical, health and hygiene care to the civilian population in remote villages.

REFERENCES

Annual Report 2002-2003, Ministry of Home Affairs, Government of India.

Ashok Krishna: Examples of Learning in Counter-Insurgency. IDSA 2000.

Bose, Sumantra: The Kashmir Challenge, Sage, New Delhi, 1997.

Bruce Elleman: Sino-Soviet Relations and the Feb 1979 Sino-Vietnamese Conflict. (20 Apr 96).

Christian. F. Ostermann: New Evidence on the Sino-Soviet Border Dispute, Cold War International History Project Bulletin Issue 5 (Spring 1995).

Col. Ahrnam Singh. Doda: Insurgency in the Wilderness. Lancer, New Delhi, 1999.

Daily Times (Pakistan), Nov. 30, 2005.

Dte General, ITBP.

Employment News.

Free Press Journal, March 13, 2000.

Gupta, Sisir: Kashmir, Asia Publishing House, Bombay, 1966.

Indian Express. March 27, 2000.

Kumar, Raj: Encyclopaedia of Military Systems in India, Commonwealth Publishers, New Delhi, 2004.

Major General Arjun Ray: Kashmir Diary, Manas, New Delhi, 1996.

Manoj Joshi: The Lost Rebellion, Penguin India, New Delhi, 1997.

Marston, Daniel P. and Sundaram, Chandar S. A.: Military History of India and South Asia : From the East India Company to the Nuclear Era, Pentagon Press, New Delhi, 2008.

Ministry of Home Affairs.

Ramesh Thakur and Carlyyle Thayer: Soviet Relations with India and Vietnam. New York. St Martin Press, 1992.

Robert A Scalapino: The Political Influence of the USSR in Asia in Donald.S.Zagoria ed. Soviet Policy in East Asia. New Haven, Yale University Press 1982.

The Hindu, Aug. 10, 1999.

The Hindu, Feb. 15, 2000.

The Tribune, Jan. 26, 2004.

Tribune, Dec. 07, 1999.

Tribune, Nov. 25, 1998.

9

Rashtriya Rifles

"Dridhta aur Virta"

Introduction

The Rashtriya Rifles (RR) is a counterinsurgency force of India. It was conceptualized by General B. C Joshi in 1990 specially for combating insurgency in Kashmir and to give support to the weak local security forces in the area. The main role of the formation is to allow the Indian Army to ensure its main job of defending the borders. The Rashtriya Rifles have 62 battalions, with additional 30 formed using regular army battalions. The effectiveness of an RR battalion arises from the fact that unlike conventional Army battalions, it has six rifle companies instead of four. Six new battalions were raised, but their fate is unclear with the Union Financial Ministry yet to sanction the move.

History

Need: The years after 1985 were predominantly bloody for Kashmir. By May 1990 it was clear that Jammu & Kashmir was in the grip of an insurgency of intensity not seen before. It started out in the urban areas and then spread to the countryside. The army which till then was the guardian of the international border and the line of control was called in to assist in Counter Insurgency operations. Based on its experience with low intensity conflicts in Nagaland, Sri Lanka and Punjab, the Indian Army was quite wary of trying to replicate strategy and tactics successfully used elsewhere. By 1993 the army had got together a doctrine for the low intensity conflict in Kashmir. In Nagaland for example, the army had learnt that physical domination of each and every village was one way to combat insurgency.

Long experience had taught the army the value of the grid system. In this system the whole terrain was divided into a grid. Each node at any given time would have a platoon worth of ready to move soldiers, the so called quick reaction team which would mutually reinforce other nodes. All would be covered with heavier fire support and have adequate logistics. However the grid often looked better on paper than on the ground. The obvious reason for this was the terrain. In the Wanni jungles of Sri Lanka where the grid had been successfully applied, civilians and villages were few and far between, and so attack helicopters and artillery could be used. This enabled heavy firepower to be brought in to support troops in the grid in minutes. Now the Kashmir valley is very densely populated and there is fear of collateral damage from using heavy fire support. So troops fighting CI had to do without it. To makeup for that the grid had to be more densely packed. This is where the army saw the need for additional forces such as the Rashtriya Rifles (RR).

Origin: The Rashtriya Rifles the prime counterinsurgency force in India. It was formed by General B C Joshi in 1990 expressly for counteracting insurgency in Kashmir. In 1990, the Rashtriya Rifles (RR) was established with six battalions and two sector headquarters. By 1993, the Indian army had expanded its role in the Kashmir Valley by deploying the Rashtriya Rifles. The 36-battalion formation, a light elite counterinsurgency force, was formed specifically to compensate for weak and untrustworthy local police and increasingly well-armed insurgents in Kashmir.

The force was further expanded in 1994-95. By 1996, as guerrilla problems grew, tens of thousands of regular army units joined the Rashtriya Rifles in the valley, further supplemented by a police counterinsurgency special task force composed principally of non-Muslim personnel not from the local area.

For the creation of this legendary force, many sacrifices had to be made by many organizations and individuals. To begin with, Headquarters

Counter Insurgency Force, a formation headquarter equivalent to a corps headquarters, was sanctioned by the Government in 1994 for the overall command and control of Rashtriya Rifles. This headquarter was trifurcated later to form two operative force headquarters in J&K and a Rashtriya Rifles Directorate at Army Headquarters, Delhi.

The Army, has made the most sacrifices. The manpower for raising the RR force was primarily drawn from the units of the Army. These units operated with reduced manpower till deficiency was made up. The reserves of the Army was used for equipping newly raised RR battalions. The regimental centres of all arms and services had also undertaken the additional task of training persons posted to RR.

A substantial amount of Army's budget was used for raising and maintaining RR till 1998. The budget of RR has been separated from defence budget since the financial year 1998-99. The relationship of the RR with the local people, civil administration and law-inforcing agencies has been of an exceptionally high order. This has been possible due to regular interaction with the locals by RR formations, units and even companies. Various core group meetings are held periodically wherein the problems of the people are looked into and acted upon with compassion.

The initial RR units performed well despite certain inherent weaknesses in their class and composition. They were raised on All India/ All Class basis with troops from all over the Army. The logic being that since the units were going to fight an insurgency, there should be no scope for vested interests in accusing a battalion of bias based on a class or regional attributes. Unfortunately, this setup created problems in the field. The initial RR units were like transit camps, with troops coming and going at regular intervals. There was little camaraderie and cohesion among troops. There were also numerous problems of administration and even of indiscipline. COs of Infantry battalions who were asked to provide manpower generally used to use that as a chance to get rid of trouble makers. If the initial battalions performed well in hostile conditions, it was mainly due to the professional competence of officers who were asked to lead them.

The initial RR battalions deployed in the terrorist-infested areas of Tarn Taran in Punjab and Anantnag in Jammu & Kashmir proved to be extremely effective. In Punjab, the deployment of the Army and RR units did contribute to the turnaround in the situation. Since then the RR has been increasingly fighting the low-intensity war on behalf of the army in

Kashmir. Casualty figures indicate that from 3 out of 44 army casualties in 1991 being from the RR, the figure has gone up to 82 out of 150 in 1996. Up to February '97, 17 RR officers (including 1 Colonel, 4 Lt. Colonels and 7 Majors), 13 JCOs and 169 ORs have made the supreme sacrifice. The officer to OR casualty ratio for the RR (at 1:9.94 till February 1997) is almost double the average for the army in the Kargil and 1971 war (at 1:20).

Many civic action programmes like construction of water points, community centres and improvement of schools, mosques, roads and tracks have been undertaken. Hundreds of school children have been taken on various RR sponsored educational-cum-cultural tours to various historical places in India. Other successes of this force include successful conduct of parliamentary and state assembly elections in 1997 and 1998 respectively, management of entire counter-insurgency and rear area security operations in J&K during operation Vijay, elimination of over 2700 militants since its raising, capture of large quantities of arms, ammunition and warlike stores, causing confusion and disarray amidst various militant cadres and improving the quality of life of the local public in their respective areas of responsibility.

In 1998, Surankot, a militant dominated tehsil of Poonch district was reeling under insurgency and drew attention of everyone in India in general and Jammu & Kashmir in particular. The common man was in a state of fear, markets were deserted and there was virtual breakdown of civil life. The civil administration too was subdued by a number of sabotage activities and made nonfunctional. The militants had even created their own capital called 'Faisalabad'. The battalions of Rashtriya Rifles (RR) were tasked to bring back normalcy in this area. In a short span, they eliminated more than 200 militants, including foreign mercenaries. Today normalcy has been restored.

It was at this stage that it was decided to raise Kay Force under the stewardship of Maj. General Nirbhay Sharma. The orders for its raising were issued on September 1, 1999 and the formation was fully operational within 20 days, with the motto "Tougher the Better." On getting operational, the formation was increasingly entrusted with a huge area of responsibility comprising most parts of North and Central Kashmir. The terrain varied from chilling snow covered heights to waterbodies, from dense forests to paddy fields and crowded villages, covering a total covering area of over 6, 500 sq km. Coupled to all this was a hostile population who were apprehensive of the security forces while at the same time being exploited by the terrorists.

By 2001 all the four force Headquarters, which include 12 sector Headquarters and 36 battalions, were deployed in J&K. While CI Force 'R' is responsible for combating terrorism in the districts of Rajouri and Poonch, CI Force 'D' has been taking care of Doda district. Likewise, CI Force 'V' is responsible for the districts of Anantnag, Pulwama and Badgam and CI Force 'K' has been deployed in the districts of Kupwara, Baramulla and Srinagar.

In April 2001 the Center exclusively earmarked more than Rs 600 crore in order to raise 30 battalions of the Rashtriya Rifles (RR) for combating militancy in Kashmir. These new battalions, comprising men and officers from within the Army, will help the present 30 Rashtriya Rifles battalions perform internal security and anti-insurgency operations in Jammu and Kashmir and some other parts of the country. Each battalion having 1, 150 men and officers will be controlled by the Army. These battalions will help the Army to withdraw its regular troops from J&K and re-train them to guard borders and fight.

Six Army battalions raised especially for Jammu and Kashmir (J-K) counter insurgency operations underwent special training, and started deployment in the state by 01 September 2001. With the entire state barring Ladakh under the Armed Forces Special Powers Act, the Army began deploying additional forces to tighten the security net, with 7, 200 soldiers of six newly-raised battalions. The battalions are assigned to the Rashtriya Rifles (RR), but parent Regiments raised them at their respective regimental centres. One of the six battalions was raised in New Delhi (Rajputana Rifles). The Maratha Light Infantry (MLI) RR battalion was raised at Belgaum, the Madras Regiment at Tiruchi, the Assam Regiment RR battalion at Shillong, the Punjab RR at Ramgarh, Grenadiers at Jabalpur and the Dogra Regiment RR battalion at Faizabad. The newly-raised battalions underwent special training at the Army's counter insurgency warfare school near Jammu. The Army had six months to raise and train the soldiers for the highly specialised operations. After that there was a four-week-long capsule course in laying ambushes in hills and mountains, detecting and disarming IEDs, carrying out cordon and search operations and carrying out operations to neutralise terrorists in heavily populated neighbourhoods.

The 59th Rashtriya Rifles Battalion (Assam) was formally raised at Assam Regimental Centre, Shillong in May 2004. This is the third RR battalion of Assam Regiment. Brig WJB Sturgeon, Commandant, 58 Gorkha Training Centre, unfurled the RR flag at a glittering ceremony held at Happy Valley, Shillong. Lt Col Suchindra Kumar has been deputed as the Commanding Officer of the battalion. The newly raised battalion comprises 24 officers, 38 JCOs and 1, 141 other ranks posted from various battalions of the Assam Regiment.

The security environment in the state of J&K is dynamic and is reviewed constantly based on threat perceptions. To reduce the commitment of Army on internal security duties, the Government had given in principle approval in 2000, to raise 30 more Rashtriya Rifles battalions, which brought up the total strength of Rashtriya Rifles troops to five Force Headquarters, 17 Sector Headquarters and 66 Rashtriya Rifles Battalions by the year 2005.

Key Dates in History

July 1990	Force came into existence
Aug. 1994	Formation headquarter was sanctioned by the Government
March 1998	Budget of RR was separated from defence budget since the financial year 1998-99
01 Sep. 1999	Kay Force setup under Maj. General Nirbhay Sharma

Present Scenario

Personnel Strength: At present there are around 50, 000 RR personnel and 66 RR battalions.

Bases: RR headquarters are located at New Delhi. The RR units are permanently located in "sectors", with each sector being the equivalent of a brigade with three battalions. The RR units come under four CI Force Headquarters. Victor Force looks after Anantnag and Pulwana districts in the south Kashmir valley, Kilo Force looks after Kupwara and Baramulla districts in the north Kashmir valley. Both these forces come under the operational control of the 15 Corps. The Delta Force looks after the Doda district and the Romeo Force after Poonch and Rajouri. These two forces come under the operational control of the 16 Corps. Each force is headed by a GOC-in-C with the rank of a Major General.

Originally comprising a total of four Counterinsurgency Forces, each responsible for an area of the Kashmir Valley and Jammu, the RR raised a fifth force 'Uniform' in 2003-04:

- Counter Insurgency Force (CIF) R / Romeo Force - Rajouri and Poonch

- Counter Insurgency Force (CIF) D / Delta Force - Doda
- Counter Insurgency Force (CIF) V / Victor Force - Anantnag, Pulwama and Badgam
- Counter Insurgency Force (CIF) K / Kilo Force - Kupwara, Baramulla and Srinagar
- Counter Insurgency Force (CIF) U / Uniform Force - Udhampur and Banihal

Organizational Structure

- General
- Lieutenant General
- Major General
- Brigadier
- Colonel
- Lieutenant Colonel
- Major
- Captain
- Lieutenant
- Subedar Major
- Subedar
- Havildar
- Naik
- Lance Naik
- Sepoy

Chiefs of Rashtriya Rifles

- General B. C. Joshi (01 Jul 1993 to 19 Nov 1994)
- General S. Roychowdhury (22 Nov 1994 to 30 Sep 1997)
- General V. P. Malik (01 Oct 1997 to 30 Sep 2000)
- General S. Padmanabhan (01 Oct 2000 to 30 Dec 2002)
- General N. C. Vij (31 Dec 2002 to 31 Jan 2005)
- General J. J. Singh(01 Feb 2005 to 30 Sep 2007)
- General Deepak Kapoor (31 Sep 2007 till date)

Duties and Functions

Motto: RR motto is ***"Dridhta aur Virta"*** meaning **'Strength and bravery"**.

Maxim: To end insurgency in Jammu and Kashmir.

Counterinsurgency operations: To reduce the commitment of Army on internal security duties, the Rashtriya Rifles (RR) has been at the forefront in counter-insurgency (CI) operations. Indian strategists believed that in the event of a war, the 40, 000-strong Rashtriya Rifles would protect the lines of communication and supplies from terrorist attacks in Jammu and Kashmir.

Made up of troops posted on deputation from the Army, the Rashtriya Rifles was meant to ensure that India's LoC divisions could do their job, engaging Pakistan, unhindered by guerrilla action. The Regiment has a distinct dress code, akin to a rifle regiment. Its badge depicts two crossed AK-47 rifles with fixed bayonets atop which is the coveted Ashoka Chakra.

Beneath, in a banner, is emblazoned the motto of this force - Dridhta Aur Virta. AK-47 is the main personal weapon of this force. Rashtriya Rifles was raised as a Paramilitary Force as it was envisaged that personnel posted to RR would comprise regular Army volunteers on deputation, ex-servicemen and lateral inductees from various Paramilitary Forces and central police organizations.

However, ever since its inception this force has comprised hundred per cent regular Army deputationists. This is the only regiment where troops from the Infantry and other arms and services operate together to combat terrorism under a common RR banner.

Each battalion comprises six rifle companies. The Infantry component comprises sixty per cent troops while that of other arms forms twenty-five per cent. The remaining fifteen per cent troops comprises task oriented troops from various services to provide the logistic back-up to the RR battalion.

All individuals, prior to joining their respective units, have to undergo a four-week rigorous pre-induction training at a Corps Battle School. This is followed by two weeks of 'on-the-job' training and a periodic refresher training cadre under sector arrangements. The reputation of Rashtriya Rifles as a specialised anti-terrorist force has a tremendous impact on the militant's psyche who avoid any kind of direct confrontation with RR troops. Secondly, due to the proactive nature of operations conducted by well-trained and well-equipped troops, militants lost a number of their cadres, arms and equipment which was a grave setback to them. Such pressures against the militants have been continuously maintained by RR troops in a relentless manner.

The motivation of all ranks to perform better has it roots in various factors such as a sense of pride to get selected in a special force with a separate identity, dress and organization. Each individual is given here the opportunity to prove his mettle in operational field..

As there is more permanence in the deployment of RR formations and units, they have a better rapport with the locals to gain more authentic flow of intelligence. As a result of all these factors, the junior leaders of RR battalions are able to take greater risks, often at the cost of their own lives to attain their operational goals. They always lead from the front, thereby setting an example for others to emulate. The fact that they have neutralised more than 7000 terrorists, captured more than 6000 weapons of all types and won more than 2000 honours and awards speaks volumes of this organization. Faced with internal security challenges in Kashmir and elsewhere, the Indian army is interested in reducing its overall strength and using available revenue for force modernization.

Some Indian spokesmen have suggested that increasing the use of light army forces, such as the Rashtriya Rifles, to fulfil missions in Kashmir and elsewhere could reduce the need for regular army forces in an internal-security role and help realize cuts. Such a move, it is argued, would better correspond to the real security issues with which India must deal. Others have suggested that the Rashtriya Rifles battalions be re-examined in light of their predominant internal-security duties and gendarme-like character. This is likely to remain a topic of close consideration and debate within the army and the government, as India re-evaluates its national-security requirements, its force-modernization priorities, and its approaches to internal security.

Acts, Rules & Regulations

Rashtriya Rifles is governed by rules and regulations of Indian Army.

Weapons and Equipments

Rashtriya Rifles have access to almost any type of small arms or specialized weapons required for a particular mission. These range from Browning Hi-Power 9 mm pistols, AK-47/74s, 9 mm Uzis, 5.56 mm M-16 A2s, 9 mm H&K MP 5-A2/A3s and locally manufactured 7.62 mm

SLR and 5.56 mm INSAS rifles. Sniper rifles like the semi-automatic H&K 7.62 mm PSG-1 and MSG-90, the SIG 7.62 mm SSG-2000 and the bolt-action Mauser SP 66/86SR are also used.

Recruitment

Ever since its foundation RR has comprised hundred per cent regular Army deputationists.

Training: All personnel, before joining their individual units, have to go through a four-week rigorous pre-induction training at a Corps Battle School. This is followed by two weeks of on-the-job training and a periodic refresher training cadre under sector arrangements.

Famous Operations

Counterinsurgency Operation in Surankot: In 1998, Surankot, a militant dominated tehsil of Poonch district was reeling under insurgency and drew attention of everyone in India in general and Jammu & Kashmir in particular. The common man was in a state of fear. The civil administration too was made nonfunctional. The militants had even created their own capital called 'Faisalabad'. The battalions of Rashtriya Rifles (RR) were tasked to bring back normalcy in this area. In a short span, they eliminated more than 200 militants, including foreign mercenaries. Today you see smiles on people's faces as normalcy is restored. National days, religious functions, sports events and marriage functions are being celebrated with impunity and greater fervour. Democratic political activity has witnessed a momentum with the emergence of sarpanchs and Panchs in the Panchayat polls.

Operation against Terrorists in Haphruda: On 02 November 1996, Lt. Col. Shanti Swarup Rana was entrusted with the task of destroying two terrorist camps in the Haphruda forest of Kupwara District in Jammu & Kashmir. Lt. Col. Rana spotted four well-fortified hideouts stocked heavily with arms & ammunition including 800 kg of explosives. In a gallant & swift strike he, with his troops, crawled towards the bunker and threw hand grenades and destroyed the hideouts.

One more hideout came to notice. During the action that followed, the terrorists resorted to heavy firing from their well fortified bunkers. Lt. Col. Rana organized his troops, crawled towards the bunker and threw hand grenades inside. Two foreign mercenaries came out firing heavily. Lt. Col. Rana killed them both instantaneously. Meanwhile the terrorists seriously injured Lt. Col. Rana in heavy firing from another location. In spite of this, the gallant officer kept on boosting the morale of his soldiers.

When one more terrorist advanced towards the soldiers, Lt. Col. Rana, without caring for his own life, charged and killed him in a face-to-face encounter. In this action, the gallant officer suffered more injuries and made the supreme sacrifice. Lt. Col. Rana thereby displayed indomitable courage, patriotism and gallantry of the highest order for which he was awarded the Ashok Chakra (posthumous).

Operation against Terrorists in Gulgandhar: On 18 April 1998, Sepoy M.G. Chittiyappa was the leading scout in an operation at the village of Guldandadhar in Doda district of Jammu & Kashmir. He spotted a group of Pakistani terrorists in the area. Undeterred & unmindful of the shower of enemy bullets, he closed in and killed one of them. The rest escaped.

Tracker Dog Rex: Yet another hero from the RR is one of its decorated Tracker Dog 'Rex'. Rex was a recipient of GOC-in-C Commendation Card for his outstanding & exemplary performance against militants. The 9A 92 Rex, a golden Labrador was born on 25 February 1993 at RVC Centre & School Meerut. After a year's training, he was posted to 14 Army Dog Unit under Delta Force and assigned the areas adjoining the town of Bhaderwah, to help troops in trailing & tracking militants. In March 1995, operating with troops of 25 RR in jungles of Badrot, South of Bhaderwah, he tracked a militant injured in an encounter for over 3 km in the thick of militant fire. In a chase that lasted for over four hours, he managed to recover one AK 56 rifles and an haversack containing 92 rounds. Recently, in April 1998, out on a patrol in area Gulgandhar, security forces killed two dreaded militants and badly injured one, who managed to escape. Picking up the scent of his blood, 'Rex' went hot on the trail and moved speedily & stealthily over strenuous undulating mountains.

After tracking over 2 km, he succeeded in tracing out the body of the militant in a hideout where he had succumbed to his injuries. Let out on yet another 'trial' with the QRT of CO 25 RR in Daraba near Rajouri, Rex suffered an unfortunate fall and sustained serious intestinal injuries. He was evacuated to the nearest Army Veterinary Hospital where he developed acute gastroentrities and finally succumbed on 22 September 1999.

Kargil War: In the spring of 1999, the Pakistani Army intruded into the Kargil heights. To deal with the situation, the army had to withdraw its battalions from CI ops in J&K. The units de-inducted included the battle hardened 8 Mountain Division which has been involved in CI ops for quite some years and which moved to Kashmir from Nagaland. During this period, the RR held the fort with the help of other Paramilitary Forces. Apart from that, RR units actively contributed to operations in the Kargil heights where they fought shoulder-to-shoulder with jawans of the Sikh, Naga, Granadiers, JAK Rifles and the Para Regiments at heights of 16, 000 feet and above. Naik Mekh Bahadur Gurung of Garhi-Dakra, Dehra Dun was one of them. Naik Gurung lost his life on 22 May 1999, while part of the first recce patrol team that had gone to check on the intruders. Before being shot himself, Naik Mekh shot down at least one of the mercenaries. Lance Naik Balaji Baburao Male of the 5 RR was killed in action in the Kargil sector. L/Nk Male originally joined the 109 Engineer regiment before he was drafted into the RR. With more and more troops being called into action, Lance Naik Male's battalion was also pressed into service in the Kargil sector to bolster the Infantry units fighting the enemy from across the border.

On Sunday, 04 July 1999, L/Nk Male's unit was called out to conduct cordon & search operations in the same sector following reports of increased insurgent activity. L/Nk Male was detailed to defuse an improvised explosive device (IED) when fate struck. Something went wrong and the explosion took away another soldier, killed in the line of duty. The 28 RR saw action in the Mushkoh Pandrass sector. Especially during the period after the Tiger Hill fell, when the Mushkoh sub-sector became the focus of attention. Lance Naik Sukhjeet Singh, was part of an Army column when he was seriously wounded in enemy shelling but did not leave his position and refused to be evacuated till his last breath. Rifleman Pradeep Kumar of the same unit laid down his life on 09 July 1999.

The next day, the unit lost Rifleman Jagjit Singh to artillery shelling. After Kargil all the RR units involved reverted back to the valley. It needs to be pointed out that the RR units who held the fort in Jammu & Kashmir while the army fought it out in Kargil were the unsung heroes of the battle. Keeping the road and lines of communications open, fighting the terrorists, taking land mine blasts, that was their job. During this period, 26 RR units were deployed in the valley and three to guard the Banihal/ Jawahar tunnel area. The sectors in the not so important areas - like Sector 9 in Kisthwar- were withdrawn and the focus was on the lines of communication and the valley. The withdrawal of the 58 army units from the CI grid, and the changes that were made, really disturbed it and stirred things up again.

They had been replaced by 14 CPRF and 6 BSF battalions. However the replacements were new to the area and also did not make up for the numbers withdrawn. A vast area like Doda for example had to do with only 8 units during Kargil from the 1996 peak of 20 units. Kisthwar and Banderwah area which was under Sector 9 was handed over to the CRPF. The end result of all this was that the insurgents had a field day. Despite the army's extreme reluctance it had to redeploy its units for CI duty. In fact even the 6 Mountain Division - inducted into the Valley during the Kargil conflict - had to be deployed on mopping-up operations in the higher reaches of north and south Kashmir. The setback was estimated to take at least a year to rectify. Keeping this in mind, after the Kargil battle, the Government decided to immediately raise 12 more battalions of the RR and 20 more battalions of the Assam Rifles. Also sanctioned were the force headquarters Kilo and Romeo.

Awards

Award	Number
Ashoka Chakra	1
Kirti Chakra,	10
Shaurya Chakra	53
Sena Medals	300

Modernization

Rashtriya Rifles has the latest weapons and equipments to fight insurgency but still it endeavour to perform better.

REFERENCES

Annual Report 2004-2005, Ministry of Home Affairs, Government of India.

Annual Report 2005-2006, Ministry of Home Affairs, Government of India.

Ashok Krishna: Examples of Learning in Counter-Insurgency, IDSA, 2000.

Bamzai, Prithvi Nath Kaul: Kashmir and Power Politics: From Lake Success to Tashkent, Metropolitan Book Co., Delhi, 1966.

Bose, Sumantra: The Kashmir Challenge, Sage, New Delhi, 1997.

Col Ahrnam Singh. Doda: Insurgency in the Wilderness. Lancer, New Delhi 1999.

Daily Pioneer, 15 Mar., 2004.

Frontier India Defence & Strategic News Service, May 2008.

General K. V. Krishna Rao: Prepare or Perish - A Study of National Security, Lancer, 1991.

Government of India, India 2004 - A Reference Manual.

Harold Wilensky: Organizational Intelligence, Basic Books, New York, 1967.

Indian Defence Review, June 1999.

Indian Express, Aug. 12, 1997.

Indian Express, Dec. 16, 1997.

Indian Express, Dec. 06, 1999.

Indian Express, July 06, 1999.

Indian Express, May 01, 2000.

Indian Express, May 18, 1999.

Baranwal J.: The Military Yearbook 1992-1993, New Delhi: Guide Publications.

Baranwal J.: The Military Yearbook 1993-1994, New Delhi: Guide Publications.

Jacob, JRF (Lt. Gen), IDR, The Defence scene and the budget: An appraisal.

Joshi, Manoj: The lost rebellion.

Ken Conboy: Elite Forces of India and Pakistan, Osprey, 1992.

Malhotra, V.P.: Encyclopaedia of Indian Army, Anmol, New Delhi 2006.

Ministry of Defence.

Ministry of Home Affairs.

Nayar K. K. (Vice Admiral): Amar Jawan - A Book of Remembrance, India Book House.

Nayar K. K. (Vice Admiral): Amar Jawan - A Book of Remembrance, India Book House.

New India Press, Mar. 15, 2004

Singh, Harjeet (Col.), Doda: An insurgency in the Wilderness.

The Tribune, Aug. 20, 1998.

Times of India, Aug. 11, 1999.

PART – IV
PARAMILITARY FORCES UNDER PRIME MINISTER OFFICE

10

National Security Guards

"One for All, All for One"

Introduction

The National Security Guards (NSG) were raised as a Federal Contingency force in the Eighties to fight the increasing menace of terrorism that was evident in the aftermath of Operation Bluestar in Punjab. That there was resistance to the idea within and outside the establishment to such a force is evident; the rationale being given that there already were forces that could be used for such forces.

The para-commandos and the Navy Commandos (Marcos) are already trained and equipped to perform such missions. The NSG was established under the National Security Guard Act of 1986. The NSG provides security to VIP's, conducts anti-sabotage checks, and is responsible for neutralizing terrorist threats to vital installations. Its missions include engaging terrorists in specific situations, responding to piracy in the air and on the land, and rescuing hostages in kidnap situations.

History

Need: In 1980s, terrorism in Punjab was at its peak. There was a need for an elite force whose main function was to check terrorism. Cabinet Secretariat passed a resolution to bring such a force into existence. Thus NSG was raised.

Origin: The National Security Guard was set up in 1984 as a Federal Contingency Deployment Force to tackle all facets of terrorism in the country. Thus the primary role of this Force is to combat terrorism in whatever form it may assume in areas where activity of terrorists assumes serious proportions, and the State Police and other Central Police Forces cannot cope up with the situation. The National Security Guard is a Force specially equipped and trained to deal with specific situations and has therefore, to be used only in exceptional situations. The Force is not designed to supplant the functions of the State Police Forces or other Paramilitary Forces of the Union of India.

The NSG was modelled on the pattern of the SAS of the UK and GSG-9 of Germany. It is a task-oriented force and has two complementary elements in the form of the Special Action Group (SAG) comprising Army personnel and the Special Ranger Groups (SRG), comprising personnel drawn from the Central Paramilitary Forces/State Police force. All the personnel are on deputation from other forces.

Key Dates in History

12 May 1988	Assault on the Golden Temple during Operation Black Thunder II
25 April 1994	Rescue of hijacked plane Indian Airlines Boeing 737 during Operation Ashwamedh
Oct. 1998	Major combat missions in Jammu and Kashmir
15 July 1999	Rescue of 12 hostages held by armed Islamic terrorists who had stormed an apartment complex in Kashmir and killed 4 people
25 Sept. 2002	Operation Vajra Shakti to free hostages held by Islamic terrorists who had killed 26 worshippers at the Akshardham temple in Ahmedabad, Gujarat.

Present Scenario

Personnel Strength: The NSG has a total personnel strength of about 14, 500. NSG is headed by an officer of rank of Director General.

NSG is divided into two groups; the Special Action Group (SAG) and the Special Rangers Group (SRG). The SAG, which comprises 54%

of the force, is the elite, offensive wing with members drawn from the Indian Army.

The SRG, on the other hand, has members on deputation from central police organizations like the Border Security Force (BSF), the Central Reserve Police Force (CRPF), the Indo-Tibetan Border Police (ITBP) and the Rapid Action Force (RAF). The primary function of the SRG is to play a supportive role to the SAF, especially in isolating target areas.

The smallest combat unit in the NSG's counter-terrorist ops is a hit which comprises of five members - two pairs, or partners and a technical support member. Four hits make a team which is under the command of a Captain. The number of hits used for an intervention job depends on its complexity and the magnitude of the operation. In hostage rescue situations, a team of 50 to 90 NSG personnel and an IL-76MD strategic transport aircraft to transport them, are stationed on alert at New Delhi's Palam AFS and are ready to deploy within 30 minutes of being informed.

Base: The NSG Training Centre is a Centre of Excellence and the National Bomb Data Centre holds international conferences. Both are located at Manesar in Haryana. The NSG Headquarters Exchange is located at Mehramnagar, Palam.

National Bomb Data Centre: National Bomb Data Centre is managed by NSG and is located at Manesar in Haryana. to fight against the ever increasing threat of IEDs, the NSG, like many other countries, has initiated the establishment of the National Bomb Data Centre (NBDC) so that the security agencies ensure close co-ordination and active support to each other to battle the menace of IED, in a joint platform.

NBDC was established at NSG, Manesar in March 2000 to create a data bank of IED related bombing incidents in India. For the NBDC to grow further we would like to call upon all the security agencies to join forces in carrying out active interaction with us so as to fight the global peril of IEDs and save the innocent victims from the ugly designs of perpetrators of terrorism.

The NBDC strives to achieve its aim by accomplishing the following tasks:

- Collect, collate, analyse and evaluate all terrorist-bombing activities reported in the country.
- Disseminate relevant information to concerned law enforcement agencies.

- Research and develop concepts for dealing with terrorist bomb threat situations.
- Remain abreast with latest technologies in the field and keep update of terrorist bombing in India and abroad.
- Compile and disseminate periodic statistical data and analytical information on terrorist bombing activities.
- Carry out research and innovation in the field of bomb disposal equipment to suit local needs and conditions.

Organizational Structure

- Director General
- Group Commander
- Squadron Commander
- Team Commander
- Inspector
- Sub-Inspector
- Head Constable
- Constable
- Sepoy

Chiefs of SPG

- Sh R. T. Nagrani (17.08.84 to 25.09.86)
- Sh M. C. Mishra (25.09.86 to 28.01.87)
- Sh K. L. Watts (28.01.87 to 31.12.87)
- Sh S. D. Pandey (31.12.87 to 31.03.88)
- Sh H. P. Bhatnagar (31.03.88 to 15.04.88)
- Sh V. P. Marwah (15.04.88 to 19.01.90)
- Sh D. V. L. N. Ramakrishna Rao (22.02.90 to 14.05.90)
  Dr S. Subramanian (14.05.90 to 31.01.92)
- Sh R. K. Wadehra (31.01.92 to 19.05.92)
- Sh B. J. S. Sial (19.05.92 to 31.07.93)
- Sh D. K. Arya (31.07.93 to 28.04.94)
- Sh A. K. Tandon (28.04.94 to 19.03.97)
- Sh R. D. Tyagi (19.03.97 to 31.10.97)

- Sh G. S. Pandher (31.10.97 to 30.04.98)
- Sh T. R. Kakkar (06.05.98 to 30.06.99)
- Sh Nikhil Kumar (01.07.99 to 31.07.01)
- Sh Gurbachan Jagat (01.08.01 to 20.08.01)
- Dr R. Rajagopalan (20.08.01 to 12.01.02)
- Sh S. C. Chaube (13.01.02 to 12.02.02)
- Sh R. S. Mooshahary (13.02.02 to 07.02.05)
- Sh A. K. Mitra (07.02.05 to 27.02.06)
- Dr G. S. Rajagopal (01.03.06 to 11.08.06)
- Sh Jyoti Krishan Dutt (11.08.06 Till Date)

Duties and Functions

Motto: NSG motto is ***"One for All, All for One"***

Maxim: Neutralization of terrorist threats.

- Handling hijacking situations in air and on land.
- Bomb disposal (search, detection and neutralisation of IEDs).
- PBI (Post Blast Investigation).
- Engaging and neutralizing terrorists in specific situations.
- Rescue of hostages.

Description of Duties: The force has seen operations in several places and differing environments. It has been involved in all types of internal security missions, including anti-hijack, counter-terrorism and other missions in strike mode. It has also been deployed as intelligence gatherers and pathfinders in places like J&K. And the NSG's most public face has been its utilization for providing VIP security. The NSG has patterned VIP security on the same lines as protection of the Prime Minister by the Special Protection Group. The initial aim was to raise a force on the lines of the German GSG-9, but given India's size and population it was realized that a force structure that could cater to India specific requirements was necessary. In fact, it was thought prudent to have three different regional units for local action, rather than have a central force that could be transported to the trouble spots as and when required.

This never happened and the NSG remained a Delhi-centric organization. The army-paramilitary mix of the force right from the start was aimed at bringing together the best of both worlds. To this end, the idea of the SAG forming the striking arm while the SRG performed associated, but equally important tasks like path-finding, intelligence gathering, logistics and so on, made eminent sense. From all appearances today, the NSG has not evolved into the cohesive fighting force as envisaged.

The force has developed over a period of time a distinctly police orientation and lacks a unified approach to combating terrorism. This is both an internal organizational problem as well as one of command and control. It may be worthwhile studying the second aspect first. The NSG as a counter-terrorism force was meant to act under the administrative and operational control of the Cabinet Secretariat. Subsequently, the elitism of the force being resented by others led to the government moving it under the Home Ministry and it became just another Paramilitary Force, which it was never meant to be. The chain of command for a counter-terrorist organization has to be clear and precise.

It is apparent the NSG cannot fight the counter-terrorist war of the next generation with weapons of the last generation. There is a certain disinclination within the organization to work towards cohesiveness. The cause of this lies in putting the SRG on VIP security duties. This bifurcation of functions takes away the force, especially the SRG from the essential task it is trained to do such as acting as a back up for the SAG.

The problem of the SRG not being able to conduct support operations has an impact on the functioning of the SAG also. In recent operations, this has hampered the pace of work simply because the SAG has a command and control problem with other police forces and is unable to better coordinate its strike mission. In circumstances where the NSG is dependent on other forces for intelligence and back-up support it is difficult for them to coordinate. This fact is well illustrated by the NSG Force decision to withdraw from the hunt for sandalwood smuggler, Veerapan. NSG only conducted the final assault but did not get involved in jungle combing, a task which the SRG should have been performing.

The suggestion by the force commanders that intelligence should be provided by the STF and local police is also an indicator that the force does not have its own intelligence assets, even though there is an officer of DIG rank looking after intelligence. But these are problems of a long-term and require analysis within the force itself. The core of the problem is the attitude of the national security establishment to the employment of Special Forces. By putting it under the head of a Paramilitary Force, the very nature, orientation and character of the force has changed. The other problem is the lack of integral assets for a force of the NSG type, which is meant to possess rapid mobility, firepower and technology. All this has been evident for decades now, but government apathy has tended to compound matters. During the mobilization for the Akshardham operation, the NSG was stuck in Delhi's rush hour traffic for a couple of hours, making it difficult for it to get from the Manesar base to Palam Airport, where an IL-76MD is always on standby to fly them to wherever is needed. Similarly, an integral intelligence capability is essential for this force.

Whether at Amritsar, or in J&K, the NSG whether being independently used or in conjunction with other forces, intelligence gathering capability internally is of paramount importance. The question uppermost in the minds is how to change things now. It is possible. Within the given constraints, the government can undertake to do some things. Minimum requirements can be met and future needs studied. It can shift VIP security duties from the NSG to the SDG, a force drawn from the CRPF, which is providing perimeter and other security to the Indian Prime Minister and other former Prime Ministers. Since there are two SAGs it stands to reason that at least two SRGs are required for each SAG, for support operations. Thus one more SRG should be raised.

Given India's size it makes sense to have integrated assets in place within the existing framework of the organization. If one wants to change things a bit and have different units co-located for regional operations, like in J&K or the north-east, then dramatic changes will be necessary. But since the NSG is training police units to perform counter-terrorists missions, like the Special Operations Group (SOG) in J&K, it seems more useful to improve inter-force communication so that the NSG can be on hand in quick time, if necessary.

Acts, Rules & Regulations

The SPG is governed by The National Security Guard Act, 1986. The Act consists 140 sections in all.

- Section 1: Short title and commencement
- Section 2: Definitions
- Section 3: Persons subject to this Act
- Section 4: Constitution of the Security Guard
- Section 5: Control, direction, etc

- Section 6: Liability for service outside India
- Section 7: Resignation and withdrawal from the post
- Section 8: Tenure of service under the Act
- Section 9: Termination of service by Central Government
- Section 10: Dismissal, removal or reduction by the Director-General and by other officers
- Section 11: Certificate of termination of service
- Section 12: Restrictions respecting right to form associations, freedom of speech, etc
- Section 13: Remedy of aggrieved persons other than officers
- Section 14: Remedy of aggrieved officers
- Section 15: Offences in relation to the terrorists and other persons in arms against the Union and punishable with death
- Section 16: Offence punishable more severely on active duty than at other times
- Section 17: Mutiny
- Section 18: Desertion and aiding desertion
- Section 19: Absence without leave
- Section 20: Striking or threatening superior officer
- Section 21: Disobedience to superior officer
- Section 22: Assault and obstruction
- Section 23: Certain forms of disgraceful conduct
- Section 24: Ill-treating a subordinate
- Section 25: Drunkenness
- Section 26: Permitting escape of person in custody
- Section 27: Irregularity in connection with arrest or confinement
- Section 28: Escape from custody
- Section 29: Offences in respect of property
- Section 30: Extortion and exaction
- Section 31: Making away with equipment
- Section 32: Injury to property
- Section 33: False accusations

- Section 34: Falsifying official documents and false declarations
- Section 35: False declaration on appointment
- Section 36: Offences relating to Security Guard Court
- Section 37: False evidence
- Section 38: Unlawful detention of pay
- Section 39: Unbecoming conduct
- Section 40: Violation of good order and discipline
- Section 41: Miscellaneous offences
- Section 42: Attempt
- Section 43: Abetment of offences that have been committed
- Section 44: Abetment of offences that have not been committed
- Section 45: Civil offences
- Section 46: Civil offences not triable by a Security Guard Court
- Section 47: Punishments awardable by Security Guard Courts
- Section 48: Alternative punishments awardable by Security Guard Courts
- Section 49: Combination of punishments
- Section 50: Punishments otherwise than by Security Guard Courts
- Section 51: Minor punishments
- Section 52: Limit of punishments under Section 51
- Section 53: Punishment of officers of or below the rank of Squadron Commanders by officers not below the rank of Inspectors-General
- Section 54: Punishment of persons of the rank of Assistant Commander
- Section 55: Custody of offenders
- Section 56: Duty of Commander in regard to detention
- Section 57: Interval between committal and trial
- Section 58: Arrest by civil authority
- Section 59: Capture of deserters
- Section 60: Inquiry into absence without leave
- Section 61: Kinds of Security Guard Courts

- Section 62: Power to convene a General Security Guard Court
- Section 63: Power to convene a Petty Security Guard Court
- Section 64: Contents of warrants issued under sections 62 and 63
- Section 65: Composition of General Security Guard Court
- Section 66: Composition of a Petty Security Guard Court
- Section 67: Summary Security Guard Court
- Section 68: Dissolution of a Security Guard Court
- Section 69: Powers of a General Security Guard Court
- Section 70: Powers of a Petty Security Guard Court
- Section 71: Powers of a summary Security Guard Court
- Section 72: Prohibition of second trial
- Section 73: Period of limitation for trial
- Section 74: Trial etc., of offender who ceases to be subject to this Act
- Section 75: Application of Act during term of sentence
- Section 76: Place of trial
- Section 77: Choice between Criminal Court and Security Guard Court
- Section 78: Power of Criminal Court to require delivery of offender
- Section 79: Presiding Officer
- Section 80: Judge Attorneys, etc
- Section 81: Challenges
- Section 82: Oaths of members, Judge Attorney and witness
- Section 83: Voting by members
- Section 84: General rule as to evidence
- Section 85: Judicial notice
- Section 86: Summoning witnesses
- Section 87: Documents exempted from production
- Section 88: Commissions for examination of witnesses
- Section 89: Examination of witness on commission
- Section 90: Conviction of offence not charged

- Section 91: Presumption as to signatures
- Section 92: Appointment paper
- Section 93: Presumption as to certain documents
- Section 94: Reference by accused to Government officer
- Section 95: Evidence of previous convictions and general character
- Section 96: Lunacy of accused
- Section 97: Subsequent fitness of lunatic accused for trial
- Section 98: Transmission to Central Government of orders under Section 97
- Section 99: Release of lunatic accused
- Section 100: Delivery of lunatic accused to relatives
- Section 101: Order for custody and disposal of property pending trial
- Section 102: Order for disposal of property regarding which offence is committed
- Section 103: Powers of Security Guard Court in relation to proceedings under the Act
- Section 104: Finding and sentence not valid, unless confirmed
- Section 105: Power to confirm finding and sentence of General Security Guard Court
- Section 106: Power to confirm finding and sentence of Petty Security Guard Court
- Section 107: Limitation of powers of confirming authority
- Section 108: Power of confirming authority to mitigate, remit or commute sentences
- Section 109: Revision of finding or sentence
- Section 110: Finding and sentence of a Summary Security Guard Court
- Section 111: Transmission of proceedings of Summary Security Guard Court
- Section 112: Alteration of finding or sentence in certain cases
- Section 113: Remedy against order, finding or sentence of Security Guard Court

- Section 114: Annulment of proceedings
- Section 115: Form of sentence of death
- Section 116: Commencement of sentence of imprisonment
- Section 117: Execution of sentence of imprisonment
- Section 118: Temporary custody of offender
- Section 119: Execution of sentence of imprisonment in special cases
- Section 120: Conveyance of prisoner from place to place
- Section 121: Communication of certain orders to prison officers
- Section 122: Execution of sentence of fine
- Section 123: Informality or error in the order or warrant
- Section 124: Pardon and remission
- Section 125: Cancellation of conditional pardon, release on parole or remission
- Section 126: Suspension of sentence of imprisonment
- Section 127: Orders pending suspension
- Section 128: Release on suspension
- Section 129: Computation of period of suspension
- Section 130: Order after suspension
- Section 131: Reconsideration of case after suspension
- Section 132: Fresh sentence after suspension
- Section 133: Scope of power of suspension
- Section 134: Effect of suspension and remission on dismissal
- Section 135: Rank Structure
- Section 136: Deductions from pay and allowances
- Section 137: Powers and duties conferrable and imposable on members of the Security Guard
- Section 138: Protection for acts of members of the Security Guard
- Section 139: Power to make rules
- Section 140: Provisions as to existing National Security Guard

Weapons and Equipments

9 mm Uzi sub-machine gun, Heckler & Koch family of 9 mm sub-machine guns, 7.62mm PSG-1 sniper weapon, Heckler & Koch 512 12-gauge shotgun, Glock 17 and Sig Sauer P226 9mm pistols. They are also armed with state-of-the-art surveillance gadgets and other sophisticated equipment.

Recruitment

Ever since its foundation SPG has comprised hundred per cent deputationists from other forces.

Training: The basic training period at the organization's training centre at Manesar, lasts 90 days. Only those who complete the entire course successfully are inducted into the NSG and given further specialised training. The probation peroid saps energy from toughest of recruits and the drop out rate is 50 - 70%. For starters there is a 26-item, 780-metre obstacle course, with a qualifying time of 18 minutes. If a person completes the course in 25 minutes, he is deemed fit. The best do it in less than nine minutes. The obstacles have to do with heights, horizontal gaps and vertical scaling and are difficult to tackle in sequence. As if this is not enough, there's a target shooting session at the end of the obstacle course meant to test the aspirants' performance under severe stress and exhaustion. Those who complete this course are recruited to the unit and sent for advanced training. Some operators are sent to Israel for advanced training. Though it is not known exactly what training they receive, it could probably be the CT/HRT course with Unit 707. The unit also cooperates with Israel's Shabach, for training in VIP protection.

Training Centre: It was Raised in 1985 at Parade Ground, Delhi Cantt by Brig SK

Nanda, the Training Centre is presently located in the salubrious surroundings of Manesar at the foothills of the Aravalis. It is equipped with a state-of-the-art infrastructure and has the best available training facilities in the country. The Training Centre trains almost 3000 personnel per annum from the Defence Forces, Central Police Forces, State Police and Friendly Foreign Countries. Its primary role is to conduct commando courses for induction into NSG (Both Army and Central Police

Forces) and secondary role is to impart training to personnel from Central Police Organization, Defence Forces, State Police and Friendly Foreign Countries in the following disciplines:

- Counter Terrorist Operations
- VIP Security
- Bomb Disposal
- Anti – extremism

Famous Operations

Operation Black Thunder I: In April 1986, 80 officers, 180 JCOs and 1, 500 NSG commandos participate in clearing the Golden Temple in Operation Black Thunder I. Temple cleared and handed over to Punjab Police on 01 May 1986. No casualties on either side.

Operation Black Hawk: In January 1988, The NSG conducted Op Black Hawk, a heliborne operation in the Mand area of Punjab. In this operation two terrorists were killed and one 7.62 mm rifle was recovered.

Operation Black Thunder II: In May 1988, 500 NSG commandos surround the Golden Temple for yet another assault, in Operation Black Thunder II. Sniper teams armed with Heckler & Koch PSG-1 rifles with night scope took up positions, including atop a 300-foot water tower. While commandos from the 51 SAG divided into assault squadrons, the SRG were used to seal off the area around the temple and for tactical support. In the three-day operation between 15-18 May 1988, the NSG cleared the temple. 30 terrorists were killed, and 217 surrendered. In mid-1990s, a NSG battalion was again deployed in Punjab to confront the Sikh rioters. There they began training the Punjab Police in counter-terrorism.

OperationCactus: In November 1988, 600 commandos of the NSG were mobilized for Op. Cactus, the airborne operation to repulse the coup in Maldives. But subsequently, they were tasked for rescue mission of hostages on board MV Progress Light.

Operation Mouse Trap: In August 1989, Op Mouse Trap was mobilized in the Tarn Taran district of Punjab, in conjunction with Punjab Police and other security forces. NSG was able to demonstrate that it was possible to achieve area dominance at night, if the strategy and tactics were right.

Operation Ani Ben: In January 1991, The NSG was involved in Operation Ani Ben, on CI tasks in Baroda, (Gujarat) where Punjab terrorists were holed up inside a house. Two terrorists were killed and two AK-47s were recovered.

December 1987: The NSG was airlifted to Andhra Pradesh after Naxalites took hostage six IAS officers on 27 December 1987, while they were returning from a tribal welfare meeting at Pulimatu. The Naxalites wanted the release of eight of their comrades in jail. The state government initially took a tough stand, but later released all eight internees and the NSG did not have a role to play.

November 1990: NSG task force flown to Kolkata to rescue hostages of a Thai airbus by Burmese students.

July- September 1991: NSG employed along with SIT in search and strike missions after the assassination of Rajiv Gandhi.

November-December 1992: 150 commandos were deployed at Ayodhya during the Ram Janambhoomi and Babri Masjid crisis.

March 1993: 52 SAG mobilised and moved to Adampur for rescue of hostages of Indian Airlines Flight IC 486.

April 1993: NSG Commandos storm a hijacked Indian Airlines Boeing 737 with 141 passengers onboard at Amritsar airport during Operation Ashwamedh. The hijacker, Mohammed Yousuf Shah, is killed before he can react and no hostages are harmed.

October-November 1993: Operations at Hazratbal Shrine in Srinagar. A task force of 20 officers, and 180 commandos was moved on 27 October 1993 to Srinagar. The operation was called off after final preparations had been made.

October 1998: As part of the implementation of the Union Home Ministry's decision to conduct pro-active strikes against militants, commando teams supported by IAF Mi-25/35 helicopter gun-ships began striking at terrorist groups deep inside the mountains and forests of Kashmir. After helicopter reconnaissance were conducted to pinpoint the militants, the commandos - comprising NSG and Rashtriya Rifles personnel - were para-dropped, along with supplies, into the area to hunt the militants. They had to rely on these supplies and their ability to live off the land until replenishment every fortnight or so. These missions are possibly ongoing.

July 1999: NSG commandos end a 30-hour standoff by killing 2 terrorists and rescuing all 12 hostages unharmed in J&K. The terrorists had attacked a BSF campus near Srinagar, killed 3 officers and the wife of another. The 12 hostages were kept locked in a room.

August 1999: After interrogating three captured terrorists, the Delhi Police Crime branch confirmed that two more terrorists were hiding in a one-storied house in Rudrapur, Uttar Pradesh. Since the terrorists were considered armed and dangerous (their colleagues were arrested with 100+ pounds of RDX), the Delhi Police sought assistance from the NSG. A 16-man team arrived at the house at 4:45 a. m. They began their assault at 5:30 a. m., before first light. The first militant managed to fire at the commandos with a pistol he kept by his bedside, but was killed an instant later. The second terrorist was shot before he had a chance to fire and died 40 minutes later. No NSG personnel were injured.

December 1999: Terrorists hijack Indian Airlines flight IC814 from Nepal, and land in Amritsar, Punjab. Within minutes of landing, the Crisis Management Group (CMG), which authorizes the use of the NSG, is informed. But the CMG wastes precious hours and by the time the go-ahead is issued, it is too late. On the other hand, the NSG team on alert was elsewhere and no other team was raised during the delay. The hijacked plane took off before the NSG reached Amritsar Airport. The plane lands in Kandahar, Afghanistan where one hostage was killed. Finally, the Indian Government agrees to the terrorists' demands to release three jailed terrorists. The hostages are released and the terrorists escape to Pakistan.

February 2000: Following the Flight IC 814 fiasco, the Indian Government decided to implement an Air Marshal programme. At least two NSG operators will be present on flights over select routes. These operators will be armed with weapons firing lethal, but low-velocity, fragmentation rounds to minimize danger to the passengers and prevent penetration of the aircraft. Another decision taken was to deploy NSG teams permanently at eight sensitive airports around the country, especially those bordering Pakistan and the North-East. This decision will cut short reaction times for the NSG and eliminate hassles involved in flying the teams to the hijack site. It is not known if this plan has been put into action.

September 2002: SAG commandos fly to the Karnataka state in India, in an effort to catch sandalwood smuggler and forest brigand Veerappan, in the wake of kidnapping of a former minister of the state cabinet, Nagappa. They pull out after suggesting that intelligence for the operation was inadequate. A small team is left behind to help, the hostage is eventually killed in December 2002.

October 2002: Two terrorists attack Akshardham temple complex in Gujarat. NSG flies in, delayed by traffic in Delhi. They carry out assaults in which one commando is killed and another one is seriously injured. But by morning the two terrorists are killed and the operation successfully completed. Op Vajrashakti.

December 2002: Terrorists attack the Raghunath temple in Jammu. NSG ready to be flown out but called back at the last minute.

Awards

Kirti Chakra,	4
Shaurya Chakra	2
Sena Medals	24

Modernization

In the prevailing internal security environment, India should expect many more terrorist strikes wherein more and more sophisticated weapons will be used. The aid of technology will be taken to force new situations on nations. The NSG is ready and on hand to counter such strikes in the future. The future suggests that the NSG should enquire into the technological and psychological aspects of terrorist actions and plan for possible counter options. It is apparent the NSG cannot fight the counter-terrorist war of the next generation with weapons of the last generation. There is a certain disinclination within the organization to work towards cohesiveness. The cause of this lies in putting the SRG on VIP security duties. This bifurcation of functions takes away the force, especially the SRG from the essential task it is trained to do such as acting as a back up for the SAG.

REFERENCES

Anil K. Jaggia and Saurabh Shukla, IC814 Hijacked: The Inside Story, Roli Books, 2000.

Asian Military Review, Oct. 1999.

Bhagwat Vishnu, Admiral (Retd): Betrayal of the Defence Forces, Manas Publications, New Delhi, 2001.

Central Police Forces in India: Bureau of Police Research & Development, New Delhi.

Bhisam H. Pal.: Central Police Forces in India, Bureau of Police Research & Development, New Delhi.

Hindustan Times, April 20, 2003.

Hindustan Times, Jan. 16, 2004.

India Today, Aug. 15, 1984.

India Today, June 30, 1984.

Indian Defence Review, Volume 16 (5) 2002.

Indian Defence Review, Jan.-Mar 1998.

Indian Defence Review, New Delhi, Jan.-March 2004.

Indian Defence Review, New Delhi, July-Sep. 2000.

Indian Defence Review, Jan., 1993.

Indian Defence Review, Vol. 8 (3), Oct. 1993.

Jack Kelley: Covert Troops Fight Shadow War Off-camera, USA Today, April 7, 2003.

Jackson A.V. William: History of India, Asia Education Services, New Delhi, Reprint 1987.

Lt Gen YN Sharma: Restructuring of the Armed Forces, Defence Management.

Lt. Gen. V. K. Nayyar: Internal Security: Some Issues and Aspects. Indian Defence Review. Jan. 1993.

Naipaul VS: India: A Wounded Civilisation, Penguin Books, England, 1977.

National Security Guards: Organization, Operations and Future Orientations, Indian Defence Review, Vol. 8 (3), Oct. 1993.

Nirmal Anjali: The Decisive Battles of Indian History, Pointer Publisher, Jaipur, 1999.

O'Hanlon Michael: Technological Change and the Future of Warfare, Brookings Institution Press, Washington DC 2000.

Omissi David: The Sepoy and the Raj - The Indian Army 1860-1940, Macmillan Press Ltd, London, 1994.

Operation Bluestar: The True Story by Maj. Gen. Kuldip Singh Brar (retd.).

Outlook, Nov. 04, 2002.

Outlook, Nov. 04, 2002.

Outlook, Nov. 04, 2002.

Outlook, Nov. 04, 2002.

Outlook, Nov. 08, 2004.

RAdm R Chopra: India's Maritime Interests and Offshore Developments, Seagull, Feb- Apr 2000.

Strategic Digest, Jul.-Dec. 1999.

Sundarji K (General): Of some consequences - A Soldier Remembers, Harper Collins, India, 2000.

The Hindu, Sep. 13, 2002.

The Hindu, Sep. 13, 2002.

The Pioneer, July 28, 2000

The Week, Dec. 28, 2003.

11

Special Frontier Force

"Bravery till Death"

Introduction

Near the end of the Sino-Indian war and towards the end of 1962, the Nehru administration ordered the raising of an elite guerrilla force composed of Tibetan refugees. Chushi Gangdruk leaders were contacted for recruitment of Khampas into this new unit. The leaders were delighted to hear of this new development and promptly agreed to it, for it was seen by them then as a means of maintaining Tibetan volunteers more formally and, moreover, a well-trained force might be of great use to Tibet in the future. A formation agreement was signed in 1962. The parties to this formation agreement were the Indian Intelligence Service (RAW), the CIA (for weaponry till 1972) and Chushi Gangdruk. Ironically, General Gonpo Tashi and Jago Namgyal Dorjee, two of the three top leaders charged and confined to Delhi in previous years for recruiting guerrillas for the Mustang base, were now to sign this three-party joint formation agreement on behalf of Chushi Gangdruk. Tibetans took main responsibility for recruiting, and an initial strength of 12, 000 men, mostly Khampas, were recruited at Chakrata, Dehradun, UP. Chushi Gangdruk sent two of the commanders to this new outfit to be political leaders inthe initial stage. Established under the direct supervision of the prime minister, the unit was named the Special Frontier Force. Its forces were trained and commanded by the Indian Army and the unit was meant to be air-dropped into Tibet in the event of another war in the Tibetan frontiers. Their main objective is the disruption of logistics and other tasks, including disruption of the enemy behind its lines.

The SFF never had a chance of being used in operations against China, but it was used against East Pakistan with the consent of His Holiness the Dalai Lama in 1971. About one-third of its full strength was developed adjacent to the Chittagong Hill Tracts as Mukti Bahini. They captured many towns and garrisons in the Chittagong Hill Tracts in continuous fighting of about one month. When East Pakistan was liberated and the cease-fire was declared on December 17, 1971, casualties suffered by the SFF were 190 wounded and 56 killed, including political leader Gyato Dhondup, one of the two commanders sent by Chushi Gangdrug, who was shot by snipers. The Indian government gave awards to 580 members of the force for their active involvement and bravery in the battles. The contribution made by Establishment 22 in liberating East Pakistan was great and the price paid by the force was also high.

The major functions of SFF in the present day scenario are Counter-terrorism, Intelligence Gathering, Combat Air Control, Close Protection and Training Foreign Military

History

Need: After the Sino-Indian war and towards the end of 1962, after much trying by Intelligence Bureau (IB), the Gobernment ordered the formation of an elite commando unit and specialized mountain divisions primarily composed of Tibetan resistance fighters. Chushi Gangdruk leaders were contacted for recruitment of Khampas into this new unit. An initial strength of 5000 men, mostly Khampas were recruited at its new Mountain Training Facility at Chakrata, Dehradun. Established under the direct supervision of the Prime Minister, the unit under the operational command of IB and later RAW, was designated the Special Frontier Force (SFF), and was primarily used for conducting clandestine intelligence gathering and commando operations along the Chinese Theatre.

Origin: Towards the end of 1962, after Indo-China war, the Govenment ordered the raising of an elite commando unit and specialized mountain divisions formed from Tibetan resistance fighters. It was estabiished under the direct supervision of the Prime Minister and under the operational command of IB and later RAW. It was designated as the Special Frontier Force (SFF).

Initial training was conducted by the CIA paramilitary officers and the Intelligence Bureau (IB) own special operations unit. In 1968 SFF with the help of the Aviation Research Centre which provided airlift facilities became fully airborne qualified and a dedicated mountain and jungle warfare unit. During this period the Indian Government also formed the Ladakh Scouts and the Nubra Guards Paramilitary Force on similar lines. SFF was later incorporated in the the Special Services Bureau (SSB) of RAW. The Special Frontier Force (SFF) was created on 14 November 1962, near the end of the Indo-China War. The Cabinet Secretariat had ordered the raising of an elite guerrilla force composed mainly of Tibetan refugees. Its main goal was to conduct covert operations behind Chinese lines in the event of another Indo-China war.

The first Inspector General of the SFF was a retired Indian Army Major General. The SFF made its home base at Chakrata, 100 km from the city of Dehra Dun. Chakrata was home to the large Tibetan refugee population and was a mountain town in the foothills of the Himalayas. Starting with a force of 12, 000 men, the SFF commenced six months of training in rock climbing and guerrilla warfare.

The Intelligence agencies from India and the US also helped in raising the force; namely CIA & RAW. The SFF's weapons were all provided by the US and consisted mainly of M-1, M-2 and M-3 machine guns. Heavy weapons were not provided. By late 1963, inter-service rivalry led to severe criticism by the Indian Army. To prove that the SFF's worth, the Inspector General sent 120 men from the SFF for a field exercise, codenamed Garuda with the Army. The exercise proved to be a dramatic success for the SFF and the Army was now less inclined to criticise the force. In 1964, the SFF led by the Inspector General, began its airborne training at Agra.

The SFF then began its own airborne training program at Sarasawan airbase near Saharanpur. By the late-1960s, the SFF was organized into six battalions for administrative purposes. Each battalion, consisting of six companies, was commanded by Tibetan who had a rank equivalent to a lieutenant colonel in the Army. A Tibetan major or captain commanded each company, which was the primary unit used in operations. Females also participated in the force and they were in the signal and medical companies. During this time, the SFF was never used against its intended enemy, China.

However, the unit did conduct limited cross-border reconnaissance operations, as well as highly classified raids to place sensors in the Himalayas to detect Chinese nuclear and missile tests. 1971 saw the SFF being used in major combat in the Indo-Pak war. Elements of the force were sent to Mizoram in late October. By November 1971, around 3000 SFF members were deployed next to the Chittagong Hill Tracts. With cross-border attacks becoming more frequent, the SFF was then ordered to attack the Chittagong Hill Tracts. For this operation, code-named 'Eagle', the SFF members were given Bulgarian AK-47s and US carbines. This operation saw the first Dapon, Tibetan equivalent of a Brigadier, to command part of the SFF task force.

With war right around the corner, the SFF was given several mission plans, including the destruction of the Kaptai Dam and other bridges.

The Inspector General urged that the SFF be used to capture Chittagong, but this was found not favourable, since SFF members did not have artillery or airlift support to conduct a mission of that magnitude. After three weeks of border fighting, the SFF divided its six battalions into three columns and moved into East Pakistan on 03 December 1971. After capturing several villages in the Chittagong Hill Tracts, the Tibetans were given mortars and recoilless rifles and also two Indian Air Force Mi-4 helicopters. With the Pakistani Lt. General A. A. K. Niazi signing the ceasefire on 17 December, the SFF had lost 56 men and nearly 190 wounded. The SFF was able to block a potential escape route for East Pakistani forces into Burma.

They also halted members of Pakistan's 97 Independent Brigade and 2 Commando Battalion in the Chittagong Hill Tracts. For their bravery and courage in battle, 580 SFF members were awarded cash prizes by the Indian Govt. In 1973, the original Inspector General of the SFF was replaced and in 1975 a new rule pertaining to the SFF was issued. This prohibited the SFF from being deployed within 10 km of the Indo-Chinese border This came about after several incidents in which SFF commandos had crossed the border and conducted unsanctioned cross-border operations. By the late 1970s, Indo-Chinese relations had eased up somewhat and the Indian Government was thinking twice about maintaining this force.

With the future of the SFF being uncertain, the force was soon given a new mission: counter-terrorism. Since the SFF consisted largely of

Tibetans, they were seen as an ideal counter-terrorist force since they were not directly related to India's communal politics. Thus in 1977, the Director General for Security dispatched 500 SFF commandos to Sarasawa for possible action against rioters during national elections. With the elections passing away without any major incidents, only 60 SFF commandos were retained for counter-terrorist duties. However, over 500 Army troops were sent to Sarasawa for counter-terrorist training.

They formed a elite new detachment, known as the Special Group and they fall under the command of the SFF Inspector General. Surprisingly, all Tibetans were removed from the Special Group and returned to Chakrata. Among the Tibetan members of the SFF, three commando battalions were raised for deployment around India; one of these battalions is normally stationed on the Siachen Glacier with the other Indian troops. The remaining SFF members were still trained for guerrilla operations in China. By early 1984, the SFF's elite Special Group became the primary counter-terrorist force in India. They participated in the assault on Golden Temple, but the mission was to prove faulty, due to a lack of intelligence on the militants' whereabouts in the temple locality.

The SFF was also used for VIP security in late 1984 around the Prime Minister following the assassination of Indira Gandhi. Currently, one SFF battalion is stationed in the Siachen Glacier. In 1985-1986 several SFF members were given bravery medals for their actions on the glacier. The current SFF force levels are around 10, 000 men. Battalions are still composed of six companies, each company consisting of 123 men. There is also a force of around 700 Gorkhas in the SFF at any given time. Training conducted at Chakrata, lasts six months and is similar to India Army training, with additional instruction in guerrilla tactics and rock-climbing.

Key Dates in History

14 Nov. 1962	Force was created
Nov.1964	ELNIT Operation with CIA in China
Oct. 1967	Operation with CIA in China to collect imformation
Nov. 1971	Operation Eagle started

Present Scenario

Personnel Strength: The current SFF force levels are around 10, 000 men.

SFF is headed by the Inspector General (IG) who works under the supervision of Director General (DG) Security, Research and Analysis Wing (R&AW) who reports directly to the Director of R&AW. The current SFF force levels are around 10, 000 men. Battalions have a strength of around 900, are composed of six companies each company consisting of 123 men. There is also a force of around 700 Gorkhas in the SFF at any given time. Transport is provided by the Indian Air Force's Sarasawa based 117 Helicopter Unit *Himalayan Dragons* which provides airlift capability with its HAL Advanced Light Helicopter (ALH) and Mi-17Sh Transport Helicopters. ARC also provides air surveillance facilities through the Chakrata Air Base near SFF Headquarters.

Base: Its Headquarters are located at Chakrata near Dehradun in India

Organizational Structure

- Inspector General
- Deputy Inspector General
- Commandant
- Deputy Commandant
- Assistant Commandant
- Subedar Major
- Inspector
- Sub-Inspector
- Asstt Sub Inspector
- Head Constable
- Constable
- Naik
- Lance Naik
- Sepoy

Duties and Functions

Motto: SFF motto is ***"Bravery till Death"***.

Maxim: Disruption of logistics and other tasks.

Disruption behind enemy lines.

To fight terrorism.

To protect at any cost.

Counter-terrorism: One Squadron is responsible for counter-terrorism duties, with a team in a constant state of alert. The four squadrons rotate through this role on a six-monthly basis. Special Group teams regularly conduct CT operations in the troubled Indian province of Kashmir against militants on specific intelligence inputs.

Special Group: The Director General (DG) Security, Research and Analysis Wing (RAW) in 1982 dispatched 500 SFF operatives along with over 500 Indian Army special forces to Sarasawa for Counter Terrorist training, it is also thought that the selected troopers thereafter were sent to Israel for highly specialized training. These men formed the nucleus of an ultra elite and highly classified new detachment, known as the Special Group.

The SFF Special Group is structured like the Special Air Service (SAS) Regiment, its Headquarters supported by an Intelligence and Planning wing, a Training wing and a specialist Signals Troop which is solely responsible for support operations. Having four Squadrons each made up of around 100 troopers, which are further divided into four Troops. Each Troop has a specialized role. The Special Group has a wide range of responsibilities, each requiring specific training and disciplines.

Intelligence Gathering: Long Range Reconnaissance Patrols or Pathfinders must be able to remain hidden under the nose of the enemy for days or weeks on an end. The outfit was trained to do this against the Chinese but in actual fact used the technique to great success in the Pakistan Administered Kashmir and the fields of the Northern state of Punjab.

Combat Air Control: With the emphasis on air power in modern warfare there comes a need for skilled combat air controllers, men on the ground calling in air strikes. There is usually a trooper specially trained to guide in attack aircraft for a strike, verbally or using Laser Designators. SFF Special Group troopers effectively demonstrated this capability during India's Kargil conflict with Pakistan in the summer of 1999.

Close Protection: The Special Group, along with the Special Protection Group (SPG) were the pioneers at close protection (CP) duties in India. Having developed many of the protocols themselves unique to the Indian Sub-Continent. Nowadays much of the VIP protection is the sole responsibility of the National Security Guards (NSG) and other specialized provincial units.

Internal Operations: SFF was used in combating communal riots in mid 70s and later was used in Operation Blue Star in 1984. It was also used briefly for VIP security in late 1984 around the Prime Minister following the assassination of Indira Gandhi. Later this role fell upon the Special Protection Group. In 1975 a new rule pertaining to the SFF was issued, this prohibited the SFF from being deployed to within 10 km of the Indo-Chinese border unless under explicit instructions.

This came about after several incidents in which SFF was found to be conducting unsanctioned cross border raids and intelligence operations. Currently, one SFF battalion is stationed in the Siachen Glacier. With warming of Indo-Chinese relations SFF has moved out of covert operation to various other fields like counter-terrorism etc.

Training Foreign Military: Over the years, the Special Group has shared their expertise with a few friendly nations like Maldives and Nepal, training their own special forces. The government also gets political benefits from such arrangements.

Acts, Rules & Regulations

SFF is governed by Indian Army rules and regulations.

Weapons and Equipments

SFF have access to almost any type of small arms or specialized weapons required for a particular mission. These range from Browning Hi-Power 9 mm pistols, AK-47/74s, 9 mm Uzis, 5.56 mm M-16 A2s, 9 mm H&K MP 5-A2/A3s and locally manufactured 7.62 mm SLR and 5.56 mm INSAS rifles. Sniper rifles like the semi-automatic H&K 7.62 mm PSG-1 and MSG-90, the SIG 7.62 mm SSG-2000 and the bolt-action Mauser SP 66/86SR are also used.

Recruitment

Officers: Officers are on deputation from other elite forces.

Other Ranks: Recruitment from other ranks is done from ethnic Tibetan community. Recruitment process is same as Indian Army.

Training: Most of the training is still conducted at Chakrata, lasting nine months and is similar to India Army training, with extensive additional courses on guerrilla tactics, mountain and jungle warfare. All commandos are parachute qualified after five jumps, with three refresher jumps every year.

SFF personnels are trained in four basic areas:

- Mountain: Experts in mountain and Arctic warfare, these men are trained to survive and fight in extreme conditions. Mountain troop's skills can be called on anywhere from the Siachen Glacier to the Himalayan ranges in the east. They are also known to have trained in the famed German Alpine Guides course at the Mountain Warfare School at Mittenwald and the High Altitude Warfare School at Gulmarg reaching proficiency levels that rivals the best climbers in the world.

- Amphibious: This Troop's combat divers are the outflts amphibious experts. In essence, it provides a comparable amphibious warfare capability to the SFF as the MARCOS provide to the Navy. While they have overlapping mission profiles, the Special Group clearly does not have as extensively maritime roles. There is close cooperation and cross-training between its amphibious troops and the MARCOS and a bitter rivalry exists between them.
- Air: Air Troop is the Special Group's free fall parachuting specialists, tasked with jumping behind enemy lines, either on their own missions or to pave the way for other squadron troops. Air Troop also employ less conventional forms of air insertion such as micro-lites and powered parachutes. For HALO/HAHO combat jumps skydivers use square-type RAM parachutes which are more maneuverable also allow for softer, controlled landings than the standard round chutes.
- Jungle warfare: Jungle operations are considered to be one of the toughest in the world and more men here fall to nature than the enemy. The Special Group's Jungle troopers are the masters in jungle craft, probably second only to the French Foreign Legion. They are skilled at carrying out deep interdiction and search and destroy operations for extremely extended periods of time.

Famous Operations

China: In 1964 intelligence reports kept indicating that China was preparing to test a nuclear bomb at its Lop Nor nuclear installation in Xinjiang. On October 16, 1964 China tested a nuclear weapon in Xinjiang. It was expected but not enough details were known. Later in November 1964, the CIA launched a U2 flight out of Aviation Research Centre (ARC)'s Charbatia Air Base in Orissa, but its return turned out to be a bit of a mishap.

The U2 overshot the runaway and got stuck in slushy ground caused by heavy rain in the monsoons. Getting it unstuck and out of India without being noticed by the Indian press, then even much more subject to leftist influences and hence antagonistic to the USA, was another clandestine operation. This gave all concerned quite a scare and it was decided to rely on other technical means. So CIA decided to launch an ELINT operation along with RAW and ARC to track China's nuclear tests and monitor its missile launches. The operation, in the garb of a mountaineering expedition to Nanda Devi involved celebrated Indian climber M S Kohli who along with operatives of Special Frontier Force and CIA most notably Jim Rhyne, a veteran STOL pilot, was to place a permanent ELINT device, a transceiver powered by a plutonium battery, that could detect and report data on future nuclear tests carried out by China.

The plan to install a snooping device was hatched far away in Washington D. C. in the offices of the National Geographic Society. Barry Bishop a photographer interested Gen. Curtis LeMay of the US Air Force with the idea. The actual efforts called for to place a permanent electronic intelligence (ELINT) device powered by a nuclear SNAP 19C power pack fuel cell. The first attempt to place this device on the Nanda Devi, by a Kohli led SFF team under the cover of a mountaineering expedition failed as the team had to retreat in the face of adverse conditions and left the device in a small unmarked mountain cave after having hauled the device to just short of the 25, 645 feet peak. When another Kohli led expedition returned the following year to recover the device, it was found to be missing. In the meantime the Chinese not only kept testing nuclear weapons at regularly intervals but also ballistic missiles.

The urgency to gather information was never greater. Another mission was launched in 1967 to place a similar device on the Nanda Kot. This mission was successful but a couple of years later another problem cropped up, snow would pile up over the antenna and render it blind. So Kohli and a SFF team was sent once again to bring it down, this time they retrieved it. In October 1967 the Chinese began testing an ICBM capable of reaching targets 6000 miles away. There was renewed urgency to find out more. So SFF mountaineers went off on one more mission in December 1969 to successfully place a gas powered device on an undisclosed mountain supposedly in Chinese controlled areas. But by the following year, the Americans had the first generation of the TRW spy satellites in place and did not have to rely on the old ELINT devices.

Indo-Pakistan War: SFF was extremely successful against Pakistan during the 1971 war on the Eastern Front. Elements of the force were sent to Mizoram in late October by November 1971, a 3000 man strong Brigade strength Task Force was deployed and conducted pre-emptive strike operations in support of the Indian army formations along the Chittagong Hill Tracts.

They trained the Bangladeshi Resistance, Mukti Bahini. For the Bangladeshi campaign, designated Operation Mountain Eagle, the SFF members were issued Bulgarian AK-47's and US carbines. SFF conducted several mission, including the destruction of the Kaptai Dam and other bridges. The Inspector General urged that the SFF be used to capture Chittagong, but this was found not favourable, since SFF members did not have artillery or airlift support to conduct a mission of that magnitude. After three weeks of border fighting, the SFF divided its six battalions into three subgroups and moved into East Pakistan on 03 December 1971, they were also loaned four Indian Air Force Mi-4 helicopters.

They also halted large portions of the Pakistani 97 Independent Brigade and the famed 2nd Commando Battalion from infiltrating into Burma by cutting off their rear defences and flanks. This operation saw the first Dapon, Tibetan equivalent of a Brigadier General to command part of the SFF Task Force. The Indian government gave awards to 580 operatives of the SFF for their meritorious conduct and valour during the Bangladeshi campaign.

Awards

Gallantry Awards

Shurya Chakra	03
Vishit Seva Medal	02
Sena Medal	05

Other Awards

Yudh Seva Medal	01
Jeevan Raksha Padak	01
Distinguished Service Medal	42

Modernization

SFF has started a dynamic transformation drive to give it more fire power. The upgrading plans of this Paramilitary Force include procuring state-of-the-art weapons and latest gadgets to boost operational efficiency of the troops.

REFERENCES

Common Wealth War Graves Commission.

Frontline, Feb. 2004.

Hindustan Times, Oct. 24, 1999.

Gupta S.C.: History of the Indian Air Force 1933-1945.

Institute for Defence Studies and Analyses, New Delhi, April 1999.

Kumar, Raj: Encyclopaedia of Military Systems in India, Commonwealth Publishers, New Delhi, 2004.

Lieutenant General K.S. Brar: Operation Blue Star - The Untold Story, UBSPD.

Major General Chand N. Das: Traditions and Customs of the Indian Armed Forces, Vision Books.

Major General Lachman Singh Lehl: Indian Sword Strikes in East Pakistan, Vikas Publishing.

Major General Sukhwant Singh: Defence of the Western Border, Vikas Publishing.

Major General Sukhwant Singh: The Liberation War, Vikas Publishing.

Major K.C. Praval: Indian Army After Independence, Lancer International.

Major K.C. Praval: The Red Eagles, Allied Publishing.

Marston, Daniel P. and Sundaram, Chandar S. A.: Military History of India and South Asia : From the East India Company to the Nuclear Era, Pentagon Press, New Delhi, 2008.

My Years with the IAF - Air Chief Marshal PC Lal, DFC.

Official History of the Indian Armed Forces in the 1971 War by Mr. SN Prasad.

Operation Vijay - Liberation of Goa by Mr. SN Prasad, Official History Cell.

Outlook, May 22, 2003.

Strategic Analysis, Aug. 2001.

Strategic Analysis, May 2001.

The Indian Express, Aug. 02, 2000.

The News, Aug. 09, 2000.

The Pioneer, July 24, 2000.

Thunder over Dacca - Air Vice Marshal BK Bishnoi AVSM VrC Bar, VAYU.

Unpublished Recollections of Serving and Retired Air Force personnel.

Vice Admiral K.K. Nayar, Amar Jawan - A Book of Remembrance, India Book House.

PART – V
PARAMILITARY FORCES UNDER MINISTRY OF RAILWAYS

12

Railway Protection Force

"Yasho Labhaswa"

Introduction

The maintenance and security of Railways, the vital artery of national communication and economic progress has been a major concern of the Government of India that goes back to the times when the Railway commenced their operations in India in 1854. The Railway Protection Force has emerged from a disorder of systems. In the beginning there were as many forms of its existence and as many modes of functioning as there were railway Companies in British India. For imparting the set-up a uniformity of working, the RPF Rules were enacted in 1959 and RPF Regulations published in 1966. In the same year, some limited powers to apprehend and prosecute offenders involved in railway property were conferred on the Force by enacting the Railway Property (Unlawful Possession) Act, 1966. Primarily RPF has been entrusted with responsibility of the safety of Railway property. But, while the provisions of RPF Act were soon found wanting for the maintenance of an effective and disciplined Force, the RPF Rules and Regulations too were found judicially unsound. The RPF Act, 1957 was accordingly modified by Parliament vide Act No.60 of 1985 on 20 September 1985 for the constitution and maintenance of the Force as an armed force of the Union. The main functions of RPF are:

- Escorting of passenger trains in vulnerable areas.
- Providing access control, regulation and general security on the platforms, in passenger areas and circulating areas.
- To remove any obstruction in the movement of railway property or passenger area; and
- To do any other act conducive to the better protection and security of railway property, passenger area and passenger.

History

Nevertheless, the genesis of such an endeavour can be traced back to 1854 when East Indian Railways employed certain staff designated as 'Police' to denote its own force by enacting the Police Act, 1861 and deployed a contingent for the security of the railway with the owner companies bearing their upkeep. The Railway Companies exercised full control over the Police Force.

The Policing System on Railways was split up in 1862, to form the Government Police, which was deployed for the benefit of the Private Railway Companies on payment of necessary charges. This paved the way for what would become the GRP in the years to come. Meanwhile, to contain the property thefts of the Company Railways, a Watch and Ward organization was formed in 1882 by deployment of chowkidars by each department. However increasing crime rate in early 1900s underlined the need for evolving a better security system by the Company Railways.

What was of extreme concern was the increasing theft of goods entrusted to the railways for carriage. The Railway Police Administration initially functioned under three different Systems viz at the District level, Provincial level and also as part of the Railway administration. The Indian Police Commission 1902-1903 in its recommendations favoured a provincial system of Railway Policing and also recommended close co-ordination between the Railway Police and the Railway Administration. Further it sought to separate Watch and Ward duties from the Railway Police.

On the recommendation of Railway Police Committee, 1872, Railway Police was organized into 'Govt. Police' (The precursor of GRP) for Law enforcement and Company Police (The precursor of RPF) for

Watch and Ward duties in Railways. The actual separation of duties came into effect in 1881. By 1882, as a result of formal division of the Police Force deployed on the railways into Government Police and Private (Companies) Police", the Railway Companies directly assumed the responsibility of protection and Security of their property as well as of the goods entrusted to them by public for carriage. For this, they appointed Chowkidars for various departments and placed them under control of their local departmental heads. With an increase in commercial traffic and consequential steep rise in the incidence of theft of goods entrusted to railways for carriage, the Chowkidar system was reorganized after the first World War onto Watch & Ward organization under a single superior officer designated as Superintendent, Watch & Ward.

Thus the Railway Police Administration functioned under three different systems viz the district system, as a part of District Police; the provincial system, for each province and the Railway Administration system, separate Railway Police for each Railway Administration inspite of recommendations of Indian Police commission, 1902-03. The provincial system found acceptance on recommendation of Railway Police Committee, 1921 and the present GRP came into existence. The 'Company Police' evolved into present RPF in 1957 passing through "Watch and Ward" phase from 1872-1954, and as "Railway Security Force" from 1954-1956. RPF was also given limited legal powers under Railway Stores (Unlawful Possession) Act.

Thus, for a full 100 years, the Force though being used for providing security to the vital artery of national communication and economic progress did not itself have any legislative status. Therefore the Govt. instituted a special enquiry through Director, Intelligence Bureau (Ministry of Home Affairs) who in his report in 1954 forcefully brought out the necessity of organising the Watch & Ward on a statutory basis. The Railway Board also appointed a Security Adviser to the Railway Board in July, 1953 to work out the details for the reorganization of the Watch & Ward department. It was decided in consultation with the Ministry of Home Affairs that there should be an integrated well organized force on the model of the Police with adequate supervisory staff specially trained to meet the particular aspects of crime that were relevant to Railway property and to work in close collaboration and act as a second line to the States Police with whom, under the Constitution, policing on Railways rested.

This led to the R. P. F. Bill for the better protection and security. It was only on 29 August 1957 that a Railway Protection Force Act was enacted by the Parliament and Railway Security Force was renamed as Railway Protection Force.

The RPF Rules were made on 10 September 1959 and RPF Regulations wee formulated in 1966. In the meantime in 1962 "Special Emergency Force" has been raised from the existing strength of RPF during Chinese Aggression, which was especially entrusted the task to protect trains in border districts. In 1965 it has been renamed as "Railway Protection Special Force". In 1966 RPF has been given legal powers for better protection of Railway property by enacting Railway Property (Unlawful Possession.) Act.

But, while the provisions of RPF Act were soon found wanting for the maintenance of an effective and disciplined Force, the RPF Rules and Regulations too were found judicially unsound.

The RPF Act, 1957 was accordingly modified by Parliament vide Act No. 60 of 1985 on 20 September 1985 for the constitution and maintenance of the Force as an armed force of the Union. For carrying out the purposes of the Act, RPF Rules 1987 was framed.

However, the One-man expert committee on Railway Security and Protection 1976 had a different set of ideas. This committee did not favour any uniformed Police Force, and recommended that GRP should continue to remain separate from District Police and that the Railways should bear 50% of the total expenditure on GRP.

The Committee however, agreed that compartmentalisation of Crime wing and Order wing of GRP should abolished and that the SPs of the District should be responsible for controlling crime on railways in their respective districts. In addition to the above, it also made two noteworthy recommendations-namely that MHA should reply to Parliamentary questions on Law & Order and Crime on Railways, thus making it amply clear as to who shall be accountable for Railway crimes. It also recommended for concurrent legal powers for RPF in matters of offences against all railway property.

Key Dates in History

Nov. 1854	Start of Company Police
Feb. 1861	Police Act, 1861
Apr. 1957	Company Police evolved into present RPF
29 Aug. 1957	Railway Protection Force Act 1957 came into act
23 Dec. 2003	Railway Protection Force Act, 1957 modified by Parliament

Present Scenario

Personnel Strength: The RPF has strength of approximately 100, 000 troops and 165 battalions. The force is led by a Director General aided by an Additional Director General. M. K. Sinha is the present Director General of RPF.

Bases: RPF Headquarters are based at New Delhi. RPF structural command is presently divided into sixteen zones which are further divided into various divisions. Various zones are;

Central, Eastern, East Central, East Coast, Northern, North Central, North-Eastern, North Frontier, North Western, Southern, South Central, South East Central, South Western, Western and West Central.

Each zone is made up of a certain number of divisions, each having a divisional headquarters. There are a total of sixty-seven divisions.

Organizational Structure

- Director-General
- Additional Director-General
- Inspector-General
- Additional inspector-General
- Deputy Inspector-General
- Assistant Inspector-General
- Senior Commandant
- Commandant
- Deputy Commandant
- Assistant Commandant
- Inspector
- Sub- Inspector
- Assistant Sub-Inspector
- Head Constable
- Constable

Chiefs of RPF

- Shri B. N. Laihri (27.07.53 to 26.07.57)
- Shri S. Parthasarthi (27.07.57 to 01.01.60)
- Shri M. M. Chudasama (02.01.60 to 24.04.61)

- Shri D. P. Kohli (24.04.61 to 25.08.61)
- Shri S. N. Aga (25.08.61 to 25.11.65)
- Shri J. Dharmaraj (26.11.65 to 07.02.66)
- Shri S. N. Aga (08.02.66 to 31.10.68)
- Shri K. V. Kasturi Rangan (01.11.68 to 17.11.68)
- Shri A. K. Dass (18.11.68 to 04.11.71)
- Shri T. Albert Mano Raj (05.11.71 to 14.01.72)
- Shri Govind Chandra (15.01.72 to 07.04.75)
- Shri Raj Dev Singh (07.04.75 to 01.07.77)
- Shri E. N. Renison (01.07.77 to 01.10.77)
- Shri M. C. Mishra (01.10.77 to 01.08.81)
- Shri M. D. Dikshit (01.08.81 to 30.06.85)
- Shri S. P. Banerjee (01.07.85 to 29.02.88)
- Shri Raja Sreedharan (19.07.88 to 31.03.93)
- Shri Kalyan Rudra (18.08.94 to 03.11.95)
- Shri Joginder Singh (10.04.96 to 31.07.96)
- Shri V. Krishna Murthy (02.08.96 to 28.02.97)
- Shri A. P. Durai (12.03.97 to 01.05.98)
- Shri H. Rao (01.07.98 to 28.02.02)
- Dr. A. K.Pandey (22.04.02 to 31.07.04)
- Shri A. K.Suri (04.08.04 to 31.01.07)
- Shri M. K. Sinha (12.03.07 Till Date)

Duties and Functions

Motto: RPF motto is ***"Yasho Labhaswa"*** meaning **"Fame is Everything"**.

Maxim: Their maxim is "We shall Protect and safeguard Railway property and goods entrusted to Railways. Promote safety and security of the travelling public on the Indian Railways".

Duties: Primarily RPF has been entrusted with responsibility of the safety of Railway property. But, while the provisions of RPF Act were soon found wanting for the maintenance of an effective and disciplined Force, the RPF Rules and Regulations too were found judicially unsound. The RPF Act, 1957 was accordingly modified by Parliament vide Act

No. 60 of 1985 on 20 September 1985 for the constitution and maintenance of the Force as an armed force of the Union.

The Committee recommended that since policing on the railways is the constitutional responsibility of the State Governments, certain matters relating to the security of railway passengers could be segregated from the policing functions and be given to the Railway Protection Force.

The Committee also recommended that the Railway Protection Force may be given the following additional duties relating to security of passengers:

- Escorting of passenger trains in vulnerable areas.
- Providing access control, regulation and general security on the platforms, in passenger areas and circulating areas.

The Railway Ministry accepted the above recommendations of the Committee. Accordingly, RPF by an amendment of the Railways Act/ RPF Act has been empowered to deal with the offences, which directly relate to the functioning of the Railways, as the Police, being preoccupied with the law and order duties, have little time for these minor offences. It was against this backdrop that the RPF Act and The Railways Act have been amended.

The main purpose is to supplement the efforts of the State Governments to reinforce the security of the passengers and the passenger areas on Indian Railways. For giving these additional responsibilities to the Railway Protection Force, the Railway Protection Force Act, 1957was again modified by Parliament vide act No. 52 of 2003 on 23rd December-2003 for providing more legal powers to RPF to provide better protection to Railway Property, Passenger area and Passengers.

In view of latest amendment RPF is entrusted with following duties:

- To protect and safeguard railway property, passenger area and passenger;
- To remove any obstruction in the movement of railway property or passenger area; and
- To do any other act conducive to the better protection and security of railway property, passenger area and passenger.

Further, it was felt that for effectively dealing with the cases under the Railways Act, the Railway Protection Force should be empowered to enquire and to launch prosecution against the persons committing offences under the Railways Act and accordingly the Railway Act has been amended to empower RPF to investigate and prosecute in offences covered under the Act.

It was necessary to make the above amendments for following reasons:

- Railway Protection Force will be legally enabled to provide . protection and safeguard to the passenger and his luggage, which will ensure better Passenger Facilitation.
- Access control to stations can be regulated in a more effective way and general security on the platforms in passenger area and circulation area will get reinforced
- Empowerment under The Railways Act will ensure more smooth train operations since many • Sections of The Railways Act aim at hassle-free train operations.
- Entrusting of new responsibilities to RPF would mean optimum utilization of human resources.
- Railway Protection Force will be able to take steps for prevention of any cognizable offence against the passengers and will also be legally empowered to apprehend any person who is involved in such offences.

With the introduction of amendment in RPF and Railways Act, RPF has been vested with the powers to investigate in Railways Act cases. RPF has accepted the challenge and 1286 important passenger trains have been provided with RPF escorts over Indian Railways.

Acts, Rules & Regulations

The CRPF is governed by the Railway Protection Force Act, 1957. The Act consists 21 sections in all.

- Section 1: Short title and commencement
- Section 2: Definitions
- Section 3: Constitution of the Force
- Section 4: Appointment and powers of superior officers
- Section 5: Classes and ranks among members of the Force
- Section 6: Appointment of enrolled members of the Force
- Section 7: Certificates to enrolled members of the Force
- Section 8: Superintendence and administration of the Force
- Section 9: Dismissal, removai: etc. of enrolled members of Fource

- Section 10: Officers and enrolled members of the Force to be deemed to be railway servents
- Section 11: Duties of members of the Force
- Section 12: Power to arrest without warrant
- Section 13: Power of search without warrant
- Section 14: Procedure to be followed after arrest
- Section 15: Member of the Force to be considered always on duty and liable to be employed in any place within India
- Section 16 Responsibilities of members of force during suspension
- Section 17: Penalties for neglect of dyty, etc.
- Section 18: Application of Act 22 of 1922 to members of the Force
- Section 19: Certain acts not to apply to members of the Force
- Section 20: Protection of acts of members of the force
- Section 21: Power to make rules THE SCHEDULE provisions as to existing Force

There were many amendments to Act of 1957, main being RPF Act 1985 and The Railways Act 1989.

Powers of RPF: Any superior officer and member of the Force may:

1. With out warrant form magistrate arrest persons found in unlawful possession of Railway Property according to section 6 of RP(UP) Act. 1966
2. Search any place used for deposit or sale of Railway Property with warrant from magistrate.
3. Summon any person whose attendance is necessary either to give evidence or to produce a document
4. Seize any vehicle used as the conveyance for carrying of stolen Railway property. Any court trying an offence under this act may order the forfeiture to Government of any property in respect of which the court is satisfied that an offence under RP(UP) Act has been committed and may also order the forfeiture of any receptacles, packages or coverings in which such property is contained, the animals, vehicles or any other conveyances used in carrying the property.

5. Arrest any person with out order from a magistrate and with out warrant according to section 12 of RPF Act 1985
   i. Who voluntarily causes hurt to or attempts voluntarily to cause hurt to or wrongfully restrains or attempts wrongly to restraint, or assaults, threatens to assault, or uses or threatens to attempts to use, criminal force to him or any member of the force in execution of his duty as such member, or with intent to prevent or to deter him for discharging his duty as such member or in consequence or anything done or attempted to be done by him in the lawful discharge of his duty as such member; or
   ii. Any person who has been concerned in (or against whom a reasonable suspicion exists of his having been concerned in, or who is found taking precautions to conceal his presence under circumstance which afford reason to believe that he is taking such precautions with a view to commit a cognizable offence which relates to Railway Property; or
   iii. Any person found taking precautions to conceal his presence with in Railway limits under circumstances which afford reason to believe that he is taking such precautions with a view to commit theft of or damage to Railway property; or
   iv. Any person who commits or attempts to commit a cognizable offence which involves or which is likely to involve imminent danger to the life of any person engaged in carrying on any work relating to Railway property.

Weapons and Equipments

RAF Personnel carry 0.303 Rifles and a single side arm of 0.32 bore.

Recruitment

Officers: The recruitment of Sub Inspectors is carried out whenever needed. The applications for the post is advertised through National Dailies, Employment Exchange and Website. Selection is through written examination, interview and physical test. These officers are also given a short prior sending them for basic training. Graduates from any stream can apply if they fall in the 19 to 25 years age group.

Other Ranks: Recruitment for Costables is done annually. Entry is through a Mental Ability Test, entrance test and an interview. Qualified candidates undergo a medical examination and those who pass are selected on the basis of merit.

Training: The Jagjivan Ram Railway Protection Force Academy, Lucknow runs Initial, Refresher, Specialized and other in-service courses. The Academy is situated at Talkatora Road, Alambagh, Lucknow at a distance of about 5kms from the Railway Station Charbagh, Lucknow. The total land area of the Academy is 46.3 acres. The Academy has a miniature range for small arms like stengun, Pistol, Revolver Firing within its campus. The status of the institute was upgrade to that of Academy in 1987 and the post of principal was again upgraded to Deputy Inspector General from Jr. Administrative Grade in the year 1988.

Initial training for constable (recruits) and refresher courses for constables are held at the Zonal RPF Training Centres.

BCTC/RPF Lines/Dayabasti/Delhi runs the specialized courses for the RPF Dogs and their Handlers. As envisaged in the Railway Protection Force Rules, 1987 "for better prevention and detection of crime" and for providing effective security to the Railway Passengers, Passengers Area and Railway Property, a Breeding cum Training Centre was established at Dayabasti Complex, Delhi.This Training Center imparts Training courses related to Explosive Detection Training for RPF Dogs, Tracker Training for RPF Dogs and Training for Assistant Dog Handlers.

Central Arms Repair Shop (CARS) Dahod, Western Railway runs the specialised courses for the Armourers. Railway Protection Force, being an Armed Force of the Union, often requires minor/ major repairs of its weaponary. for carrying out these jobs, as the result of which, the Central Arms Repair Shop (CARS) was commissioned w.e.f. 21.11.1966, in the premises of Railway Workshop/Dahod/WR. Furthermore, over the years, RPF/RPSF armourers were being imparted training of their cadres in the Training Centers / Work Shops of Indian Army and other paramilitary organizations. With the passage of time, the need of exploring the possibility of conducting different courses of this cadre within the Force itself, was felt. Hence, consequent upon the availability of necessary infrastructure and other essential facilities, it was finally decided to establish our own training Center for conducting various courses related to this cadre, as the result of which, RPF's own Training Center was established, which started functioning from July 2001, at the existing Central Arms Repair Shop (CARS)/Dahod. At present, it is being utilized for imparting training, exclusively to those RPF/RPSF personnel, who are desirous to become Armourer.

Awards

President's Police Medal for Distinguished Service	24
Police Medal for Meritorious Service	56

Modernization

RPF is almost on par with other Paramilitary Forces like BSF, CRPF, CISF etc. RPF has been awfully deficient in modern weaponry, means of communiaction and transport facilities. Now a remarkable change was bought in the spheres of Transportation, Communication, CCTV, Wireless network, training infrastructure/aids, electronic aiming devices, LCD projectors, Cameras, Finger print kits, Security Gadgets, Riot Gear equipment, Materials required for accident sites like Folding chairs, folding stretchers, folding tables, Loud hailer, Nylon rope, Tent single fly, Night Vision Devices, Passive Night Vision goggles, Passive Night vision binoculars, Bullet proof jacket, Bullet proof jacket against carbine, Dragon search light, Over head projector, Hand held metal detector, Door frame metal detector, Wireless communication system, Walkies Talkies, Fax machines, Computers, Vehicles and weaponry.

These steps have given the Force professio

nal efficiency and have doubtless made the Force very effective. The recent amendments in 2003, in the Railways Act 1989, and the RPF Act 1957 have conferred additional powers on the RPF to tackle petty offenders in railways and towards maintenance of orderliness in railway premises.

This however, is not to state that an ideal situation has been achieved in solving the security related problems in Railways. There still remain certain vital areas that have to be covered in the fight against crimes and lawlessness on Railways. Security of rail passengers and prompt registration of baggage thefts on the trains have been the biggest areas wanting in this regard.

REFERENCES

Allport, R.J.: Developing World Transport, London: Grosvenor Press International. Armstrong-Wright, A.: Urban Transit Systems—Guidelines for Examining Options, Washington, The World Bank, Technical Paper No. 52.

Arrowsmith, B.: The Dock and Harbour Authority, London: Foxlow.

B.Prasad ed., Official History of the Indian Armed Forces in the Second World War - Expansion of Armed Forces and Defence Organization, Combined Inter-Services Historical Section - India & Pakistan 1962.

Business Standard, New Delhi, June 10, 2008.

Crone, G. R.: Maps and Their Makers: An Introduction to the History of Cartography.

Frontline, Volume 20-Issue 15.

Government of India, India 1996 - A Reference Annual.

Government of India, India 1995 - A Reference Annual.

Guinness Book of World Records-2005.

Hare, F. K.: The Restless Atmosphere.

Indian Railways Archives.

Lt.Gen. M.L.Chibber: Paramilitary Forces - USI Paper 4, United Services Institution 1979.

Ministry of Commerce & Industry.

Prasad: Expansion of Armed Forces and Defence Organization.

Presidents Secretariat.

Rail Sainik, Jan.-Mar 2005.

Rail Sainik, July-Sept 2005.

Statistical Summary-Indian Railways.

The Hindu, March 19, 2004.

The Tribune, Nov. 14, 2004.

Times of India, Feb. 24, 2006.

Wood, H. J.: Exploration and Discovery.

Wooldridge, S. W.: The Spirit and Purpose of Geography.

PART – VI
PARAMILITARY FORCES UNDER STATE GOVERNMENTS

13

Home Guard

"Nishkam Sewa"

Introduction

The role of the Home Guard is to service as an auxiliary to the Police in maintenance of law, order and internal security, help the community in any kind of emergency such as an air-raid, an earthquake, etc., help in the maintenance of essential services, promote communal harmony, assist civil administration in protecting weaker sections, participate in socio-economic and welfare activities and perform civil defence duties. The Home Guard are trained to use 303 Rifles and Sten guns. They are also trained in fire fighting. Some also have access to light machine guns. Home Guards are of two types - rural and urban. In border states, Border Wing Home Guard battalions have also been raised, which serve as an auxiliary to the Border Security Force (BSF). The total unauthorised strength of the Home Guards in the country is at 472,000 however the actual strength is at 416,000 personnel. The organization is spread over in all states and union territories except in Arunachal Pradesh and Kerala.

The Home Guard was raised in 1946 under the Home Guard Acts & Rules of States/Union Territories. They are recruited from various cross sections of people such as doctors, engineers, lawyers, teachers, employees of public & private sector organizations, college & university students, agricultural & industrial workers, etc., who give their spare time to the organization for betterment of the community. All citizens of India, who are in the age group of 18-50, are eligible to become members of the Home Guard. Normal tenure of membership in Home Guards is three to five years. A Home Guard, whenever called up for duty/training, is paid duty/training allowance at prescribed rates to meet out of pocket expenses.

Members of Home Guard with three years services in the organization are trained in the Police in maintenance of law and order, prevention of crime, anti-dacoit measures, border patrolling, flood relief, fire fighting, prohibition, elections and social welfare activities. In the event of a national emergency, some portion of civil defence work is also entrusted to the Home Guard. The Ministry of Home Affairs formulates the policy in respect of role, target, raising, training, equipping, establishment and other important matters of the Home Guard. Expenditure on Home Guard is generally shared between the Centre and State Governments as per the existing financial policy.

Apart from carrying out training measures during peacetime, Home Guards are also deployed, on voluntary basis, in various constructive activities including assistance to the administration, relief & rescue work during natural calamities like floods, earthquakes, cyclones, droughts, etc. by the administration of the State Governments/Union Territories of their own. Training is conducted in the country on a three-tier concept, i.e. Local/Town level, at State level and National level.

History

Need: In the wake of Chinese aggression in 1962, the Centre advised the States and Union Territories to merge their existing voluntary organization into one uniform voluntary force known as Home Guards. The role of Home Guards is to service as an auxiliary to the Police in maintenance of law and order and internal security, help the community in any kind of emergency such as an air-raid, fire, cyclone, earthquake, epidemic etc, help in maintenance of essential services, promote communal harmony and assist the administration in protecting weaker sections, participate in socio-economic and welfare activities and perform Home Guard duties.

Origin: The Home Guard Policy of the Government till the declaration of emergency in 1962 was confined to making the States and Union Territories conscious of the need of Home Guard measures and to ask them to keep ready Home Guard Paper Plans for major cities & towns under the then Emergency Relief Organization (ERO) Scheme. Two major incidents gave reason to the development of Home Guard in India; the 1962 Indo-China and the 1965 Indo-Pak conflicts. This led to a considerable rethinking about the policy & scope of Home Guard and as a result the Home Guard Policy as it exists today, was evolved and Home Guard legislation was enacted in the Parliament in 1968. In the 1971 Indo-Pak War, the Home Guard acquitted itself commendably. Home Guard aims at saving lives, minimising damage to the property and maintaining continuity of industrial production in the event of a hostile attack.

The Home Guard Act of 1968, is though applicable throughout the country, but the organization is only raised in such areas & zones which are tactically and strategically considered vulnerable from enemy attack points of view. At the moment Home Guard activities are restricted to 135 categorised towns spread over 32 States/Union Territories. To meet the early warning communication requirement for an impending hostile attack, a reliable and flexible network, both on telephone lines and radio/wireless, have been established in most of the categorised Home Guard Towns.

Communication facilities, on telephone lines & radio, has also been planned and established in most of the Home Guard towns for the purpose of command, control, coordination & liaison and also for mutual aid and cooperation. Home Guard is primarily organized on a voluntary basis except for a small nucleus of paid staff and establishment which is augmented during emergencies.

Key Dates in the history

Apr. 1946	Home Guard came into existence
Dec. 1968	Home Guard legislation was enacted in the Parliament
Dec. 1971	Home Guard performance appreciated during war

Present Scenario: Home Guards are raised under the Home Guards Acts and Rules of the States/Union Territories. They are recruited from various cross sections of the people such as doctors, engineers, lawyers, teachers, professionals, Government Servants, employees of public and private sector organizations, college and university students, agricultural and industrial workers etc., who give their sparetime to the organization for betterment of the community. All citizens of India, who are in the age group of 18-50, are eligible to become members of Home Guards.

Normal tenure of membership in Home Guards is three to five years. A Home Guard, whenever called up for duty/training, is paid duty/training allowance at prescribed rates to meet out of pocket expenses. Members of Home Guards with three years services in the organization are trained in police in maintenance of law and order, prevention of crime, anti-dacoity measures, border patrolling, flood relief, prohibition, fire fighting, elections and social welfare activities.

In the event of national emergency, some portion of Civil Defence work is also entrusted to the Home Guards. The Ministry of Home Affairs formulates the policy in respect of role, target, raising, training, equipping, establishment and other important matters of Home Guards. Expenditure on Home Guards is generally shared between Centre and State governments as per the existing financial policy. During 1996-97, Rs. 28 crore had been reimbursed to States on raising and training of Home Guards and their deployment for various purposes including that of Lok Sabha/Vidhan Sabha elections. For 1997-98, a budget of Rs. 28 crore has been catered for, which is likely to be fully utilised during current financial year.

Personnel Strength: The present force of Home Guard volunteers is 472,000 personnel in 135 towns in 32 states.

At present the Home Guard is being headed by an officer of the rank of Additional Director General of Police-cum-Commandant General Home Guards and Director Civil Defence of respective States.

Department has following organizational structures:

- Commandant General Home Guards & Director Civil Defence.
- Deputy Commandant General Home Guards & Director Civil Defence.
- Divisional Commandant General Home Guards.
- Battalion Commanders for battalions.
- Commandant Combined Home Guards & Civil Defence, Training Institutes.
- District level officers designated as District Commanders in States.

Organizational Structure

Organizational setup of Home Guard from top to bottom is:

- Commandant General
- Deputy Commandant General
- Divisional Commandant General
- Battalion Commanders
- Commandant
- District level officers

Duties and Functions

Motto: Home guard motto is ***"Nishkam Sewa"*** meaning **"Selfless Service"**.

Maxim: To serve as an auxiliary to the police and assist in maintaining internal security.

- To assist the community in any kind of emergency - in air raid, a fire, a flood, an epidemic and so on.
- To organize functional units to provide essential services, such as, motor transport, pioneer and engineer groups, fire brigades, nursing and first aid, operation of water and power supply installations.
- To promote communal harmony and give assistance to the administration in protecting weaker sections of the Society
- To participate in socio-economic and welfare activities, such as, adult education, health and hygiene, development schemes and such other tasks as are deemed useful.

Duties: Civil defence is an effort to prepare civilians for military attack. It uses the principles of emergency operations: prevention, mitigation, preparation, response, or emergency evacuation, and recovery. Programmes of this sort were initially discussed at least as early as the 1950s but only became widespread after Indo-China war.

Since the end of the War, the focus of civil defence has largely shifted from military attack to emergencies and disasters in general. The new concept is described by a number of terms, each of which has its own specific shade of meaning, such as crisis management, emergency management, emergency preparedness, contingency planning, emergency services, and civil protection. In some states, the all-encompassing nature of civil defence is denoted by the term "total defence". The name suggests committing all resources, hence the term total, of the nation to the defence. It can be compared to total war.

Relatively small investments in preparation can speed up recovery by months or years and thereby prevent millions of deaths by hunger, cold and disease. According to human capital theory in economics, a country's population is more valuable than all of the land, factories and other assets that it possesses. People rebuild a country after its destruction, and it is therefore important for the economic security of a country that it protect its people. Also, reducing fear and uncertainty via civil defence helps people's quality of life and has positive economic benefits. According to psychology, it is important for people to feel like they are in control of their own destiny, and preparing for uncertainty via civil defence may help to achieve this. If the people are not in control, and the preparations ineffective, the government loses its credibility and the respect of its citizens.

Home Guard main aim is to support and supplement efforts at national, regional and local level with regard to disaster prevention, the preparedness of those responsible for civil protection and the intervention in the event of disaster. To establish a framework for effective and rapid cooperation between different civil protection services when mutual assistance is needed (police, fire service, healthcare service, public utility provider, voluntary agencies). To set up and implement training programs for intervention and coordination teams as well as assessment experts including joint courses and exchange systems. To enhance the coherence of actions undertaken at international level in the field of civil protection especially in the context of cooperation. To contribute to the information of the public in view of increasing the level of self-protection of citizens. To collect and disseminate validated emergency information. To pool information on national civil protection capabilities, military and medical resources. To ensure efficient information sharing between the different authorities.

The functions to be performed by Home Guards are listed below:

- To serve as Auxiliary to the Police and generally help in maintaining internal security.
- To help the community in any kind of Emergency—such as on Air-raid_precautions or on any natural Calamity.
- To function as an Emergency Force intended for special tasks directly or indirectly connected with the defence of the country.

- To maintain functional units to provide essential services such as motor transport, Engineering groups, Fire brigade, Nursing and First Aid, Operation of Power supply, Water installations and Communication systems etc.
- The Border Wing of 18 battalions assists the Border Security Force.
- Marine Units function as an Indian Coast Guard auxiliary.
- The Fire Wing assists the Indian Fire service.

Acts, Rules & Regulations

Home guard is governed by The Civil Defence Act, 1968. It has 20 sections in all.

- Section 1: Short title, extent and commencement
- Section 2: Definitions
- Section 3: Power to make rules for civil defence
- Section 4: Constitution of Civil Defence Corps
- Section 5: Appointment of members and officers
- Section 6: Dismissal of members of Civil Defence Corps
- Section 7: Appeal
- Section 8: Functions of members of Civil Defence Corps
- Section 9: Power to make regulations
- Section 10: Provisions of the Personal Injuries
- Section 11: Penalties
- Section 12: Effect of Act and rules, etc:, inconsistent with other
- Section 13: Ordinary avocations of life to be interfered with as little as possible
- Section 14: Savings as to orders
- Section 15: Act not to apply to measures taken for the protection of the Armed Forces
- Section 16: Limitation of prosecutions
- Section 17: Power to delegate
- Section 18: Protection of action taken in good faith
- Section 19: Authorised persons and members of the Corps to be public servants
- Section 20: Rules and regulations to be laid before Parliament

Weapons and Equipments

The Home Guard is equipped with and trained to use older weapons such as the 303 Lee Enfield SMLE rifle, Sten and Bren guns.

Recruitment

Personnel are recruited from various people to include doctors, lawyers, teachers, employees of public and private sector organizations, college and university students, agricultural and industrial workers and others who give their spare time to their communities. All 18 to 50 year old citizens of India are eligible for membership and normally serve from three to five years each. Members are paid an allowance when called up for service. All members, after their first three year term of service, are eligible to be trained by the police in the maintenance of law and order, crime prevention, anti-dacoit measures, border control, disaster relief, fire prevention and firefighting, election and social welfare activities.

Officers: The recruitment of officers is carried out through general selection. The applications are advertised through National Dailies and Employment Exchange. The preliminary selections of the candidates is conducted at district level centres by conduct of Mental Ability Test and an Interview.

These officers are also given a short course on personality development prior sending them for basic training. The qualifications required to become an officer is graduation

Other Ranks: Recruitment to the OR is done when needed. Candidates can join one of many branches. Qualified candidates undergo a medical examination and those who pass are selected on the basis of merit. Candidates undergo a written test followed by an interview.

Training: Central Civil Defence training centres were established in various states to impart training to both Civil Defence and Home Guards personnel. The training consists of individual as well as team training. After Independence the task of Civil Defence training was revived only after 1962.

National Civil Defence College, Nagpur is a subordinate office of Director General Civil Defence Ministry of Home Affairs, Government of India, established for fulfilling the training requirement of Civil Defence Organization. The College does not charge any course fee for its training programmes. However boarding and lodging charges are borne by the candidates.

The NCDC expects the nominating authorities to select candidates as per laid down eligibility conditions so that the training obtained by them is employed to further multiply the number of trained Civil Defence personnel.

Trainee officers for all courses should be medically fit and in good health so as to be in position to pursue practical training exercises which include extensive outdoor jobs. Those not in possession of a Medical examination certificate will not be accepted by the college for undergoing any of the below given courses.

- Civil Defence Instructors Course.
- Flood / Cyclone Disaster Response Course.
- Earthquake Disaster Response Course.
- Basic Life Support Course.
- Training of Trainers in Radiological Emergencies.
- Chemical Disaster First Responders Course.
- Biological Incident First Responders Course.
- Auxiliary Fire Fighting Course.
- Advanced Search & Rescue Course.
- Unexploded Bombs & Explosive safety.
- Incident Management & Command System Course.
- Emergency Response to Rail Transport Accident

Awards

There are provisions in Home Guards & Civil Defence to confer honour to any staff member or volunteer either individually or collectively in recognition of conspicuous good work, work of outstanding nature, gallantry, devotion to duty, etc. in various forms as per following details:

- Cash Awards: Upto Rs. 1000/- per head by DGCD of the Ministry and upto Rs. 500 per head by DCDs & CGHGs of the States/UTs.
- DGCD's Commendation Certificate Disc: The recommendation for these are to be initiated by an officer not below the rank of District Commandant or Controller of Civil Defence and are required to be suitably endorsed by DCDs & CGHGs of the State. No momentary grant is attached to this certificate.

- Medals: Two types of Gallantry Medals and two types of Service Medals have been instituted in October, 1974 by a presidential Notification for Home Guards & Civil Defence.

Gallantry Medals

President's HG & CD Medal for gallantry	4
HG & CD Medal for gallantry	12

Service Medals

President's HG & CD Medal for Distinguished Service	63
HG & CD Medal for Meritorious Service	42

REFERENCES

Austin J. Ruddy: To The Last Round: The Leicestershire & Rutland Home Guard 1940-1945, Breedon Books, 2007.

Civil Defence Act. 1968.

Civil Defence Journal of the Civil Defence Services: Editor Col. Kr. D. S. Rawal, 1970 No. 1.

Datta, Civil Defence - Problems & Prospects.

David R Orr: Duty Without Glory-The story of Ulster's Home Guard in the Second World War and the Cold War, Redcoat Publishing, 2008.

Govt. of India, Ministry of Defence Annual Report 1995-1996.

Home Guard Pocket Manual.

India, A country Study of the Library of Congress.

K.Mathur, Administration of Police Training in India, Gian Publishing House, 1987.

Lt.Gen. Thapan, Review of the Organizational Pattern of the Indian Army - Seminar held at the United Service Institution of India on 26 March 1976.

Maj. S. Bhaduri, Weapons Overview' in Indian Defence Review - July 1991.

McReynolds, David: Ralph DiGia, 1914-2008. The Catholic Worker LXXV, March-April.

Norman Longmate - The Real Dad's Army - The story of the Home Guard.

P.Singh, Civil Defence in the Nuclear Age, Army Educational Store 1972.

Prasad R.: India's Civil Defence in the Nuclear Age.

MacKenzie S. P.: The Home Guard — A Military and Political History, Oxford University Press, 1995

Ghosh S. K. & Rustamji K. F. ed., Encyclopaedia of Police in India, Ashish Publishing House 1994.

S.P.Baranwal, Measures of Civil Defence in India.

Tom Wintringham: How to Reform the Army, Fact Monographs, 1939.

PART – VII
ORGANIZATIONS ASSISTING PARAMILITARY FORCES

14

National Cadet Corps

"Ekta aur Anushashanta"

Introduction

National Cadet Corps is a Tri-Services Organization, comprising the Army, Navy and Air Force, engaged in grooming the youth of the country into disciplined and patriotic citizens. National Cadet Corps (India) is the Indian military cadet corps. It is open to school and college students on voluntary basis.

The National Cadet Corps in India is a voluntary organization which recruits cadets from high schools and colleges. The Cadets are given basic military training in small arms and parades. The officers and cadets have no liability for active military service.

History

The origin of NCC can be traced back to the University Corps, which was created under the Indian Defence Act 1917, with the object to make up the shortages of the Army. National Cadet Corps is a Tri-Services Organization, comprising Army, Navy and Air Force, engaged in grooming the youth of the country into disciplined and patriotic citizens. In 1920, when the Indian Territorial Act was passed, the 'University Corps' was replaced by the University Training Corps (UTC). The aim was to raise the status of the UTC and make it more attractive to the youth.

It was a significant step towards the Indianization of the Armed Forces. In 1942, the UTC was re-christened as the 'University Officers Training Corps'. During the Independence movement, leaders of our nation had realised need to create a national level youth organization, to train and groom young boys as responsible citizens and future leaders of our great country in all walks of life, including the defence forces. Consequently, a committee under Shri HN Kunzru was set up in 1946 under the directives of the first Prime Minister, Pandit Jawaharlal Nehru, to consider the establishment of a nationwide cadet corps, which was born through the Act of Parliament on 15th July 1948.

The first Prime Minister of India, Pandit Jawahar Lal Nehru presided over the function of raising the first NCC Unit at Delhi on the last Sunday of November 1948. This day is traditionally celebrated as the 'NCC Day'.'

During the 1965 and 1971 wars with Pakistan, NCC cadets were the second line of defence. They organized camps to assist the ordnance factories, supplying arms and ammunition to the front, and also were used as patrol parties to capture the enemy paratroopers. The NCC cadets also worked hand in hand with the Civil Defence authorities and actively took part in rescue work and traffic control. After the 1965 and 1971 Indo-Pak wars the NCC syllabus was revised. Rather than just being the second line of defence, NCC syllabus laid a greater stress on developing qualities of leadership and Officer-like qualities. The military training which the NCC cadets received was reduced and greater importance was given to other areas like social service and youth-management.

It is a voluntary organization and neither officers nor cadets are under any obligation or compulsion to centre active military service. NCC consists of three divisions, Senior, Junior and Girls with Army, Navy and Air Wings. It has 16 Directorates, 2 Training Schools, 92 Group Headquarters, 11.93 lakhs Cadet Strength, 7000 Schools, 4,500 Colleges.

As Director General (NCC) wrote in his message on completion of 51 years of NCC, the National Cadet Crops made a humble beginning in 1948 with less than 2 lakhs cadets. Today it has a strength of 1.2 million covering the urban and rural areas including remote areas across the length and breadth of the country.

The NCC has undergone many changes i.e. from a purely military oriented organization it has changed to a true youth development organization spread over in all States of the Country in the true spirit of its motto unity and discipline.

Today, the NCC offers a wide spectrum of activities classified into five main area. Institutional training is paramount amongst these and it includes conduct of Annual Training Camps. Flying, Sea Training and familiarisation training with various Services institutes like Indian Military Academy at Dehradun and Officers Training School at Chennai.

Community Development is another area in which cadets have set an example by involving in various activities viz. adult literacy, anti-drug, anti-leprosy campaigns, planting of trees to conserve ecology etc.

Of late, the scope of adventure and sports activity has been enlarged bringing in its ambit events like para-sailing, scuba-diving, car and motorcycle rallies and expeditions designed to explore the national heritage of India, beside the conventional activities like mountaineering.

The NCC has also sent a number of cadets to Singapore, Sri Lanka and UK on youth exchange programme. These programmes give the youth of our nation an enhanced understanding of the international environment and help them to become effective leaders in the future.

Key Dates in History

15 July 1948	NCC founded
Dec. 1971	NCC performance appreciated during war

Present Scenario

Personnel Strength: The NCC has strength of approximately 1025,000 troops.

The Headquarters of the NCC is in New Delhi and is commanded by a Director-General of the rank of Lieutenant General. At New Delhi, a Central Advisory Committee has been set up with the RM / RMM as Chairman to advise the Government on all matters of policy and administration of the NCC. Each state also has a State Advisory Committee. The NCC is administered directly by the Ministry of Defence. The Director General has a staff which is drawn from the three services - Army, Navy and Air Force.

The NCC is divided into 16 directorates, similar to brigades, in which each state or group of states forms a directorate. The smaller states and union territories are attached with directorates of the bigger states. Each directorate is under the command of an Officer equivalent to the rank of a Brigadier. The directorates are further sub-divided into groups, which varies according to the size of the state, each under the command of an Officer equivalent to the rank of Colonel. A group consists of NCC battalions and NCC Air Force & Naval units. Other than the Commanding Officer, each Group Headquarter has an Administrative Officer and a Training Officer with ranks of either a Lieutenant Colonel or a Major.

The groups are further sub-divided into battalions, each commanded by an Officer equivalent to Lieutenant Colonel, and an Officer in the ranks of Lieutenant Colonel or Major as the Administrative Officer. Each battalion also has a JCO in the rank of Subedar Major as the Senior JCO. Each company consists of 160 cadets from a college/technical institute.

The Company Commander in the NCC is a lecturer who teaches in the college. They receive three months training at the Officer's Training College in Kamptee, and are considered as Officers Commanding. Each troop consists of 100 cadets from a single school. A Troop Commander in the NCC is a teacher who teaches in the school. They receive three months training at the Officer's Training College in Kamptee and are considered as JCOs. Lecturers of NCC companies and troops are known as Associated NCC Officers (ANO).

The NCC Army units include Infantry, Armoured Corps, Artillery, Engineers, Signals, etc. Naval and Air Force units have also been organized along the same lines. The Auxiliary Cadet Corps (ACC) was a supplement of the NCC and enrolled boys and girls between the ages of 13 to 16.

There are four distinct divisions in the NCC:

Senior Division for boys (SD) — This consists of cadets recruited from colleges and are under the command of a lecturer called the Associated NCC Officer (ANO). This is called a company and consists of a maximum of 160 cadets.

Junior Division for boys (JD) — This consists of cadets recruited from high schools and are under the command of an ANO who is a teacher in that school. This is called a group and consists of a maximum of 160 cadets.

Senior Wing for girls (SW) — This is similar to the SD and consists of girls recruited from colleges.

Junior Wing for girls (JW) — Cadets in the JW are girls recruited from schools.

The divisions are further divided into Army, Navy and Air force wings. For example a school could have a naval junior division (JD) squad commanded by an ANO.

Directorates: The NCC is divided into regional directorates as part of its organizational structure. Each directorate is under the command of a Deputy Director General (DDG) of the NCC. These are:

- Andhra Pradesh
- Bihar
- Delhi
- J&K
- Punjab, Haryana and Himachal Pradesh
- Gujarat
- Karnataka & Goa
- Kerela & Lakshadeep
- Madhya Pradesh
- Maharashtra
- NER
- Orissa
- OTAs
- Rajasthan
- TN & P
- UP
- UA
- WB & Sikkim

Organizational Structure

Cadets: Cadets are divided into two groups:

Senior Division & Senior Wing:

- Senior Under Officer (one in a Company)
- Junior Under Officer (three in a Company)
- Company Sergeant Major (one in a Company)
- Company Quarter Master Sergeant (one in a Company)
- Sergeant (three in a Company excluding the CSM and CQMS)
- Corporal (ten in a Company)
- Lance Corporal (fifteen in a Company)
- Cadet

Junior Division & Junior Wing:

- Troop Sergeant
- Company Quarter Master Sergeant (one in a Company)

- Regimental Sergeant Major (RSM)
- Regimental Quarter Master Sergeant (RQMS)

Associate NCC Officers: Associate NCC Officers (ANOs) are teachers or lecturers who have been given formal military training for the purposes of leading NCC organizations locally in institutions.

- For Colleges (in charge of SD & SW cadets)
  1. Major
  2. Captain
  3. Lieutenant
  4. 2nd Lieutenant
- For schools (in charge of JD & JW cadets)
  1. Chief Officer (equivalent to Subedar Major)
  2. First Officer
  3. Second Officer
  4. Third Officer

Duties and Functions

Motto: ***"Ekta aur Anushashanta"*** meaning **"Unity and Discipline"** is NCC motto.

Maxim: The maxim of the National Cadet Corps is:

- To develop qualities of character, courage, comradeship, discipline, leadership, secular out look, spirit of adventure and sportsmanship and the ideals of selfless service among the youth to make them useful citizens.
- To create a human resource of organized, trained and activated youth, to provide leadership in all walks of life including the Armed Forces and always available for the service of the nation.

Description of Duties: One of the important aspects of National Cadet Corps training is community development, which aims at bringing about an awareness of the social problems and forge them into pragmatic social workers. Activities include; Planting of Tree Saplings, Adult Education, Blood Donation, Earth Day Awareness Campaign, Anti Dowry Pledge, Cheshire Home, Eye Donation, Health Education, Shramdan, Pulse Polio Immunization Programme, Assistance in Disaster Management

Activities: Since 1970, NCC has conducted 40 Mountaineering expeditions, of which 22 were for boys and 18 for the girls. 49 vacancies are allotted to NCC cadets on basic and advance mountaineering courses conducted at Himalayan Mountaineering Institute Darjeeling, Nehru Institute of Mountaineering Uttarkashi and Mountaineering & Allied Sports, Manali.

Various trekking expeditions are organized during in which many cadets participate.

Cycle and Motor Cycle Expeditions were organized at the national and state levels.

124 Para Sails are presently held by different NCC Directorates and regular launches are organized by them.

Every year 20 boys and 20 girls NCC cadets are trained at Para Training School, Agra.

10 Senior Division and 10 Senior Wing cadets are trained in slithering to participate in the demonstration during the PM's Rally.

Scuba Diving is carried out at Delhi, Mumbai, Vishakhapatnam and Kochi and has gained great popularity amongst NCC cadets. Till date hundreds of cadets have qualified in this adventure activity.

Republic Day Camp: The culmination of the annual NCC activity takes place during the Republic Day Camp at Delhi every year. The one month programme, which is attended on an all India basis by more than 1700 candidates - both boys and girls - from all states, has the prestigious Prime Minister's Rally as its last event. The selection of cadets for the various Youth Exchange Programmes conducted by the NCC with other countries is done from amongst the cadets who attend Republic Day Camp.

Acts, Rules & Regulations

National Cadet Corps is governed under National Cadet Corps Act (No. XXXI of 1948) enacted by Parliament.

Weapons and Equipments

NCC cadets are trained in basic weapons. They use older weapons such as the 303 Lee Enfield SMLE rifle, Sten and Bren guns.

Recruitment

The NCC is open to all regular students of schools and colleges on a voluntary basis. The officers and cadets have no liability for active military service.

Training: NCC training is given through the regular parades conducted at the colleges on the weekends. The parades start at 9 am and ends at 1 pm. During the parades the cadets are given training in drill (both free hand and rifle), map reading and classes are conducted on topics like Indian history & geography, Indian military history, general knowledge, leader-ship qualities and man-management.

These parades are conducted for maintaining the discipline of the unit and also for imparting the theory part of the syllabus. Ceremonial parades are conducted during the Republic Day, Independence Day and the NCC day.

Camps: NCC camps are conducted through out the academic year. Camps are of various types and each serves a different purpose. The camps are of 10-12 days duration and the cadets receive intensive practical and theoretical training.

In camps they under stand the merits of community living and also learn more about the Army way of organising people and places; like sentry posting and manning the quarter guard. Camps are organized in a pattern exactly similar to the Army camps, with drill, physical training and fatigue works. The rigorous routine in the camps also make the cadets more disciplined and organized.

The Annual Training Camps are the most frequently organized camps. It is mandatory for every cadet to at least attend two annual training camps to qualify for the examinations. In these camps, every aspect of NCC training is covered. Cadets are trained in the usage of 22 rifles, 7.62mm SLRs and LMGs and also thorough practical training in map reading and military subjects. They also receive good training in free hand and arms drill. The annual training camps can be conducted separately for girls and boys or some times combined annual training camps are held for both girls and boys. Annual training camps are conducted during school and college vacations.

The Army Attachment Camps are conducted once every academic year. Here selected cadets from every NCC battalion are sent to the regular Army regimental centers for training. In this camp, the cadets receive the similar training which a recruit gets. Cadets get excellent training in the use of automatic weapons, and in the advanced part of map reading like night-marching and star-navigation.

Trekking Camps are conducted in an All-India basis. The camp can be conducted any where in India, and cadets from every directorate takes part in it. The cadets who attend these camps are less in number since the camp is organized at the National level. They receive no special training in these camps except that they trek across hills and valleys.

National Integration Camps are also conducted on a National basis. Unlike Annual Training Camps, these camps give importance to letting the cadets know more about the place in which the camp is organized. The cadets are taken for sight-seeing trips, cultural programs and competitions are conducted inside the camps. These camps are conducted for the cadets to know more about their country, other states and the life styles of various places. The Republic Day camp and the Basic Leadership camp is conducted in New Delhi. The selection to these camps are done from various Annual Training camps conducted in the different states. The NCC contingent which marches during the Republic Day parade is formed up by the cadets who attend the RD camp.

The cadets who attend RD camp are given excellent training in drill, and can also be selected to the Youth Exchange program. A Basic Leadership camp, is a competition camp in which the best shooters and also map-readers of the various directorates compete with each other.

As per the new syllabus of the NCC social service is given importance in all these camps. Cadets as part of their fatigue duty are to build roads in rural area and also clean and maintain the camp premises and surroundings.

The NCC provides a pool of disciplined and trained manpower that could be of service to the country in the event of any emergency. It has actively taken parts in the three wars with Pakistan (1948, 1965 and 1971). The NCC was used mainly in the transporting of supplies and capturing enemy para-troopers.

32 Vacancies per course have been reserved for the NCC 'C' Certificate holders for Permanent Commission through the Indian Military Academy, and 50 vacancies per course have been reserved for NCC 'C' Certificate holders for Short Service Commission (Non Technical) through OTA Chennai with exemption from UPSC written examination.

For the Navy, six vacancies per course with exemption of UPSC Examination and for Indian Air Force 10% vacancies in all course including Flying Training Course. Here too the cadets need not attempt the UPSC Examination and only will have to attend the SSB Interview. The scheme has been proved a great success. A change in the outlook towards life and its problems is already noticeable in the NCC youth. A healthy development of character will go a long way in improving the quality of future soldiers.

Certificates

Senior Division and Senior Wing:

- C-Certificate is the highest recognition of training and qualification of a Senior NCC cadet
- B-Certificate is the initial recognition of training and qualification of a Senior NCC cadet

Junior Division and Junior Wing:

- A-Certificate is the main recognition of training and qualification of a Junior NCC cadet

Commendations

The regional and national chiefs of the NCC recognize exceptional merit and achievement by deserving cadets through an award of a commendation letter. These are usually issued by the Deputy Director General (DDG) for regional award or even by the Director General (DG) in the case of awards at a national level.

Miscellaneous

- A cadet holding C certificate in B grade gets entitled to apply for direct commission in the defence services.
- A cadet holding B or C certificate can aspire to be enrolled as ASI in the State Police.
- Preferential advantage in seeking admissions in professional course at all India level.

REFERENCES

Annual Report 2002-2003: Ministry of Home Affairs, Government of India.

Annual Report 2006-2007: Ministry of Home Affairs, Government of India.

B. Prasad ed., Official History of the Indian Armed Forces in the Second World War - Expansion of Armed Forces and Defence Organization,(Kanpur : Combined Inter-Services Historical Section - India & Pakistan 1962).

Datta, Civil Defence - Problems & Prospects.

Dte General, Indian Coast Guard, New Delhi.

Government of India, India 1995 - A Reference Annual, New Delhi: Ministry of Information & Broadcasting 1996.

Government of India, Ministry of Defence Annual Report 1995-1996.

Indian Defence Review, June 1999.

Indian Express, July 06, 1999.

Indian Express, May 01, 2000.

Indian Express, May 18, 1999.

Indian Express, May 08, 1999.

J.Baranwal, The Military Yearbook 1993-1994, New Delhi: Guide Publications.

Jackson AV William: History of India, Asia Education Services, New Delhi, Reprint 1987.

Kumar, Raj: Encyclopaedia of Military Systems in India, Commonwealth Publishers, New Delhi, 2004.

Lt Gen. YN Sharma: Restructuring of the Armed Forces, Defence Management.

Lt. Gen. VK Nayyar. Internal Security: Some Issues and Aspects. Indian Defence Review. Jan. 1993.

Prasad, Expansion of Armed Forces and Defence Organization.

R. Datta: Civil Defence - Problems & Prospects, Sehgal Publishers 1991.

Prasad R.: India's Civil Defence in the Nuclear Age, Prakash Book Depot 1988.

Baranwal S. P.: Military Yearbook 1974, Guide Publications 1974.

Baranwal S. P.: Measures of Civil Defence in India.

The Hindu, Oct. 16, 2004.

The Tribune, Jan. 26, 2004.

The Tribune, Nov. 25, 1998.

Vayu Aerospace Review, VI, 1993.

World Military Aircraft Inventory: Aerospace Source Book 2007, Aviation Week & Space Technology, Jan. 15, 2007.

15

Border Roads Organization

"Shramena Sarvam Sadhyam"

Introduction

The Border Roads Organization [BRO] plays a very vital role in connecting the inaccessible border areas. BRO was raised on May 7, 1960 with the mission of developing communication in hither to forlorn areas of the north and North-East states of India and also fortification of the turbulent borders. BRO, the brain child of first Prime Minister Pandit Jawaharlal Nehru came into existence on May 7, 1960 as a pioneer road construction agency. With a humble beginning of two projects the organization has grown vast and vibrant. The organization has till date constructed 28,342 kilometres of formation cutting, 32,885 kilometres of surfacing, 12,200 metres of permanent bridges and has undertake Rs. 2039 crore worth of permanent works. Today, BRO is diversifying in various other areas from road construction to airfields, building works and construction of model hospitals, bridges etc.

Border Roads Organization, popularly known as BRO, is a civil engineering institution responsible to provide civil (construction) engineering cover to the Armed Forces of India, during war and peace.

The organization is manned partly by civil engineers drawn from Corps of Engineers of the Army, but mainly by those recruited exclusively for BRO. The latter complement of manpower is called General Reserve Engineer Force (GREF). The organization is under Ministry of Defence for specific deployment but placed under Ministry of Highways for general administration. The GREF troops, like soldiers of other Armed Forces, are governed by Army Act, 1950, though with a difference. The difference pertains to the method of the recruitment and the terms of salary, pension, leave, retirement benefits etc.

History

Need: The requirement of raising BRO was felt during fifties when it was found that the lofty Himalayas was no longer effective as a natural protective wall. Pak-sponsored marauders had already played havoc in Jammu and Kashmir in 1948. The possibility of an aggression from Chinese side was also imminent. Positioning of Indian troops farthest in Himalayas had thus become obligatory but there were no means of communication for their deployment and maintenance in the mountainous tract. Setting up of a network of new roads was essential in the so far inaccessible highlands. The State PWD could hardly tackle the massive task. It was at that juncture that the Indian Parliament decided to raise BRO/GREF under the stewardship of the Engineer-in-Chief of the Corps of Engineers.

Origin: BRO was raised on May 7, 1960 with the mission of developing communication in forlorn areas of the north and north-east states of India and also fortification of the turbulent borders. BRO, the brainchild of first Prime Minister Pandit Jawaharlal Nehru came into existence on May 7, 1960 as a pioneer road construction agency.

With a humble beginning of two projects the organization has grown vast and vibrant. The organization has till date constructed 28,342 kms. of formation cutting, 32,885 kms. of surfacing, 12,200 metres of permanent bridges and has undertake Rs. 2039 crore worth of permanent works. Today, BRO is diversifying in various other areas from road construction to airfields, building works and construction of model hospitals, bridges etc. Border Roads Organization, popularly known as BRO, is a civil engineering institution responsible to provide civil (construction) engineering cover to the Armed Forces of India, during war and peace. The organization is manned partly by civil engineers drawn from Corps of Engineers of the Army, but mainly by those recruited exclusively for BRO. The latter complement of manpower is called

General Reserve Engineer Force (GREF). The organization is under Ministry of Defence for specific deployment but placed under Ministry of Highways for general administration.

The GREF troops, like soldiers of other Armed Forces, are governed by Army Act, 1950, though with a difference. The difference pertains to the method of the recruitment and the terms of salary, pension, leave, retirement benefits etc. The requirement of raising BRO was felt during fifties when it was found that the lofty Himalayas was no longer effective as a natural protective wall. Pak-sponsored marauders had already played havoc in Jammu and Kashmir in 1948. The possibility of an aggression from Chinese side was also imminent Positioning of Indian troops farthest in Himalayas had thus become obligatory but there were no means of communication for their deployment and maintenance in the mountainous tract. Setting up of a network of new roads was essential in the so far inaccessible highlands.

The civil engineering element of State resources viz PWD could hardly tackle the massive task. It was at that juncture that the Indian Parliament decided to raise BRO/GREF under the stewardship of the Engineer-in-Chief of the Corps of Engineers. The auspicious event took place on May 7, 1960. Initially, only two projects were raised, one at Srinagar in West and the other at Tezpur in the East. At that time the organization was intended to be only a temporary outfit. As the time passed, requirement of roads in the mountainous terrain soared and the outfit delivered satisfactorily.

The organization went on expanding. Today, BRO has 13 projects, each commanded by a Brigadier of Engineers or a GREF Chief Engineer of a rank equivalent to Brigadier. The organization was assigned just about 700 km of new road-formation to be cut in sixties but today they have nearly 40,000 km of hills and plain roads in their charge. Most of the roads assigned to them are in remote Himalayan heights—from Saichen Glacier in the west to the Blue Mountain in Mizoram in the east.

It is, therefore, no surprise that India Today in one of its special issues published on August 19, 2002, acclaimed BRO as the fifth most important asset of the nation. BRO usually works in remote to very remote mountainous areas along the international border which are inhabited mostly by tribal people. All these tribes are very happy with BRO. There are two reasons for that. One, by cutting new roads in difficult to most difficult tribal areas, the BRO has brought about tremendous change in communications leading to marked improvement in economy and the living and working conditions of the tribals. Two, the expenditure incurred by BRO on various roads comes from the Government of India funds saving the limited State funds for execution of other developmental activities.

Take the case of Himachal Pradesh. In and around this state, the organization has project Deepak. The project looks after some of the most sensitive roads like Hindustan-Tibet road from Wangtu to Shipikila; Manali-Serchu road and Dhami-Basantpur-Kingal road.

The project has quite a few roads and strategic canals in Punjab, Haryana and Uttranchal also. The Himachal Government is now inclined to hand over Karcham-Chitkul road also to BRO. Project Deepak came into existence in May, 1962. It has given a very good account of itself. The BRO men are able to build roads on war-footing within a short notice. On the night of August 17, 1997, the Himalayan ranges forming upper catchment of river Satluj in Shimla district of Himachal Pradesh, had a cloud burst.

The flow of the river was blocked near Wangtu. As a consequence, the valley had in no time turned into a lake — nearly 6.5 km long and 600 to 800 mtr wide. Some 5 km length of the road was either submerged in the lake so formed or completely washed away. Kinnaur district was completely cut off. The tribal area needed a lifeline road most for carting out cash crop of apples and other fresh and dry fruits and for stocking ration, oil, petroleum products and construction stores. There was an untold pressure on the civil administration to restore the communications. There being no other link to the Kinnaur valley, it was essential to build the alternative relief road as early as possible. BRO was given a target to cutting 3 km-long new formation from Tapri side to the point where a new high level suspension-cum-bailey bridge was proposed to be launched. Time allotted was just five months.

The BRO troops, unmindful of the hardships, worked round-the-clock in three shifts and cut the new road in just about two-and-a-half months. Even prior in 1997 certain high altitude areas of Himachal Pradesh had been exposed to a number of calamities. BRO has all along been helping the civil administration in relief operations, especially in opening up of the paralysed communications by building new roads on highest priority. BRO played amajor role during operation Vijay.

The Srinagar - Sonamarg - Kargil - Leh and Manali - Sarchu - Leh axes were opened well in advance facilitating the movement of armed forces. Many other operationally important airfields and road sectors were also opened and maintained for mobilisation of troops and provision of stores. Snow clearance continues to be one of the most unique tasks performed by BRO. The daredevils slog day and night in subzero temperatures and in conditions almost beyond human endurance to keep Changla and Khardungla open throughout the year and keep the hostile border in constant touch and vigil. Opening of Zojila, Rohtang, Baralachala and Tanglangla much ahead of schedule are testimony to the tireless and dauntless efforts of the BRO.

It is only due to efforts of the BRO that Ladakh, higher reaches of Himachal, the Kashmir Valley and the dizzy heights of the North-East are connected to the rest of the country. The BRO's task is not a cake walk. The job takes a heavy toll in terms of human lives. During 1999 BRO lost 445 of its valiant men to militancy, natural calamity and road accidents in difficult terrains.

Targets for the year 1999-2000 have already been achieved. A total 715 kms of formation cutting, 1574 kms of surfacing, 1410 metres of length of bridges and Rs 21715 lakh of permanent works have been successfully completed during the financial year.

Road under maintenance by BRO is 16872 kms. In 1987, the BRO was entrusted with the construction of roads and fencing the Indo-Bangladesh border in the states of Tripura, Meghalaya and Mizoram. The Ministry of Home Affairs sponsored the construction of roads and fencing along the borders Bangladesh. These are commonly known as Indo-Bangladesh Border Roads or IBB Roads. Out of 910.1 Kms of roads, 733 kms have been completed.

The budget for 1999-2000 was approximately Rs 13 crore. As to the question on Indo-Bangla border fencing, 749 kms of IBB roads and 960 kms of fencing have been identified which is to commence in the year 2000-2001.

The year 2000 was also dedicated to the General Reserve Engineering Force (GREF) Pioneer and the Casual Paid Labourer, the backbone of the organization. Keeping pace with Information Technology (IT) in the fast changing era, BRO will be introducing IT to enhance decision-making. The future vision for BRO is to become a leading construction organization, undertaking a diverse range of construction works across the length and breadth of the country with speed, quality and cost effectiveness.

Key Dates in History

7 May 1960	BRO came into existence
Apr 1960	Project Beacon started
May 1961	Project Dantak came into being
May 1961	Project Deepak started
June 1962	Project Chetak started
May 1962	Project Deepak started
Jan. 1975	Project Sampark started
June 1990	Project Udayak started

Present Scenario

Personnel Strength: At present there are around 75,000 BRO personnel. BRO is led by the Director General of Border Roads (DGBR), as it Executive Head, who is of the rank of Lieutenant General.

Today, BRO has 13 projects, each commanded by a Brigadier of Engineers or a GREF Chief Engineer of a rank equivalent to Brigadier.

Organizational Structure

Organizational setup of BRO from top to bottom is:

- Director General
- Additional Director General
- Inspector General
- Deputy Inspector General
- Additional Deputy Inspector General
- Commandant
- Deputy Commandant
- Assistant Commandant
- Subedar Major
- Inspector
- Sub-Inspector
- Asstt Sub Inspector
- Head Constable
- Constable
- Naik

- Lance Naik
- Follower

Duties and Functions

Motto: BRO Motto is ***"Shramena Sarvam Sadhyam"*** meaning **"With hard work every thing is possible".**

Maxim: Nation's most reputed, multifaceted, transnational, modern construction Organization committed to meeting the strategic needs of the armed forces with enlightened leadership, a strong, skilled and committed work force, a well ingrained value system and a strong environment conscience. Playing a national role in socio economic development through its large scale contribution to infrastructure development.

Mission: To support the armed forces meet their strategic needs by committed, dedicated and cost effective development and sustenance of the infrastructure.

To achieve international levels of quality excellence and time consciousness in a diversified sphere of construction activity in a cost effective manner.

Optimise potential and expertise through increased involvement in agency, transnational and national development projects.

To attain leadership in development, adoption, assimilation and use of state of the art technology.

To create the environment for accurate, real time and effective decision making through optimising use of information technology.

Through a focus on core competencies; ensure highest level of skill and proficiency in construction activity.

To sustain a sense of values in the Organization that will ensure a high level of self esteem in each individual and immeasurable synergy in the Organization.

To help enrich the quality of life of the community and ensure all round growth.

Functions: BRO usually have projects in hostile and difficult environment, where private companies are not willing to work, due to various factors including security & harsh climate. They have projects in other countries like in Tajikistan, Afghanistan, Myanmar and Bhutan. The Zaranj-Dilaram highway in Afghanistan, to be completed by 2008 as its personnel cannot work night shifts due to security considerations. The restoration of the Ayni-Farkhor Air Base, near Tajikistan's capital Dushanbe. The BRO also played a vital role in reconstruction in the aftermath of the tsunami in TamilNadu, India and the October 8 earthquake in Kashmir, India.

Acts, Rules & Regulations

BRO is governed by rules and regulations of Indian Army.

Equipments

Beside using normal equipments, BRO uses some specialized machinery such as; Rubber Tired Pavers, Track Mounted Pavers, Milling Machines, Recyclers, Road Wideners, Asphalt Distributor Trucks, Windrow Elevators, Material Transfer Vehicles, Skid Steer Loaders, Chip Spreaders, Brooms, Excavators & Cranes, Compactors, Loader Backhoes, Wheel Loaders, Motor Graders, Dozers & Crawler, Loaders, Scrapers and Water Tankers

Recruitment

All recruitments are done through Indian Army. All rules and regulations are followed. Technical officers having required qualifications are also selected through Indian Army.

Famous Projects

Project Beacon: Raised in April 1960 at Srinagar, Beacon is the Pioneer Project of BRO. Brig BP Wadhera, the first Chief Engineer, coined the slogan "Beacon Bole Changla". Work commenced on Sonamarg–Leh and Chushul roads in 1961. The Jammu – Srinagar stretch of NH-1A was taken over from PWD in 1965, and upgraded to double lane. The Project was also made responsible for the 200 Kms stretch of road Leh – Manali, between Upshi and Sarchu. Due to increased workload, two new Projects viz. Sampark and Himank were carved out of Beacon by transferring some of its Sectors.

Some of its major achievements are construction of Thoise Airfield, resurfacing of Airstrip at Rajouri and Airfields at Leh, Awantipur, Srinagar and Jammu, Centrally Heated General Hospital at Leh and rehabilitation of Jawahar Tunnel. During "OP Vijay" Beacon once again rose to meet the challenge of opening the Zojila Pass on 07 May 99 against all odds and kept the communication line through, for the unprecedented induction of men and material. Beacon has developed 2500 Km of roads in J&K, and is presently maintaining 1584 Km of roads. It is also upgrading 585 Km existing roads to NH double lane specifications. Beacon has earned a place for ıtself in history by its immense contribution to the development of the State of J&K by building a vast network of roads.

Project Chetak: Raised in June 1962 at Dehradun for construction of Joshimath-Malari-Rinkin Road and named after the legendary mount of Maharana Pratap, its jurisdiction today is spread across the States of Rajasthan, Haryana, Punjab, Maharashtra and Goa. In October – November 1962, during the Chinese aggression, the Project helped the Army by providing transport service on the Rishikesh-Joshimath-Malari axis.

After the peace was restored, the Project paid attention to the field of development. The famous pilgrim route from Rishikesh to Badrinath was substantially developed by the Project and opened in June 1965. It has been a great boon for the devoted pilgrims visiting Hemkund Sahib and Badrinath Shrine. The Tanakpur-Tawaghat Road was opened in 1966, which facilitated pilgrims' visit to Mount Kailash and the Holly Lake of Mansarovar in Tibet.

The Project was disbanded in 1966 and raised again in 1980 to undertake construction of General Staff Roads in the sandy deserts of Rajasthan. Construction and improvement of strategically important General Staff roads and roads for Indira Gandhi Nehar Project in Rajasthan, construction of two lane NH 4B from Panvel to Nhava - Sheva Port near Mumbai, Two lane Khoni- -Taloja Highway for Maharashtra Industrial Development Corporation, four laning of National Highway 17B in Goa and resurfacing of Naval Airfield at Goa and Pune are hallmark achievements of Chetak

Project Dantak: Bhutan is a beautiful country nestling in the Eastern Himalayas. Its snow capped peaks, turbulent rivers with wide green valleys at high altitudes, steep hilly terrain and thick forest over, create a magnificent landscape. Bhutan has an area of 46,620 Sq km and lies between the parallel ranges of the outer Himalayas in the north and inner Himalayas in the south. Annual rainfall varies between 500 mm to 2,000 mm in the northern region and from 2,000 mm to 5,000 in the south. The southern ranges are broken gorges scoured out by the main rives of Bhutan, the Amochu (Torsa), the Wangchu (Raidak), the Mochu (Sankosh) and the Dongme Chu (Manas) which flow mostly in the north-south direction and being snow fed carry substantial flow during the non-monsoon months.

The mountain spurs run in north-south direction and descend from heights of over 6,000 m to the foothills near the Indo-Bhutan border. By the end of year 1960, Bhutan had realized the need to planned social and economic development. Therefore, His Majesty the late King Jigme Dorji Wangchuck launched the First Five Year Plan (1961 – 1966) in July 61. Until 1960, Bhutan had no motorable roads. It was connected only by footpaths and mule tracks. As development of roads and transport system play a vital role in the economic and social development of the country, primary importance was given to these sectors during the first three Five Year Plans of Bhutan. Total grant of development of roads was 58.7% in First Five Year Plan, 34.9% in Second Five Year Plan, 17.8% in Third Five Year Plan, 11.6% in Fourth Five Year Plan, 15.3% in Fifth Five Year Plan, 9.3% in Sixth Five Year Plan and 7.8% in Seventh Five Year Plan.

It was against this background that Project Dantak came into being. Project Dantak was raised in May 1961 at Samdrup Jongkar in Eastern Bhutan. A humble beginning was made in bamboo huts and thatched roofs. Since then Project Dantak has not looked back. It has contributed to economic growth of Bhutan by not only developing roads and tele-communication net works but also other prestigious works throughout Bhutan. Over the years, Project Dantak has constructed 1500 Km of roads, airfield at Paro and Yangphula, number of helipads, tele-communication net work in Bhutan, Indo-Bhutan Microwave link, Bhutan Broadcasting Station, the prestigious India House Complex, Chukha Hydel Housing Complex, Hydel Sub-stations, river training works, Schools and Colleges.

The list of accomplishments is endless and in the coming years it is hoped that works like Infrastructure for Kurichu Hydel Project, Dungsum Cement Plant and Tala Hydel Poject will be added. The year 1995-96 saw a flurry of activities. In Eastern Bhutan, the Bulk Petroleum Storage Installation was completed and handed over to RGOB in February 1996. In Western Bhutan, the Paro Air Control Tower was handed over to Druk Civil Aviation. Two bridges were constructed in Thimphu and handed over to PWD, RGOB. The year 1996-97 saw Dantakites battling the fury of nature.

The Sorchen Slide on Phuentsholing – Thimphu Highway posed a challenge to the human endurance and technical skill. The slide prone areas were ultimately bridged by constructing a 120 feet Bailey Bridge. This feat is still fresh in the minds of people who saw Dantak rising to call of duty and worked day and night to restore the only life line to Thimphu. Roads Sibsoo-Tendu land Dewothang-Bhangtar have been completed as per schedule. These works executed far are given in succeeding paras.

Project Deepak: Raised in May 1961 primarily for construction of Hindustan-Tibet Road, the Project is looking after a road length of about 1863 Km, 182 Km long Ditch Cum Bund & the strategic roads from Indo-Nepal Border in the East to the Indo-Pak Border in the West, in the states of Uttaranchal, Himachal and Punjab. Deepak played an important role in 'OP Vijay' by clearing the Manali- Sarchu Road ahead of schedule and keeping it open to unprecedented vehicular traffic.

The project took active part in 'OP White Horse' for relief operations at Malpa. It contributed significantly in the earthquake relief measures in Uttarkashi-Gangotri-Nelong belt of Garhwal region. Besides construction/improvement of roads, the project has constructed 20 Nos 1076 Mtrs length of permanent bridges up to 31 March 2001. One of the most arduous and challenging job before the Project is annual snow clearance to remove huge accumulation of frozen ice through a road stretch of over 600 Kms. Project Deepak is a boon to the pilgrims visiting Badrinath and Hemkund Sahib. 'The Glowing Lamp' Deepak is very popular among the local population and State Governments for its dedicated service to nation building for over four decades. The Project marches ahead inspired by the motto "Sada Age-Sabse Age".

Project Sewak: Raised at Naga Hills Tuensang Area (NHTA) in July 1961 and located at Dimapur. Area of responsibility included Nagaland, Manipur, Mizo Hills and Lohit division of NEFA. At present Project is responsible for roads in Nagaland, Manipur and MEA Road in Myanmar. Construction of prestigious 160 Km Tamu-Kalemyo-Kalewa Road in Myanmar in a record time of three years, construction, double laning and maintenance of NH 39 from Dimapur to Maram, NH 53 from Imphal to Jiribam, construction and maintenance of Kohima-Jessami-Ukhrul, Churachandpur-Tipaimukh, Zunheboto-Aghunato-Kiphire and NEC Roads Akhegwo-Waziho-Washelo, Kohima-Leike, Maram-Peren, Wokha-Bokajan, Longmatra-Likimro are some major works of the Project.

Besides construction of allied works for the Likimro Hydel Project, Earth Satellite Station at Kiphire, accommodation for an Inf Batallion at Rangapahar and for Manipur Police in Imphal, Helibase at Leimakong, and Raj Bhawan Annexe at Kohima are the land mark construction by the Project. Prestigious work of construction of a township for Assam Rifles at Kaithalmanbi is in progress. The Project continues to earn accolades for its dedicated services and provision of reliable and smooth road communication in both the States, both for Army as well as the people of the States of Nagaland and Manipur inspite of insurgency and inclement weather.

Project Pushpak: Raised in May 1967, primarily to accelerate and intensify road development activities in the state of Mizoram. The 'Wonder Orchid' of the East is one of the biggest Project of the Border Roads Organization and is responsible for the development and maintenance of roads encompassing the states of Mizoram and South Cachar region of Assam. Pushpak executes works on NH –53, NH -54 and a number of other roads funded by General Staff, North-Eastern Council and Ministry of Home Affairs. The Project has successfully completed major roads like Udharband-Jatinga, Seiling-Tipaimukh, Serchhip-Thenzawl, Phailang-Marpara, and Kawlkulh-Mimbung and handed over to the State PWD.

Construction of 285 m long Kaladan Bridge, the longest bridge in Mizoram and located in a most difficult area is yet another feather in the cap of the Project. It is also actively involved in the construction of roads and fencing along the Indo-Bangladesh border in Mizoram. Pushpak contributed significantly in the 1971 Bangladesh Operation, building and restoring the communication lines.

Challenging odds like adverse terrain, frequent floods, limited working season uncongenial climatic conditions, never deterred the Pushpakians from achieving their goals. Pushpak is a house hold name in Mizoram, true to the slogan "Mizoram and Pushpak are made for each other".

Project Himank: Raised in August 1985 exclusively for the development of road infrastructure in Ladakh due to the ever-increasing workload of the BRO in J & K. The Project provides the necessary wherewithal to keep the lines of communication open through out the year, not only in Ladakh, but also in the operationally sensitive Siachin sector. Battling tough terrain and extreme climatic conditions, coupled with a short working season of four months, Himank has carved a niche for itself in the Ladakh district of J & K and can rightfully claim the title "The Mountain Tamers". Project Himank has the unique distinction of maintaining and improving roads over the three highest passes of the world viz. Khardungla, Tanglangla and Changla. The highest Bailey Bridge in the world was constructed at Khardungla but has been subsequently replaced by a causeway. Himank has made a singular contribution to 'OP Vijay' by opening the road axis to Leh and Kargil in the first week of May 99.

This was instrumental for the induction of force level meeting the Op requirements of Kargil war. The memorial at Headquarter Himank acknowledges the Supreme sacrifice made by Himankites who laid down their lives on the altar of duty to the Nation, in the dizzy heights of snow clad Himalayas. Project Himank salutes their courage and dedication.

Project Setuk: Raised in September 1989 exclusively for bridging the mighty rivers in the Eastern Sector of the country and named 'Setuk' after the sanskrit word Setu meaning a bridge, the Project was later entrusted with other construction activities such as roads and buildings. It is involved in the development and maintenance of roads in the States of Meghalaya, Assam and Tripura.

The Headquarter of the Project is located at Shillong, the picturesque capital of Meghalaya. National Highway-44 which is the lifeline of the states of Tripura, Mizoram, Manipur, South Assam and South Meghalaya is being kept open for vehicular traffic throughout the year, by the Project, despite the difficult hilly terrain, incessant rainfall and problem of insurgency. Construction of roads and fencing along the Indo Bangladesh border is an important task being carried out by the Project.

National Highway-51 connecting Karimganj to Sutarkandi and Raghna Bazar maintained by the Project, is a key trade route between India and Bangladesh. National Highway -44A from Manu in Tripura to Sairang in Mizoram is yet another important road links under Setuk's jurisdiction. Strengthening of the prestigious Agartala airfield was completed in a record time. Setuk today is a household name in the North-East as it strives for the infrastructural development and strategic needs of the country inspite of constant threat by militants in many sectors of the Project.

Project Sampark: Raised in January 1975 due to ever increasing work load of BRO in Jammu region, the Project has grown from strength to strength and the work load has increased from 843 Km of roads in 1975 to 2310 Km of roads and 145 Km of Ditch Cum Bund in 2000-01.

The Project has so far completed 2146 Km equivalent Cl-9 of formation cutting, 2078 Km of surfacing, 3457 Km of periodic renewal of road surface, 35 major permanent bridges, strengthening and overlaying of Pathankot and Agra air fields and Rajouri Air Strip. Other major achievements of the Project are construction of Roads Budhil-Mohr-Gul,

Basoli-Bani-Bhaderwah, Nagrota By Pass; strengthening and improvement to NH double lane specification of the Roads Jammu-Rajouri-Poonch, Chakki-Dhar-Udhampur, Rajouri-Kandi-Budhil-Mohr-Gul.

The Project has been assigned the task of four laning of National Highway Pathankot-Jammu and is thus the first Project of BRO to be selected to participate in the development of the North-South corridor, the ambitious plan of the Prime Minister. The Project has rendered yeomen service in providing effective communication in militancy affected areas near the Line of Control and turbulent International Borders. Acts of militants aided and abetted from across the border and enemy shelling have failed to dampen the spirit of the daredevils of Sampark.

Project Udayak: Raised in June 1990 to execute works in the states of Arunachal Pradesh, Nagaland and Assam in northeastern sector. The Rivers Brahmaputra and Lohit split the Project sector into three distinctive parts. With a total bridge length of more than 16 Km over a road length of 1260 Km in Arunachal Paradesh.

Udayak probably has the highest bridge to road length ratio in the entire world. Apart from looking after about 2100 Km of roads, 'The Rising Sun' has constructed a 80 Bed Hospital at Pullong, resurfaced and strengthened the Dibrugarh Air Field and is engaged in construction of buildings for residential JNV School at Tissa and Chare. Improvement of NH-52 in Aruncachal Pradesh has been a major achievement of the Project. The Project has been entrusted with four important roads in Arunachal Pradesh which are being constructed by attempting multiple attack points through Air Maintained Detachments.

Inspite of limited fair weather and difficult accessibility due to river Lohit, the Project has managed road construction by inducting dozers, road rollers, compressors and tippers utilising MI-17 helicopters. The 'Rising Sun' has become a house hold name in North-Eastern sector & is all set to transform road communication in the far North-Eastern sector true to its motto "Uttam Kam Pragati Mahan – Udayak Kam Hai Mahan".

Project Vartak: Raised in February 1960, Tusker was the first Project of the BRO which was renamed as Vartak in June 63. Deployed in the states of Arunachal Pradesh and Assam, the Project is poised to undertake and manage works to the tune of Rs 120 Crore per year. Vartak has constructed 2776 Km of new roads, 150 permanent bridges and prestigious building projects.

The Project has 1690 Km of roads under construction & 2134 Km under maintenance. Number of permanent bridges, prestigious building works for North-East Regional Institute of Science and Technology Itanagar, University of Tezpur and Navodaya Vidyalayas are under construction. First to start construction of hill roads and permanent married accommodation for all ranks, Vartak also led BRO in construction of well foundations for permanent bridges & to commence departmental construction of bridges in 1972.

Four Bailey Suspension Bridges of 400 feet span and over 340 Equipment Bridges have been launched successfully. In 1999, started construction of OP priority Roads in remote areas by air-induction of dozers and personnel. With its motto 'Patience, Perseverance and Performance' Vartak dauntlessly continues to keep road communications trafficable; despite incessant rains and heavy landslides. Vartak is a name to reckon within the economic progress of Arunachal Pradesh.

Awards

Gallantry Awards

Ati Vishist Sewa Medal	04
Shaurya Chakra	10
Sena Medal	05
Vishist Sewa Medal	03
Jeevan Raksha Padak	02
Other Awards	54

Future Plans

Ministry of Shipping, Road Transport & Highways has approved special accelerated road development programme (SARDP) under which all districtHeadquarters of North-Eastern states are to be connected with double lane roads with state capital. Out of total 32 routes View of Completed NH-17B under this scheme. BRO is to complete 12 routes by 2010 under Phase-A and 20 routes under Phase-B, which caters for 498 Kms of roads in Phase-A and 2200 Kms of roads in Phase-B for improvement.

The Planning Commission has decided to entrust a number of road infrastructure projects to the BRO in the North-East, as part of PM's package instituted for the development of many backward districts in the North-East.

Some future plans of BRO are:

BRO intend taking on above mentioned projects as entrusted and complete them within the committed time frame and estimated cost.

Modernize and upgrade technology through the introduction of a vast variety of construction equipment on trials in various project sectors and the training of 354 personnel of BRO organization by various equipment manufactures.

Specialized training to a team of GREF officers and supervisors in Germany, for the operation and maintenance of state of the art snow cutters introduced into service last year.

Up-gradation in the field of information technology through the provision of state of the art computer hardware and design of application software to meet the organization

requirement up to the grass root level.

Design of a BRO web site and establishment of an infrastructure for a WAN for thirteen CE Projects and its sub units.

Improvement in the overall quality of life of families in various stations through the construction of married accommodation with dedicated allocation of funds.

As BRO moves ahead in the coming years, it would be dedicating itself to achieve a level of professionalism and excellence with honesty and integrity, to make this organization a cost effective and leading construction Agency.

REFERENCES

Annual Report 2006-2007: Ministry of Home Affairs, Government of India.

Verghese B. G.: India's Northeast Resurgent: Ethnicity, Insurgency, Governance, Development, Konark, 1997.

Verghese B. G.: Reorienting India: The New Geo-politics of Asia, Konark, 2001.

Bangkok Post, Dec. 03, 2001

Deccan Herald, March 28, 2003

Deccan Herald, April 11, 2002.

Defence Aerospace, May 27, 2003

Economic Times, March 22, 2007

Financial Express, June 11, 2008

Govt. of India, Ministry of Defence Annual Report 2005-2006.

Gulshan Sachdeva, Economy of the North-east: Policy, Present Conditions and Future Possibilities, Konark, 2000.

Hindustan Times, March 27, 2006.

Major K.C. Praval: The Red Eagles, Allied Publishing.

MoD Press Release, June 02, 2006.

MoD Press Release, March 07, 2002.

MoD Press Release, May 09, 2004.

MoD Press Release, May 15, 2006.

MoD Press Release, May 16, 2006.

MoD Press Release, June 27, 2005.

Prasad, Expansion of Armed Forces and Defence Organization.

Stephen Peter Rosen: Strategic Traditions for the Asia-Pacific Region, Naval War College Review, 2001.

Strategic Analysis, Aug. 2001.

The Hindu, April 06, 2002.

The Tribune, June 28, 2007

The Tribune, May 29, 2002

Bibliography

Arnold Job: *Letter to Frank Moore*, Duke University, 1866.

Athearn, Robert C.: *Forts of the Upper Mississippi*, Prentice-Hall, 1967.

Bahadur, Lal: *Struggle for Pakistan*, Oriental University Press, London, 1988.

Bahargava, G.S.: *South Asian Security After Afghanistan*, Lexington Books, Toronto, 1983.

Bamzai, Prithvi Nath Kaul: *Kashmir and Power Politics: From Lake Success to Tashkent,* Metropolitan Book Co., Delhi, 1966.

Bellairs, Edgar G.: *As It Is in the Philippines*, Lewis Scribner & Company, New York, 1902.

Bellias, Georth Athan: *George Washington's Generals,* William Morrow, New York, 1964.

Berryman, S. E., R. M. Bell, and W. Lisowski: *The Military Enlistment Process: What Happens and Can It Be Improved*, Rand, Santa Monica 1983.

Birdwood, Lord: *A Continent Decides*, Robert Hale, London, 1953.

Blikenberg, Lars: India–Pakistan: *The History of Unresolved Conflicts*, Dansk Undenrigspolitik Institute, Copenhagen, 1972.

Bokhari, Imtiaz H. and Thornton, Thomas Perry: *The 1972 Simla Agreement: An Asymmetrical Negotiation,* The Johns Hopkins University Press, Washington D.C., 1988.

Bose, Sumantra: *The Kashmir Challenge*, Sage, New Delhi, 1997.

Brecher, Michael: *The Struggle for Kashmir*, Oxford University Press, New York, 1953.

Brezinski, Zbigniew: *Power and Principle: Memoirs of the National Security Adviser 1977–81*, Farrar-Straus-Giroux, New York, 1983.

Brown, Dee: *The Gentle Tamers: Women of the Old Wild West*, University of Nebraska Press, 1958.

Bull, Headley: '*The new environment: sea power and political influence' in Sea*

Power and Influence; Old Issues and New Challenges edited by Jonathan Alford, The International Institute for Strategic Studies, London, 1980.

Burke, Davis: *George Washington and the American Revolution*, Random House, New York, 1975.

Campbell, D. D.: *Pakistan: Emerging Democracy*, N.J. Van Nostrand, Princeton, 1963.

Campbell-Johnson, Alan: *Mission with Mountbatten*, Robert Hale, London, 1953.

Chaudhuri, K. C.: *History of Ancient India*, Central, Calcutta, 1982.

Cheema, Pervaiz Iqbal: '*Arms procurement in Pakistan: balancing the needs for quality, self-reliance and diversity of supply' in Military Capacity and the Risk of War: China, India, Pakistan and Iran* edited by Eric Arnett Sipri, Oxford University Press, Oxford, 1997.

Cheema, Pervaiz Iqbal: *'Economic trends, national security and defence spending in Pakistan' in Regional Economic Trends and South Asian Security* edited by

Iftekharuzzaman, Regional Centre for Strategic Studies, Colombo, 1997.

Cheema, Pervaiz Iqbal: '*India's Kashmir policy' in Perspectives on Kashmir*, edited by K.F. Yusuf, Pakistan Forum, Islamabad, 1994.

Cheema, Pervaiz Iqbal: *'Growing defence expenditure and its implications for economic development in South Asia' in Regional Security in South Asia* edited by Sridhar K. Khatri, Centre for Nepal and Asian Studies, Katmandu, 1987.

Choudhury, G.W.: *Pakistan's Relations with India 1947–1966,* Pall Mall Press, London, 1968.

Commager, Henry Steele: *The Blue and the Grey*, Fairfax Press, New York, 1982.

Connell, John, Auchinleck, Cassell, 1959.

Das Gupta, J.B.: *Indo–Pakistani Relations,* Djambatan, Amsterdam, 1960.

Das, S.T.: *Indian military—its history and development*, Sagar Publications, New Delhi, 1969.

Defence Implications of a Partition of India into Hindustan and Pakistan, East and West Publishing Company, Karachi, 1976.

Fernandez, R. L.: *Enlistment Effects and Policy Implications of the Educational Assistance Test Program,* Rand, September, 1982.

Ganguly, Sumit: *The Origins of War in South Asia*, Westview Press, Boulder, 1986.

Gauhar, Altaf, Ayub Khan: *Pakistan's First Military Ruler,* SangeMeel Publications, Lahore, 1994.

Gunaratna, Rohan: *Indian Intervention in Sri Lanka, South Asian Network on Conflict Resolution*, Colombo, 1993.

Gupta, Anuradha S.: *Memoirs of the Army Days,* Trishul, Noida, 2000.

Gupta, Sisir: *Kashmir,* Asia Publishing House, Bombay, 1966.

Haq, Mahbub ul: *Human Development in South Asia 1997*, Oxford University Press, Karachi, 1997.

Harrison, Selig S. and Kemp, Geoffrey: *India and America After the Cold War*, The Carnegie Endowment, Washington, 1993.

Hoover, James W.: *Men Without Hats : Dialogue, Discipline and Discontent in the Madras Army, 1806-1807,* Manohar, New Delhi 2007.

Human Development Report 1997, United Nations Development Programme, New York, 1997.

Ismay, Lord: *Memoirs,* Heinemann, London, 1960.

Jalal, Ayesha: *Democracy and Authoritarianism in South Asia,* Sang-eMeel Publications, Lahore, 1995

Johnston, William C.: *'Jammu and Kashmir 1947–49' in Challenge and Response in Internal Conflict* edited by D.M. Condit, Best H. Cooper Jr. and others, Centre for Research in Social Systems, The American University, Washington D.C., 1968.

Khalidi, Omar: *Khaki and the Ethnic Violence in India : Army, Police and Paramilitary Forces During Communal Riots,* Three Essays, New Delhi, 2003.

Kumar, Raj: *Encyclopaedia of Military Systems in India,* Commonwealth Publishers, New Delhi, 2004.

Kunju, N.: *Army Life: A Fast-Forward Review,* Reliance, New Delhi 2006.

Lamb, Alastair: *Kashmir: A Disputed Legacy*, Oxford University Press,

Lamb, Alastair: *The Kashmir Problem*, Praeger, New York, 1966.

Malhotra, V.P.: *Encyclopaedia of Indian Army,* Anmol, New Delhi 2006.

Marshall,S. L. A.:*The American Heritage History of World War I*, American Heritage Publishing Company, New York, 1964.

Marston, Daniel P. and Sundaram, Chandar S. A.: *Military History of India and South Asia : From the East India Company to the Nuclear Era,* Pentagon Press, New Delhi, 2008.

Michel, A.A.: *The Indus Riveis,* Yale University Press, Princeton, 1967.

Mittal, Attar Chand: *Defence Modernisation, Secret Deals & Strategy of Nations : A Global Study of Army, Navy, Air Force & Para-Military Forces* (2 V) Delhi 1989.

Mosley, Leonard: *The Last Days of the Biitish Raj*, Weidenfeld Si Nicholson, London, 1961.

Musa, General (Retd.) Mohammad: *My Version: India-Pakistan Wai 1965*, Wajidalis, Lahore, 1983.

Palit, DK: War in High Himalaya : *The Indian Army in Crisis-1962*, Lancer Publishers & Distributors, New Delhi 1991.

Praval, KC: *Indian Army After Independence*, Lancer Publishers & Distributers New Delhi 1987.

Sareen, T.R.: *Indian National Army : A Documentary Study*, Gyan, New Delhi, 2004.

Sarkar, Bhaskar: *Outstanding Victories of the Indian Army - 1947-1971*, Lancer Publishers & Distributers New Delhi.

Sharma, Gautam: *Soldier's Memoirs : Army Narratives,* Reliance Publication, New Delhi, 2005.

Simpson, Arnow Harriette: *Flowering of the Cumberland,* Macmillan, New York, 1963.

The Army Family. White Paper 1983 by the Chief of Staff, U.S. Army, 15 August 1983.

Vansittart, Eden: *Gorkhas,* Compiled under the order of the Government of India Delhi 1991.

Wood, W.J.: *Leaders and Battles : The Art of Military Leadership*, Lancer Publishers & Distributers, New Delhi, 1996.

Yadava. S.S.: *Forgotten Warriors of Indian War of Independence 1941-1946* : Indian National Army, Hope India Publication, Gurgaon, 2005.

50 Years of Peacekeeping, Inter Services Public Relations, Rawalpindi, 1998.

Index

B

C

N

S